BRITISH-INDIAN ADULT CHILDREN OF DIVORCE

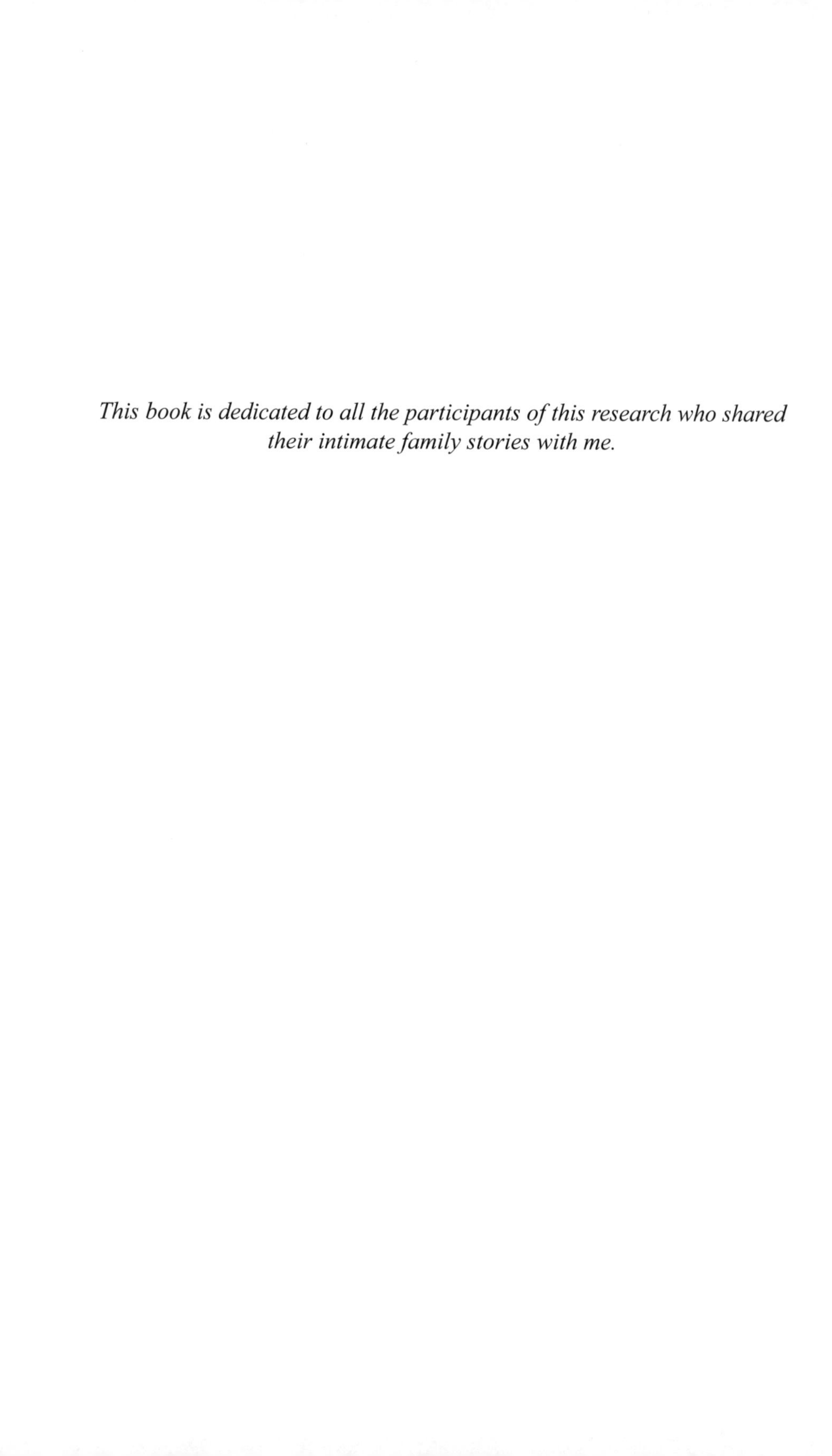

*This book is dedicated to all the participants of this research who shared
their intimate family stories with me.*

British-Indian Adult Children of Divorce
Context, Impact and Coping

CHAITALI DAS
Queen's University Belfast, UK

ASHGATE

Published by
Ashgate Publishing Limited
Wey Court East
Union Road
Farnham
Surrey, GU9 7PT
England

Ashgate Publishing Company
Suite 420
101 Cherry Street
Burlington
VT 05401-4405
USA

www.ashgate.com

British Library Cataloguing in Publication Data
Das, Chaitali.
 British-Indian adult children of divorce : context, impact
 and coping.
 1. Adult children of divorced parents--Great Britain.
 2. Adult children of immigrants--Family relationships--
 Great Britain. 3. South Asians--Great Britain--Social
 conditions.
 I. Title
 306.8'9'089914041-dc22

Library of Congress Cataloging-in-Publication Data
Das, Chaitali.
 British-Indian adult children of divorce : context, impact and coping / by Chaitali Das.
   p. cm.
 Includes bibliographical references and index.
 ISBN 978-1-4094-0824-6 (hbk) -- ISBN 978-1-4094-0825-3 (ebook)
 1. Divorce--Great Britain--Cross-cultural studies. 2. Adult children of divorced
parents--Great Britain--Cross-cultural studies. 3. East Indians--Great Britain. I. Title.
 HQ875.D37 2011
 306.89089'914041--dc22

                                                                                    2010048802

ISBN 9781409408246 (hbk)
ISBN 9781409408253 (ebk)

Printed and bound in Great Britain by the
MPG Books Group, UK

Contents

List of Figures and Tables

Figure

Tables

Preface
Research on Divorce and Identified Gaps

In current societies, various family forms exist which depart from the traditional notions of the family. Family and marriage are being reshaped and redefined in terms of its values and its functions and one sees a split between marriage and parenthood (Cere 2003). Contemporary British families reflect this with family forms ranging from cohabiting families, divorced families, remarried families, step-families, single-sex families, adopted families, and single-parent families. Over the last four decades, divorce has played a significant role in the reshaping of the family. Divorce, in Britain as well as other western countries, has had a significant impact on families and their transition into other family forms, such as single-parent families, remarried, and step-parent families.

In spite of a vast array of literature and research available on the subject, there is scope to further develop understanding of divorce processes and address some gaps. For instance, researchers have indicated the scope of studies within cross-cultural contexts, and in societies that are in transition to further inform our understanding of divorce (Berardo 1990, Kitson and Morgan 1990, White 1990, Goode 1993, Cherlin 1999, Simons et al. 1999). In addition, while studies on mainstream populations in the western contexts do exist, there is little that has explored divorce in other ethnic and non-white populations that have migrated and/or are resident in these countries. The understanding of divorce, its consequences, impact and processes for ethnic families have remained understudied.

As indicated above divorce studies have primarily been informed by a white-western perspective since most research on divorce has focussed on white communities using predominantly white samples (Mitchell 1985). Though these research findings have contributed to the understanding of divorce processes, there is a need to validate these findings with other racial and ethnic groups, particularly because the fact racial and cultural differences permeate across all life experiences (Bigle and Kaufman 1983, Smart 2000, Reynolds 2002). Cultural perspectives are in fact critical in studying families of ethnic groups and findings from one culture cannot be generalised onto others (Berry 2006). Most studies on divorce have largely ignored cultural influences of other non-white ethnic groups (Dilworth-Anderson and McAdoo 1988). Divorce introduces very complex arrangements for families and child care. Simplistic, generalised and causal relationships may not hold true across different contexts (Smart and Shipman 2004) and need to be understood through research that includes diverse ethnic and racial groups, and study the processes and factors that are salient in the lives and experiences of minority ethnic groups.

In addition, though divorce studies have been highly informed by quantitative studies, particularly in the United States of America, there is scope for further understanding divorce processes qualitatively. Rodgers and Pryor's (1998) review of studies of divorce in the United Kingdom (UK), also identified the lack of qualitative research as a gap. A number of qualitative studies since, have greatly promoted the understanding of a range of issues that take into account children' experiences, roles of grandparents, issues of communication and contact, and sibling relationship in the divorce environment. Some qualitative studies (not an exhaustive list) include Smart and Neale (1999), Dunn and Deater-Deckard (2001). Trinder et al. (2002), Smart and Wade (2002); Abbey and Dallos (2004) and Buchanan (2009). However, there remain very limited qualitative or quantitative studies that have been informed from an ethnic or racial perspective. Singh's (1998) study on lone Asian mothers in London which included a sample of divorced women, is among a few exceptions to this. Similarly, while there is recognition for the inclusion of children's voices and their narratives, within the divorce context, there is limited representation of the divorce experiences of children from diverse ethnic groups.

While studies on causes and consequences of divorce are able to indicate some important and significant aspects, it is hard to ascertain definitive outcomes of divorce for children. Two reasons can be afforded to this. First, the variety and complexity of the process of divorce, associated environment factors and individual differences, make generalisations for impact of divorce, difficult (Popay et al. 1983, Kroll 1994, D'Cruz and Bharat 2001). Thus, while divorce may be regarded positively by children in cases of domestic violence, abusive, high conflict and dysfunctional families (Nye 1957, Landis 1960, Despert 1962, Jekielek 1998), children still reportedly miss their absent parents, may want their parents to remain together in spite of the conflict and sometimes even consider the pre-divorce situation to be better than the post-divorce situation (Wallerstein and Kelly 1980, Walzack and Burns 1989). Individuals and families are embedded within their social, environmental, legal, emotional, and financial contexts. Since divorce processes interact with and have an impact across these various contexts, it is often hard to predict the outcomes of these interactions. Furthermore, the interaction, reactions and agency of individual members in families within such situations can be hard to predict and measure. But these are, nonetheless, critical in determining outcomes. Second, studies conducted in the past cannot predict changes that are recent and responsive to divorce as a social phenomenon. In other words, past research may not necessarily represent contemporary contexts (Mitchell 1985). Indeed, a brief historical analysis of divorce studies indicates how perspectives and studied outcomes of divorce have seen shifting (Berardo 1990, Smart 2000). Early studies of divorce that focussed on divorce as an event have given way to the view of divorce as a process of family transition (Ahrons and Rodgers 1987, Burgoyne et al. 1987, Kitson and Morgan 1990, Smart 2000). While divorce studies in the 1980s and 1990s indicated a high negative impact of divorce on children and families, more recent research stresses the management of the divorce process. Children of divorce may face higher risks of maladjustment and negative outcomes but this does not necessarily indicate actual maladjustment and negative outcomes for children, as most children adjust without severe negative outcomes (Cherlin 1992, Wyman et al. 1999). More recent studies also suggest that initially predicted negative outcomes of divorce have diminished over time as communities and families have learnt to manage divorce better (Amato and Keith 1991a, Faust and McKibben 1999, Pike 2003)

Most children of divorce show high resilience in coping with the difficult transitions, adversities and change that divorce brings. However, resilience of children depends on various environmental and ecological factors. While some environmental factors present challenges and risks, other factors present opportunities and protective features. Examining children's interactions with these protective and risk factors is therefore one way to understand divorce processes, general patterns as well as individual outcomes of divorce.

Focus and Aims of this Book

This book aims to fulfil, in part, this gap by adding the voices of British-Indian children of divorce, to understand the processes and conceptualisation of divorce from a different ethnic perspective.

The book presents a study that seeks to understand of the impact of divorce on British-Indian adult children by documenting and describing the family accounts of twenty-one British-Indian adult children who experienced parental divorce. These twenty one, British-Indian adult children of divorce who have informed this study and whose accounts are presented willingly volunteered to participate in the project. They have been referred to as participants throughout the book.

Participants' accounts were collated and analysed to reflect the processes, dynamics and experiences of divorce in terms of the context of parental divorce, their perceived impact of divorce and their accounts of coping with divorce. Participants' stories reflected a range of diverse experiences as well as some common frameworks through which the impact of divorce was felt by them. The book analyses and seeks to interpret and understand these findings within the historical, cultural and social contexts which form the ecological context of British-Indian families. Bronfenbrenner's ecological framework is used to identify the larger contexts within which participant narratives are interpreted. In doing so, the processes and interconnections between macro structures, community relations, ideology and individual agency, that produce specific impacts for children and the resources and strategies for coping for children in this community are highlighted. Positive protective features and risks inherent within these processes and factors are also considered.

The study is retrospective and the interviews with participants' obtained accounts of their childhood experiences of divorce, the events that occurred, their impact and subsequent coping as well as their current understanding, feelings and thoughts. The study in this sense explores the continuity of family history through time. This continuity also provides to some extent insights into the inheritance of both risk and protective features that have an impact on children.

Intended Readership

The focus of the study is on the British-Indian community and presents an understanding of risks and resilience within a particular contextual perspective. The study highlights why this contextual perspective is important and how the experiences of children in this community differ from experiences of mainstream children. A similar approach can be replicated in understanding children's and community experiences in different contexts. This can further inform culturally competent policies and practices such that risks and protective factors that apply to specific communities can be considered appropriately. The subject matter is relevant to those who are engaged in working or studying ethnic families, cultural studies and family transitions. It may also be particularly relevant to parents, families and children that may be experiencing divorce and enable a better understanding of the divorce processes and how to manage it.

Outline of Chapters

The first chapter presents an overall synopsis of divorce studies and the general overview of our understanding of divorce. It presents the causes, consequences and the effects of divorce for individuals and children. However, children also show resilience and many individual, familial and community characteristics help children to cope and mitigate negative outcomes for children. For children of divorce, risks and protective factors present in their environment can affect their development. Children's environment consists of their families, communities and the society at large that contributes directly or indirectly to child development (Bronfenbrenner 1979). Children's environment is contextualised using Bronfenbrenner's into micro, meso, exo and macro systems. The theory of resilience is used to indicate the different risks and protective factors present for children of divorce across these systems

The second chapter provides an insight into the British-Indian community towards understanding the current status and development of the community in the UK. It considers the historical development of the British-Indians in the UK, from their arrival in the 1940s, the development of their community, adaptation in the UK, continuation of traditions, socio-economic achievements and status, and the continuing trends of acculturation patterns in subsequent third and fourth generations. This chapter presents a closer view of the historical, socio-economic and cultural contexts for British-Indians since these factors shape their ecological environment. The literature also explores the recorded experiences of divorce within this community and its implications of divorce for this community. This chapter lays the foundations for considering resilience within a historical framework for British-Indians to illuminate the inheritance of processes, and the development of actions and reactions, that shape the risks and protective factors, that have an effect on children of divorce in British-Indian families.

One of the key reasons of the lack of research with Black and other minority ethnic groups is often cited to be the difficulties in gaining access and obtaining participation. The third chapter considers some of these issues of access, rapport building as well as the insights obtained from the community and the researcher's experiences in the field. All participants were from Hindu and Sikh communities. The reasons for this was the particular selection criteria that was outlined at the beginning of the study The profiles of participants whose narratives inform this book are provided in more detail. Finally, the author presents a reflexive account and her engagement with the subject matter and the research processes.

The second part of this book presents the voices of the participants. This part is divided into four chapters and documents participants' accounts of the context of parental divorce, the impact of divorce on them and their strategies and resources for coping.

Chapter 4 presents accounts of how and why participants' parents divorced. This forms the main text of this section and includes participants' family situation both before and after the divorce. The perceived reasons for the parental divorce, custody issues, living and care arrangements and introduction of step-families. The narratives present the issues of arranged and love marriages, domestic conflict and violence, the resistances to divorce due to stigma as well as care of children. The change in family practices, economic status as well as custody arrangements are presented, their step-families and participants' relationships with their custodial and non-custodial parents are also explored. Most fathers remarried while mothers were more likely to remain unmarried due to reported cultural reasons. The gender dimensions of divorce as a family transition within the British-Indian cultural context are also discussed. Chapter 4 also presents participants' perspectives on marriage and divorce and how these have been informed by their own experiences of parental divorce.

In Chapter 5, detailed findings and analysis of participants' accounts of how the divorce and the family transition affected their lives in a variety of ways are presented. These various impacts are discussed under five categories namely physical impact, emotional impact, financial impact, education/career impact and social impact. Participants' stories highlighted the losses and emotional impact, as well as the changes in their social lives due to parental divorce. Subsequently, many participants indicated how the divorce affected their educational involvement and achievements. Participants also described the economic poverty and the loss of social, economic, educational as well as inter-generational resources as a consequence. Accounts of the physical displacement, instability in care arrangements are presented. Changing family roles and the tensions this created are also analysed. Vivid accounts of how the stigma of divorce affected their lives are also presented. Particularly striking are international child care arrangements through the diaspora, issues of loyalty conflicts between larger extended family relations and the overwhelming impact of stigma of divorce which often had a lasting impact and consequences. This chapter helps interlink these different impacts and illustrates how children's lives are indeed embedded in context and singular impact cannot be isolated. The chapter attempts to indicate key risks that children of divorce in the British-Indian community face.

Chapter 6 presents insights into the coping and resilience of participants. Participants outlined various strategies which are categorised into physical strategies, psychological strategies and social strategies to cope. They gave various accounts of staying away from their families to distance themselves from the difficult family environment. Some reported engaging in aggressive behaviours or used substances to cope while others used psychological and mental strategies. Many of the participants interviewed also talked about their resolve and ability to build productive social relationships and use social resources to cope. Various coping resources, formal and informal, also featured in their narratives. Participants were also active agents in helping their parents seek both formal and informal resources for coping individually and as a family. The chapter concludes by identifying particular protective features in the community that can support children of divorce to cope.

Chapter 7 systematically outlines the risks and protective factors highlighted by the data in Chapters 4, 5 and 6 across Bronfenbrenner's (1979) ecological systems. The chapter also considers risk and protective factors as dynamic, dependent on the interactions across the ecological contexts within which a community is situated. Thus, risk and resilience is conceived within processes that are dependent on system dynamics and have historical continuity.

The final chapter uses the findings to emphasise the need for culturally competent practice with minority ethnic communities that recognises the wider context of the development of children in these communities and are able to support them in a meaningful and inclusive manner. A case for culturally competent services thus that imbibes knowledge of communities, their cultures and histories, skills to engage and understand needs, supported by values that do not judge them in a deficient manner, is made. Knowledge of the ecological context of families, individuals within families, their culture and histories are crucial for such practice. It remains imperative for policy to flexibly adapt and meet the diverse needs of different people whilst protecting rights of the most vulnerable groups in society. There is a need to contextualise children's development within their environments and integrate support and services that consider the needs of families and parents. Work in partnership with communities to identify needs, provide services and plan appropriate access remain crucial for successful cultural competent practice and policy development.

Acknowledgements

First and foremost, I would like to thank the participants who participated in this research project. I would also like to thank the many people in the British-Indian community who shared their thoughts and opinions and helped me to develop a deeper understanding of their lives in the UK.

I would also like to thank my supervisor, Professor Ravinder Barn, and my colleagues at Royal Holloway, where I completed the research; as well as colleagues at Queen's University Belfast, where I wrote this book.

In addition, my thanks to the editors and staff at Ashgate for their support in publishing this book.

Finally, special thanks to Dr Christopher Cohrs and Dr Harsimran Singh who read various drafts of the book and gave constructive comments.

PART I
Understanding Divorce
and its Impact

Chapter 1

What We Know About Divorce: Causes and Impact

Divorce is intricately linked with the family and has been widely studied, both in terms of causes and consequences. The ways in which the family has been conceptualised has greatly influenced studies of divorce. With changes in family forms and structures, the notion of divorce has also seen shifting perspectives which have led to changing ideas, research methodologies, outcomes and interpretations.

Early understanding of the family was based on the family as a functioning unit that served a variety of purposes such as care of its members, reproduction, recruitment and socialisation of new members, maintenance of order, and provision of services and goods by and for members (Goode 1964, Ahrons and Rodgers 1987, Thornton 2009). Marriage was considered as the first step towards the initiation of the family. Marriage thus constituted the family that was oriented towards fulfilling functions of exclusive sexual partnership, reproduction and socialisation of children (Gray 2005, Thornton 2009). Divorce from this understanding of the family represented a malfunctioning and crisis for the family and was regarded as a pathological event, as 'deviance', or a 'crisis'.

Divorce is, nonetheless, one of the first movements towards disassociating marriage from the family. Divorced families indicate a conceptual shift in terms of thinking about families distinctly from marriage. With rising divorce rates and alternative family forms, marriage has increasingly lost its unique position as the only socially acceptable way to establish intimate relationships, fostering childbirth and establishing a family (Gonzalez-Lopez 2002). Divorce is now common and regarded as a process through which the family changes. The Office for National Statistics (ONS) (2007a), recorded that divorce rates rose from approximately 75,000 in 1971 divorces to 120,000 divorces in 1972, in the UK. Divorce rates have since been steadily rising, peaking again in 1985 at around 160,000 and then tapering to about 145,000 in 1999.

Moreover, within the UK, many diverse family forms now exist, lone-parent families, remarried step-families, cohabiting families, divorced families, same-sex families to name a few. According to the 2001 census, there were 0.7 million step-families with dependent children of which 0.4 million were married step-families while 0.3 million were cohabiting step-families (ONS 2007a). Between 1996 and 2006, the number of married families had fallen by four per cent, cohabiting couples had risen by 60 per cent and lone-mother households had increased by 11 per cent (ONS 2007a). The rise in cohabiting couples and lone-parenthood, increasing divorce and lower rates of remarriage indicate that families in Britain are increasingly conceived without marriage. However, it is important to note that in spite of the diversity of family forms that now exist, marriage remains one of the most common forms of partnership for men and women in the UK. In 2005, according to the Office of National Statistics, there were 284,000 (of which more than 60 per cent first marriages and 40 per cent remarriages) marriages in the UK. Thus while other forms of family are becoming increasingly more normalised within society, the married family form retains significance.

The trends could be interpreted to suggest that while divorce is accepted as a process of family change and negative attitudes have decreased, the marriage partnership continues to be significant. There may be ambivalence towards divorce as suggested by some American scholars (Cherlin 2009, Thornton 2009) and the case may be similar in the UK.

This transformation of the family and changing conceptualisation of marriage and divorce seems to be a result of various social movements, changes in the mode of production, increasing women's participation in labour market, and increasing emphasis on individualism within cultures. Some of these associations are considered below.

Divorce and Culture

There is some support to suggest that some cultures are more permissive towards divorce. However, research that can systematically isolate cultural factors amidst other continual, social, economic and historical processes are difficult to conduct. Though more comparative and/or cross cultural research could shed more light on this, conducting comparative research across contexts is not easy. Goode (1993) has presented an analysis of different contexts and the conceptualisations of marriage and divorce in different countries, however, he has also acknowledged problems of consistent measurements, tools and analysis. The transferability of concepts can pose challenges and make the emergence of a clear picture that implicates culture in any specific way, difficult. In addition, the definition of culture in itself can be problematic and it can be argued that changes in culture make its articulation in research difficult. Finally, in increasingly diverse societies where cultures amalgamate, culture cannot be conceived as fixed and measurable. The problem of culture as a moderating factor is thus difficult to pin-point.

Nonetheless, some elements of culture have been put forward as influencing divorce. Some researchers suggest that structural changes in the macro environment have led to post-modern capitalism and a culture of individualisation which has made relationships less stable, less normative and more negotiable (Davies 1950, Weitzman 1985, South and Trent 1989, Reynolds and Mansfield 1999, Amato and Rogers 1999, Gonzalez-Lopez 2002, Crow 2002, Birgit and Birgit 2002). The culture of individualisation, has replaced the earlier companionate marriage of the 19th century. Within this new culture with a sharp focus on self growth and self development, one can leave a marriage if one is unhappy rather than continue in a loveless marriage out of the necessity to fulfil one's duty (Cherlin 2009). Toth and Kemmelmeier (2009) in their research with 22 countries (most of them in the western hemisphere) also supported the idea that divorce was viewed more favourably in individualised societies, independent of context, whereas attitudes to divorce in more collectivist societies were less favourable and more sensitive to context.

Joplin et al. (2003), in their research across five countries (Hong Kong, Singapore, China, Mexico and USA), implied that there is a relationship between culture and family change and/or family transition. They suggested that different countries combine different cultural values that support or resist family change in the face of macro environmental pressure such as changes in economy, labour markets, legal provisions, etc. Their results and discussions indicated that Singapore and Hong Kong combined more of eastern and western values and hence showed less resistance to family change in response to macro environmental pressures. However, in China, the family was more resistant to change and encountered more conflict with the macro system. According to Gonzalez-Lopez (2002), diversity in values and gender expectations seems to play a role in the organisation of family life across western countries even if they show similar economic integration and equality of women. Gonzalez-Lopez's from her analysis of western countries (namely: USA, Canada, Norway, Finland, Sweden, Germany, Italy, France, Spain, Belgium, Portugal, Britain, and Austria) in the 1990s indicated that culture and policy both play a role in understanding differences in family choices and family patterns in these countries. Toth and Kemmelmeier (2009) also support the idea that attitudes towards family matters are embedded in culture. Culture thus may have an influence on family patterns and may affect divorce rates.

There is however, much more research and data on the economic and labour systems that seem connect macro environments to the incidence of divorce. One of the key factors that are co-related to divorce is the presence of women in society, their economic participation and agency.

Divorce and Women in the Economy

Globalisation and modernisation have opened the labour market to enable more participation of women in economic activities. Real earnings of women seem to have increased due to their labour participation, reducing the gains for women from marriage. Studies of women's participation in labour are often interpreted to mean that women's increased independence through labour participation has led to more choices and decision making power for women This increased economic independence gives women more agency and personal choice to leave unhappy marriages, thus raising the divorce rates (Davies 1950, Nock 2001, Astone et al. 2002).

South and Trent (1989) through their studies of women's participation in labour across 66 countries suggested that divorce rates may also be linked to sex ratios where less availability of women decreased divorce rates. South and Trent

(1989), in ascertaining the relationship between family changes and the macro environment, found that higher socio-economic development, higher female labour participation and more women in the sex ratio showed higher divorce rates.

Evidence thus suggests that developments that empower women may lead to an increase in divorce rates as women may find the marital institutions as disadvantageous and at the same time have alternative life opportunities outside of marriage.

Though increasing economic participation of women due to modernisation may allow women more agency and perhaps more freedom, feminists like Walby (1990), however, contend that this economic participation of women does not necessarily mean emancipation. Walby (1990) presents that in the new capitalist order women's labour is exploited across different races and classes. This capitalism continues to dominate women in conjunction with patriarchy to exploit women's labour across different dimensions using different modes.

Some research suggests that presence of children in families can also influence women's agencies to divorce, particularly when husbands are abusive (Burgoyne et al. 1987, Amato and Preveti 2003). Amato and Preveti (2003) noted that women with children were more likely to report abuse as reasons for divorce and suggested that the presence of children and their security concerns may motivate women to leave abusive husbands.

Other socio-demographics such as teenage marriage, pre-marital births, premarital conception, premarital and previous cohabitation, previous partnership breakdowns, parental divorce, lower education and poor economic conditions also seem to contribute to the potential for divorce (White 1990, Amato and Keith 1991c, Clarke and Berrington 1999, DeGarmo and Forgatch 1999, Amato and Preveti 2003). Higher potential for divorce in lower socio-economic contexts, when macro studies suggest that divorce rates seem to increase with more labour opportunities for women, may indicate that more opportunities for labour may be available for women in the lower socio-economic strata.

Divorce studies thus seem to indicate that divorce is influenced by macro and microcontexts. At the macro level, institutional frameworks and culture are implicated while at the micro level, socio-economic conditions, history, nature and experience of previous relationships seem to affect divorce.

Impact of Divorce

Though divorce is now common in the UK, it still presents significant implications for individuals and societies. The married family remains deeply embedded within social processes, social structures and systems. Due to this centrality of the married family unit within society (Waite 2000, Cere 2003), changes and transitions in the family form present significant implications for individuals and social provisions at large. Family transitions such as divorce involve substantial changes in the legal, financial and social statuses of individual members and severely impact on the lives of family members. Family members have to renegotiate their relationships with each other, make adjustments in their everyday lives and plan for the future in response to the multiple changes of divorce. At the macro societal level, divorce presents significant policy implications as it disproportionately affects women and children, indicating a feminisation of poverty, leading to higher rates of poverty and dependence among divorced women and lone-mother families. Studies across various countries have implied this feminisation of poverty as a consequence of divorce and it is only after cohabitation and/or that many lone-parents are able to recover their pre-divorce financial status (Weiss 1975, Furstenberg and Cherlin 1991, Amato 1994, Goode 1993, Maundeni 2000, Morrison and Ritualo 2000, Smart 2000).

In the UK, divorce particularly affects the lifestyles and economic class of women compared to men (Walzack and Burns 1989, Carbone 1996). Lone-parents, as a consequence of divorce, often face poverty due to the transition in their families and the loss of their spouse's financial income. Women more often than men fall into the category of lone-parents and face severe financial constraints, are among the most disadvantaged and show more child poverty (McKay and Rowlingson 1998, McKendrick 1998). In 2007, 21 per cent of all families with dependent children were lone-mother families, compared to two per cent lone-father families, in the UK (ONS 2008a). These figures have been more or less consistent since 1997. Households headed by lone-mothers are more likely to be unemployed or in part time employment than households headed by lone-fathers (Winchester 1990, Walling 2005). Women also report difficulties and barriers from employers due to the presence of children which may reduce work opportunities available to them (Goode 1993, Carbone 1996). According to the report presented to the House of Commons on Child Poverty in the UK (2004), 2.6 million children were living in poverty in 2002-2003. Of these, 1.62 million children in poverty were in lone-parent households, and 1.88 million in workless families of which two thirds were lone-parent families. In 2002-2003, 29 per cent of children were living in poverty as a consequence of family transitions (House of Commons Report 2004). Poverty is also likely to make divorced and lone-parent families more vulnerable and dependant on welfare provisions. In 2006/07, 90 per cent of lone-parent families with dependent children received income related benefits and 69 per cent received income support and/or families tax credit (ONS 2008a). The macro picture thus suggests that lone-parenthood (particularly and mostly women), unemployment and child poverty are inter-related.

The government's strategy to address this poverty has been through addressing workless-ness. The government aimed to enable 70 per cent of lone-parent families to enter work by 2010 (House of Commons Report 2004) through programmes such as the *New Deal for Lone Parents* that support lone-parents through personal advisors and provide flexible work opportunities (Brewer and Gregg 2001). However, McKendrick's (1998) research on the quality of life of 275 lone-parents in Scotland showed that the majority of working lone-parents (71 per cent) share a quality of life similar to non-workers. This may be due to the availability, affordability and accessibility of child care related provisions. There has also been some concern that this government agenda does not adequately consider the social norms and expectations of lone-parents. Lone-parents are often prompted to prioritise parenting roles over their desire or obligation to work and conform to social care norms (Himmelweit 2002, Reynolds 2002). Child-care commitments as well as the inability to meet costs of alternative childcare may be reasons for lone-parents' reluctance to join the labour force and their poorer quality of life.

Winchester (1990) argues that the design of policy largely rests on the ideology of a family with the male as the breadwinner and the female as the unpaid carer and that policy may in fact be contributing to this feminisation of poverty. There is a need to address and reward the contribution of child care work appropriately and support care work that is consistent with social values and desired child welfare outcomes.

Impact of Divorce on Spouses

It is important to take into account the special context and processes of divorce within which family change occurs. These include the deliberate decision to divorce by marriage partner/s (Ahrons 1980). It is likely to be unscheduled, and structural changes occur at multiple levels resulting in ambiguity of roles and relationships. Furthermore, the prevailing family identity is shattered and divorce results in a series of life changes that have a continuing impact long after the legal event of divorce has occurred (Ayoub et al. 1999). These include remarriage, increased mobility as a consequence of remarriage (South et al. 1998), introduction of new family members and the reconstitution of the family through step-families, and the renegotiation of relationship boundaries (Simpson 1998).

Divorce in most circumstances involves a separation from one's spouse in a variety of everyday living arrangements which include almost all aspects of one's life. Ayoub et al. (1999) add that divorce occurs at multiple levels, there is a social divorce, emotional divorce, financial divorce along with the legal divorce that affects all family members and can resemble a crisis phase during the phase of separation.

Divorced spouses face the consequences of divorce on a daily and recurring basis and have to adjust to the demands of their new life and circumstances. In most cases, divorce is a painful reality where the hopes and dreams that one had for the marriage have to be reconsidered (Simpson 1998). Divorce is an emotional process but also one that is generally associated with conflict between spouses that generally precedes divorce. Often this conflict can linger for years prior to and after the divorce (Weiss 1975, Wallerstein and Kelly 1980, Ahrons and Rodgers 1987, Furstenberg and Cherlin 1991). The emotional impact of divorce is universal and divorcing spouses have to manage a range of emotions. Spouses have to consolidate a range of powerful emotions: anger, grief, loss and fear to rebuild their lives independently of each other.

Changes in financial status as a result of divorce has a significant impact as discussed previously. It produces physical effects of living in poverty, and psychological and social effects of having to live outside the day-to-day cultural and political life of the community.

Adjustments are also required to accommodate changes in housing, work circumstances, changing financial situations as well as altered domestic roles (Burgoyne et al. 1987). In terms of physical displacement, most women in the West, following divorce, tend to remain in their homes with men moving out of the house while in other cases women move out temporarily, to live with their parents, before seeking out independent housing (Walzack and Burns 1989, Furstenburg and Cherlin 1991). These changes affect the lives of divorcing spouses as well as children involved.

The social impact of divorce can also be rather marked. Divorced couples often report a loss in social friendships (Burgoyne et al. 1987). Terhell et al.'s (2004) longitudinal study on 104 people who divorced in 1987 in the Netherlands showed a marked change in the social networks of all divorcees. For some, these changes were short term or temporary while for others they were more permanent as observed over 12 years. Divorced women seemed to manage their social networks better and men reported more losses. However, all divorcees lost the network relationships they had with their in-laws. Researchers in the 1980s recognised the stigmatisation of divorce, disapproving attitudes by society and disadvantages of lone-parent families (Popay et al. 1983, Ahrons and Rodgers 1987, Gerstel 1987). McKendrick (1998) demonstrated in his research that lone-parents in Scotland, on the whole, showed more dissatisfaction with housing services, health and people's attitudes towards them. However research also documents decreasing negative attitudes towards divorce over time (Faust and McKibben 1999).

In the face of these multiple changes and adjustments, it is of little surprise that divorce and lone-parenthood are associated with negative health implications. Single and divorced men and women in the UK have among the highest suicide rates (ONS 2009). According to the 2001 census, lone-parents in Britain reported the poorest health across all other family categories. These health implications may result from additional stress of marital breakdown and bereavement of loss, financial poverty, as well as the loss of protective features available in a marriage such as emotional and physical support, intimacy, interaction and companionship.

It is clear that the impact of divorce as a transition within a family is multiple, multifaceted and interlinked across a range of social, economic, emotional contexts. Divorce has an impact at various levels, from the micro individual level where individual and families have to cope with the impact of multiple changes that ensue, to the macro level, where divorced families and lone-parenthood are increasingly associated with poverty, poor health, and dependence.

Impact and Outcomes for Children of Divorce

It is not surprising that divorce severely affects children in the family. The transition to a divorced family is often preceded by conflict and tensions between marital spouses. These conflicts provide a difficult environment for adapting to the post-divorce situation. In many families, post-divorce conflicts over children are common and include disagreements over custody, visitation, school decisions and so on. Children are affected by these conflicts situations which often directly involve children and have an impact on their relationships and contact with their custodial and non-custodial parent (Wallerstein et al. 1989, Kline et al. 1991, Ayoub et al. 1999, Dunn and Deater-Deckard 2001, Smart et al. 2001, Welsh et al. 2004). In addition, this conflict also indirectly affects children by diminishing partnerships between parents, reducing parents' emotional capacity to engage with their children and their capacity to parent (Weiss 1975, Burgoyne et al. 1987, Furstenberg and Cherlin 1991, Buchanan et al. 1996). Indeed, most researchers have indicated that children exposed to conflict show higher levels of depression, deviance, substance abuse, distress and maladjustment (Amato and Keith 1991c, Ayoub et al. 1991, Kline et al. 1991, Cherlin 1992, Amato 1993, Mo-Yee Lee 1997, Buchanan et al. 1996, Fergusson and Horwood 1998, Simons et al. 1999, Bream and Buchanan 2003).

Divorce often demands adjustments to multiple changes that can overwhelm children and diminish their capacity to cope. Buchanan et al. (1996) suggest that increasing number of life changes in the lives of children affect their abilities to adjust. These life stresses, which are common to many children of divorce, include poverty, changing homes and neighbourhood, new social environments, changing social roles and responsibilities in the new family context and entry of new members in the family through parental remarriage or re-partnering.

Children feel the loss in the financial status of their family as a consequence of divorce have to live with fewer material goods (Furstenberg and Cherlin 1991). Divorce sharply increases children's mobility rates from their homes and communities in the short term and this mobility tends to be to poorer neighbourhoods due to the economic impact of divorce on families (South et al. 1998). This mobility and physical displacements has an impact on children's social lives and they may resent losing their friends in neighbourhoods and having to re-establish their lives. Furthermore, children face more family transitions through introduction of step-parents, step and half-sibling through remarriage of their parents (Freeman 1996, Amato and Zobolewski 2001). These changes have an impact on the social life and social roles that children play, as family dynamics and relations are renegotiated.

Many researchers have noted that children from divorced families increasingly take up activities of care-giving or sharing of responsibilities within the house to support the parent, encouraging premature maturation in children from divorced families (Weiss 1975, Wallerstein and Kelly 1980, Mitchell 1985, Wallerstein 2000, Smart et al. 2001). Though many children willingly support and help their parents, some children may also be resentful of the additional responsibilities and may indeed struggle to meet the expectations of support that their parents may want from them. The emotional impact of divorce is as significant for children as it is for adults. Many children suffered from fears and anxieties about being rejected by their parents (Mitchell 1985, Smart and Wade 2002). They may be worried about their parents' welfare, available support and resources of the single-parent to meet their needs (Wallerstein and Kelly 1980, Furstenberg and Cherlin 1991, Wallerstein et al. 2002). School-age and adolescents worry and are disturbed by the sexual activity and/or re-partnering of their parents after the divorce (Wallerstein and Kelly 1980, Smart et al. 2001). Furthermore, children of divorce often feel torn between warring parents and face issues of divided loyalties when they are directly and indirectly urged by one or both parents to take sides and are exposed to inter-parental conflict (Ahrons and Rodgers 1987, Furstenberg and Cherlin 1991).

These multiple changes are often linked and aggregate the cumulative impact of changes on children. For example, studies have indicated how loss of pre-divorce financial status affects children's behaviour, their adjustments, academic achievements, self esteem and confidence (Keith and Finlay 1988, Walzack and Burns 1989, Furstenberg and Cherlin 1991, Amato 1993, Morrison and Cherlin 1995, South et al. 1998, Wallerstein 2000).

Children of divorce may struggle to cope with these changes and show lower competencies across a range of developmental outcomes. They are more vulnerable to mental illness and psychological distress (Popay et al. 1983, Amato and Booth 1996). Amato (1993) reported that children of divorced showed lowest well-being scores compared to both bereaved and intact families. The 2001 census reported that children between ages of 0-15 in lone-parent families recorded the second highest relative risk of long term mental illness (ONS 2007a). In many studies, children of divorced seemed to show lower educational achievements and lower competencies, more distress and learning deficiencies as compared to children in intact families (Wallerstein and Kelly 1980, Amato and Keith 1991c, Amato and Booth 1996, Feng et al. 1999). Evans et al. (2001) studied national data sets of children in Australia whose parents had divorced and their findings reported that on average these children received seven tenths of a year less education than children from intact families. They also reported that 48 per cent of children from intact families completed secondary school while the figure is at 23 per cent for children of divorce.

Amato and Booth's (1996) study suggested that children of divorce were significantly more dependent, noncompliant, and unpopular with peers. Studies have also reported that many children of divorce seemed to exhibit problematic behaviour and have difficulties adjusting. These are often reflected in externalising problem behaviour such as delinquency, disobedience, and aggression (Popay et al. 1983, Burgoyne et al. 1987, Grych et al. 1992, Hetherington et al. 1992). Children of divorce also seem to have increased engagement with substance abuse (Needle et al. 1990).

Though a range of risks and negative outcomes are associated with children of divorce, most are able to adjust and are able to adapt to the new family structures and processes. For most children, negative outcomes diminish from about two years after the divorce (Buchanan et al. 1996, Jekielek 1998, Wallerstein et al. 2000). Research in the late 1990s, shows lower negative impact on children.

However, for many children the emotional and psychological impact of divorce may continue long after the divorce and into their adulthood. Often consequences of divorce and impact seem to manifest only in later adulthood. For children, reconciliation with their familial experiences and family conflicts can carry on into their adult lives (Glenn and Kramer 1985, Walzack and Burns 1989, Christenson and Brooks 2001). Wallerstein (2000) suggests that impact of divorce does not occur during adolescence or childhood but reaches a crescendo in adulthood and when they begin searching for life partners.

Outcomes for Adult Children of Divorce

Parental divorce seems to be a predictor for negative outcomes for children even in their adulthood. American studies indicate that adult children of divorce show lower scores on measures of psychological, social, and marital well-being as compared to other adults (Duran-Aydintug 1997, Amato and Sobolewski 2001). Studies have also suggested poorer physical health, more behaviour problems, lesser education and lower financial status for adult children of divorce (Amato and Keith 1991a, Amato and Keith 1991b, Ross and Mirowsky 1999, Amato and Sobolewski 2001). One possible explanation for this is that divorce affects the educational states and choices for children, thus presenting consequences on adulthood (Ross and Mirowsky 1999). Rodgers and Pryor's (1998) review of divorce studies in the UK also indicated that adult children of divorce achieve less in socio-economic terms as compared to children from intact families.

Adult children of divorce also seem to experience more emotional and inter-personal problems, and have poorer parent-child relationships. In Cherlin et al.'s (1995) study, adult children of divorce showed more emotional problems even up to ages of 33 years and their life courses seemed to diverge considerably compared to adults whose parents had not divorced (Cherlin et al. 1998). Johnson et al.'s (2001) study indicated that adult children of divorce were more emotionally cut off from significant others than adult children from intact families; exhibited more emotional reactivity and achieved less fusion in their interpersonal relationships. Children of divorce in the UK tend to leave home early, report more depressive symptoms and show higher levels of smoking, drinking and other drug use (Hope et al. 1998, Rodgers and Pryor 1998). The relationship of children of divorce leaving home early may be linked with differences in parent-child relationships in divorced families. Some studies have indicated that adult children of divorce seem to have poorer parent-child relationships, lower self-esteem and elevated distress (Amato 1996, Amato and Booth 1996, Amato and Sobolewski 2001). Amato and Booth (1996), in their longitudinal study in the USA found that divorce decreased contact and closeness of adult children with their parents. Buchanan and Flouri's (2001) longitudinal study with 10,686 persons from divorced families in Britain also found that for male adult children and those who experienced public care were less likely to use their family as a first source of emotional support. Amato et al. (1995) reported the results of another study on a national USA sample wherein adult children of divorce offered less support to fathers, gave more but received less support from single-mothers, and gave less and received more support from mothers who are remarried. Adult children of divorce were also less likely to see their parents as supportive and available to help (Amato et al. 1995, Amato and Booth 1996).

Studies of attitudes towards divorce in USA seem to indicate that children of divorce have more liberal attitudes and lower inhibitions towards divorce. Choudhary (1988) suggests that this may be due to perpetuation of mores of divorce from one generation to the next. Research evidence of divorce attitudes does suggest that children of divorce have more positive attitudes towards divorce and are more likely to divorce and easily consider divorce in terms of their own marriages if problems arise (Greenberg and Nay 1982, Glenn and Kramer 1985, Glenn and Kramer 1987, Amato 1996, Feng et al. 1999). Children of divorce are also more sceptical of marriage. Wolfinger (2003) in his study found that children of divorce were disproportionately less likely to marry after the age of 20 than their peers from intact marriages and more likely to choose other alternatives to marriage such as co-habitation. Children of divorce show more resistant towards marriage, exhibit a lower commitment to marriage and were less optimistic about the successes of their own future marriage (Duran-Aydintug 1997). These attitudes and perceptions of marriage may be affected by parental separation and divorce (Landis 1960, Wallerstein and Kelly 1980, Wallerstein 2000).

Pro-divorce attitudes of children of divorce correlate with demographic data on their own divorce. American data suggest that children of divorce seem to experience more marital or relationship instability in their own marriages (Amato and Keith 1991a, Amato and Sobolewski 2001). Wolfinger's study (2000) supported the the inter-generation view of divorce, and his results showed that children of divorce are in fact more likely to undergo divorce in their own marriages irrespective of economic and educational factors. Wolfinger (2000) believes that multiple family transitions increases the likelihood of poor marital/family outcomes in the marriages of children of divorce. Tallman et al. (2001) in their research on newly married couples over three years concluded that newly married couples where both husband and wife came from divorced families experienced most deterioration in their relationship and communication patterns, over time. They suggest that persons from divorced families incorporate feelings of mistrust by their socialisation process and through their observation of their parents. However they also suggest that this socialisation is not permanent and that adults can and do partake in re-socialisation processes, particularly when their partner is able to foster it. This is also supported by Amato's (1996) explanation of transmission of inter-generational divorce where higher divorce rates between adult children of divorce may be attributed to inter-personal problems, poor modelling of dyadic behaviour from parents, and predisposition to mistrust and lack of commitment, rather than attitudes or socio-economic status. Amato and Cheadle (2005) in their comparison of divorce and child well-being over three generations concluded that the effects of divorce on children does not necessarily decrease over time and in fact divorce can impact children who are not yet born. They explain that divorce among grandparents can present outcomes for grandchildren who were not born at the time of grandparent divorce. The researchers suggests that effects of divorce in the first generation can in fact extend up to three generations in terms of marital quality, marital discord, divorce, lower psychological tension and poor parent-child relationships. This is consistent with research that suggests long term continuing effect of divorce on children.

This intergenerational transmission of divorce seems to emphasise social learning theories that children of divorce learn patterns of behaviour, and communication from their divorced parents which may not necessarily support family processes in a married family unit.

While most studies seem to indicate the high likelihood of negative outcomes for children of divorce, most children of divorce do not exhibit the pathological picture suggested by these studies. There is increasing evidence that in spite of difficulties that can follow well into the adulthood, most children cope and show positive adjustments (Vance and Sanchez 1998, Wallerstein 2000, Hetherington 2003, Kelly 2003, Neale and Flowerdew 2003). Cherlin (1992) seems to support this view and notes that while divorce does seem to trigger an initial period of stress, but children can and do adapt to a normal course of development over time and only a few children experience long-term psychological problems.

Children are capable of self righting themselves and develop competencies and confidence even in 'at-risk' conditions (Howard et al. 1999). Wyman et al. (1999) and Cherlin (1992) suggest that the risk of maladjustment and negative outcomes for children is not the same as actual maladjustment and negative outcomes. Thus, even though impact of divorce on children is substantial, many mediating and protective features operate within children's contexts to provide them with resources and opportunities to develop strategies to cope with adversities.

Resilience and Ecological[1] Contexts of Children

It is clear that parental divorce affects children as their development is embedded in the family and social systems. These systems present the framework which children interact with and use their own agencies to dynamically interact with these systems. These systems define particular contexts for children and present risks as well as opportunities/protective features. As explored earlier, though children are exposed to significant risks in the context of divorce, many children cope positively. Thus while the context of divorce exposes children to many vulnerabilities and risks; children's resilience or protective factors in the environment may mitigate these risks. This concept of resilience can be usefully employed to understand processes

---

1 Ecological contexts throughout the book refers to Bronfenbrenner's model of bioecological systems comprising of the micro system, meso system, exo system, macro system and chrono system.

through which parental divorce produces risks and protective factors for children within their social and developmental environments (Strohschein 2005).

Resilience refers to a dynamic process of encompassing positive adaptation within the context of significant adversity (Luthar et al. 2000). Risks in the environments can undermine coping or resilience of children, while protective factors or opportunities in the environment increase the likelihood that a child will resist or recover from exposure to adversities (Newman and Blackburn 2002). Risk is indicative of environmental factors which singly or in combination limit a child's ability to thrive. Protective factors on the other hand, are internal and external factors that can help negotiate risk factors and promote coping. These can include factors that reduce risk, reduce negative chain reactions, promote positive self esteem and efficacy, and/or provide new relationships or directions in life.

Children who are able to negotiate the risks present in the environment of divorce through support and protective factors may be more likely to cope with the changes and adversities presented by divorce. Conversely, children whose environments are fraught with risk factors may find it more difficult to cope. Though individual children's capacities and qualities are important in terms of resilience, environmental factors can also affect resilience and can aid and support positive child development. These protective environmental factors can imbibe a range of systems, and influences. To further conceptualise these risks and protective factors in children's environments, Bronfenbrenner's (1979, 2004) model of ecological systems for child development can be usefully employed (see Figure 1.1).

Bronfenbrenner's model suggests that child development is shaped by four nested systems with which children interact directly or indirectly. The inner most system represents the micro system which involves places, persons, and situations with which the child interacts directly. These interactions include the child's family, friends, school interactions, and so on. The next system is the meso system which includes interactions between the various micro systems of the child. For example: interaction of parents with teachers. The child may not be directly involved but interaction in the meso system has an effect on the child. The exo system is third system which comprises the connections and interactions between the child's micro system and other environmental features. These interactions may not directly involve the child. For example, the interaction of a child's parents at their work places reflects the exo system that can play an important role in the life and development of the child through parents. Finally, the largest unit of the ecology is the macro system which consists of larger social structures such as the national laws and policy, culture and attitudes. The macro system incorporates the overarching ideologies, and organisations of social institutions. Time is another feature of development that has been later incorporated in the model. The chrono system has been used to encompass dimensions of time. This dimension reflects the historical continuity and is able to consider that dynamic development of children through time.

One of the key benefits of this model is that it allows a focus on direct and immediate interactions that impact on child development such as the child's

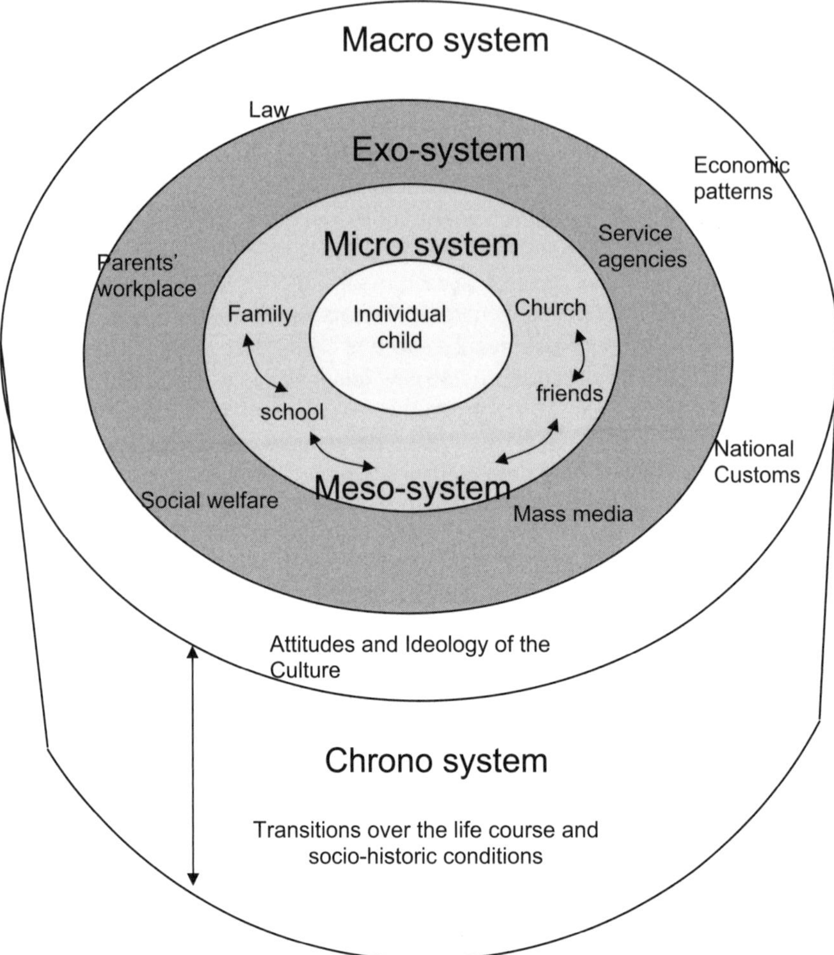

Figure 1.1   Bronfenbrenner's ecological system of child development (adapted from Parquette and Ryan, 2001; Hutchins and Sims, 1999)

interaction with his/her parents, peers, and school systems, as well as the more distant cultural environment, such as the political or economic systems (Gabarino et al. 1982). The model recognises that children develop in a dialectical and transactional process where care-giving systems and contextual elements influence children's development and experiences (Wyman et al. 1999) and essentially enables an understanding of how the whole society functions and contributes to child development. Within this understanding of children's ecological system, resilience in terms of risks and opportunities that are present for children of divorce can be investigated within each system (Gabarino et al. 1982).

The various risks and protective factors for children of divorce, as indicated through various literature and research are identified below.

Risks and protective factors in the micro system   The micro system encompasses the direct interactions that children have with their environment that can aid or hamper their development. Loving, enduring, trustworthy and consistent relationships provide opportunities for development and resilience building. Subsequently, violence and abuse in the child's micro system present severe risks for children that can greatly undermine their capacity to cope.

For children of divorce, as explored previously, conflict associated with divorce (pre and post) presents considerable amount of changes, conflict, inconsistency and incapacity that has an impact on the nurturing environment. Divorce directly affects the relationships that children have with their parents (custodial and non-custodial). Divorce also affects parents capacities and availability for children. In addition, changes in housing, schools etc have a direct impact on children's micro systems. All these present risks for children. In addition, children of divorce are exposed to a high number of transitions and this affects their psychological well being and long term adaptation (Amato and Zobolewski 2001). This is significant as it is not 'which' risks the child has encountered but rather 'how many' risks the child is exposed to and what protective factors are available for support that can determine children's resilience.

However, in spite of the prevalence of these risks, many protective factors can be fostered to help children cope. Addressing severe conflict situations appropriately is a significant protective factor. For many children in conflict-ridden and dysfunctional families, divorce can, in fact, be a positive development (Nye 1957, Landis 1960, Despert 1962, Hetherington et al. 1978, Wallerstein and Kelly 1980, Jekielek 1998, Morrison and Coiro 1999, Kavemann 2004).

Increased awareness and capacity of single-parents to provide alternative resources and opportunities for their children in the divorced context are protective factors and mitigate negative outcomes for children (Pike 2003). Good quality contact and relationship with non-custodial parent (and absence of inter-parent conflict) has positive indications for children. Good access arrangements and a good relationship with part-time parent which had the blessings of the custodial parent lead to better acceptance of the divorce, less stress and happier outcomes (Hess and Camara 1979, Wallerstein and Kelly 1980, Rowlands 1981, Walzack and Burns 1989, Simons et al. 1999). In addition, other family members, particularly grand-parents can be a great source of support to children. Buchanan and Flouri's research on grandparents' role and involvement in child well-being indicates that grandparents can serve as a protective factor for children, particularly for adolescents in non-intact families and can assist in better adjustments for children (Buchanan 2008).

Finally, open communication with children to help them understand the meaning and processes of divorce is also a protective factor. Recognition of children's ability to understand, enabling them to express themselves and be involved in decision making process, agencies and supports positive coping for children (Wallerstein and Kelly 1980, Luther 1991, Maundeni 2002, Hawthorn et al. 2003, Stewart 2003, Banyard and Canter 2004, Buchanan and Ritchie 2004). However, for many families this is challenging and few children feel able to get information about the divorce and ask questions (Dunn and Deater-Deckard 2001, Hawthorn et al. 2003).

In addition, children's access to other sources of support in their micro environment such as surrogate families of friends or extended family support can also bolster their resilience to cope (Wallerstein and Kelly 1980, Buchanan et al. 1996). The presence of grand parents and their interaction with children of divorce can also be particularly useful in reducing adjustment difficulties for children in non-intact families (Buchanan 2008).

Risks and protective factors in the meso system   The meso system reflects the relationships and connections between the different micro systems. Stronger positive connections and links between the range of diverse micro systems of the child can serve as protective factors, for example: strong connections or communications between the child's family and the child's school, the child's family and child's play group, relationships between the child's parents and extended family can serve as protective factors for children.

Within the divorce context, inter-parental conflict can have an impact on parents' communication with each other. Divorce also results in loss of contact with in-laws and this can indicate a weakening of relationships between sets of parents and extended family relatives. These present as risks factors or lower the protective links in the children's development system.

Nonetheless, management of conflict and good inter-parental communication can serve as protective factors. Good communication links between parents and schools, particularly in the context of divorce can also support children's development by sharing concerns and strategies for the child's welfare. Strong links between extended families and parents can also bolster parental capacity and enrich the child rearing environment.

Risks and protective factors in the exo system   The exo system includes situations and contexts which affect parents or other significant adults in ways that can help them to cope or diminishes their opportunities or resources. Thus parents or significant carers' involvement and the quality of interaction with their child/ ren can suffer in situations where they face work stresses, inflexible working, or unemployment. Within the exo system, risks or protective factors can also be implicated in decisions that affect the child's environment directly, for example: changes in environmental setting such as parks which the child accesses.

Risks factors in the exo system, for divorced parents, are inherent in the difficult context and changes that divorced parents have to navigate in terms of housing, social roles, finances, etc. As discussed, divorced spouses have to make a variety of changes and adjustments in the legal, financial, emotional, and social contexts.

These issues have an indirect impact on children by diminishing parents' capacity and availability for parenting. Decisions made by parents regarding changes in housing etc also have an impact on children and their micro system.

Some protective factors can include links with spiritual and faith systems that help divorced persons to cope with the emotions of divorce and help find meaning to the divorce event (Krumrei et al. 2009). Social capital and resources available to parents and carers can also serve as protective factors. Social capital is a useful concept to understand the ways in which community, cultural and social, resources within the social environment are available for families and children. Social capital refers to connections among individuals and composes of social networks based on the norms of reciprocity and trustworthiness that arise from them (Putnam 2000). Social environments are important as they also promote positive family environments and help develop capacities of individuals. Halpern (2005) and Putnam (2000) also record that individuals in communities with more networks and social capital gain more economic and educational benefits. Good parenting and cohesive communities also enhance social capital for families and can present better outcomes for children (Coleman 1987, Edwards et al. 2003).

Risks or protective factors within the macro system   The macro system reflects ideologies or cultures that can impoverish or improve children's micro systems, meso systems or exo systems. Thus political support and policies that can help support parents and parenting are regarded as protective factors in the macro system; whereas racists or sexist values that demean parents and children, reflect risks in the macro systems Thus lack of support services, lack of appropriate job opportunities, lack of child care arrangements for single parent families, all present risk factors as they trap divorced and single families in poverty.

Nonetheless, positive changes in legislation that are geared towards meeting the needs to single parent families are positive factors. Changes in legislation that integrate services for children and families can be protective for single parent families. Finally, decrease in negative attitudes towards divorce and improved management of divorce in the culture can serve as protective factors as they do not stigmatise children and also make support available within the larger culture (Amato and Keith 1991a, Faust and McKibben 1999).

While some of the ways in which systems interact for children of divorce is outlined, it is important to note that these are interconnected and dynamic. Positive supportive networks in the community and family (micro, meso and exo), wide web of positive relationships in the micro system, low levels of conflict, positive direct communication with children and protective policies for divorced families and children are protective factors. Risks factors include high parental conflict, risk of abuse, lack of support and networks, stigmatisation, poverty and multiple changes.

Many characteristics of individual children, families and communities can enhance systems and their interactions. Communicative, friendly, and humorous children seem to be able better able to access support around them (Hetherington

2003). Similarly, families and communities that are characterised by long-term relationships, family cohesion, educational aspirations, mutual support, religious involvement, strong networks, close and regular meeting with friends, school and neighbourhoods, seem to implicate better socio-economic adjustments and outcomes for children (Furstenberg and Hughes 1995).

However, it is also important to note that for different families, risks and protective factors will differ based on the specific dynamics within the family and community within which they are embedded. Though these risks and protective factors identified provide a broad understanding of the various environmental factors that matter for children in their ecological environments, they do not consider the specific context of children from other ethnic groups.

Most of the research on impact, resilience and coping inform the development of children in western contexts but not for children whose familial, social, and cultural systems may differ from western norms. For most children from other ethnic groups, contexts of inequality and discrimination shape their experiences and may present different risks and protective factors within the macro, exo, meso and microcontexts. In addition, experiences of immigration and histories of family migration can have an impact on their adaptation, development and availability of resources that can be accessed. The histories of migration also shape the intergenerational resources, social connections and social capital available to children of migrant and minority ethnic communities. It is within these contexts that parenting and care arrangements are determined and they may differ from western mainstream families. What impact do these have on the experiences of development for children of divorce? Risks of poverty, discrimination, lack of services, loss of social capital, which are identified as risk factors may exist for minority ethnic families. How do these risk factors affect children of divorce in these communities? What are the protective factors that are present and how do risks and protective factors interact for children of divorce from minority ethnic communities ? What is then the impact of divorce on children of divorce from minority ethnic communities? The following chapter considers the ecological context of British-Indians as a distinct ethnic group in the UK towards identifying their specific ecological context and their interactions with the system.

Summary

This chapter outlined some of the discourses of divorce through history. Divorce was previously regarded as a deviant or pathologised family form. However, more recent perspectives consider divorce as a process through which the family changes.

Though divorce is common now, it facilitated a shift from the traditional married family form. This shift, arguably, has been influenced by changes in the modes of production, cultural contexts and women's participation in labour. However, due to the centrality of the family unit, transitions in the family present significant impact for individuals as well as the larger macro and political context. Divorced and lone-parent families are identified as being vulnerable to poverty, have limited access, flexibility and participation to labour opportunities and show high rates of dependence. This reflects the impact of divorce individuals and families. Divorcing spouses, particularly women, have to contend with the multiple impact of divorce across many dimensions of their lives: physical, emotional, social, legal, and financial.

These various dimensions and levels of impact also affect the development of children of divorce, directly and indirectly. Most studies indicate the high risks and multiple negative outcomes for children of divorce. For many children, the impact of divorce is long standing and even affects their adult life outcomes and opportunities. However, this picture is not complete. Many children cope positively and show high resilience. This positive coping is considered within the notion of resilience of children of divorce and is discussed by considering the various risk and protective factors that are present in children's environments that mediate the effects of divorce. Bronfenbrenner's ecological model is used as a framework to identify the various levels and interconnections of the social systems that influence development of children. Risks and protective factors are considered within these social systems to understand impact and outcomes for children.

Inter-parental conflict, diminished parenting capacity, and the multiple changes that follow divorce, present risks for children. However, various personality factors, familial and environmental systems can mitigate these risks and serve as protective factors. Some protective factors include positive relationships in the family, contact with non-residential parents, involving and communicating with children about divorce, positive involvement of grand-parents, good social networks and social capital in the community.

While literature and research has substantially informed the dynamics of divorce process in western mainstream white communities, these processes for children in minority ethnic families whose socio-cultural contexts are different, are unknown. It is likely that the various protective and risks factors interact differently within the British-Indian context due to different histories of immigration, adjustment, adaptation and dynamics of race relations that shape the ecological environments of British-Indians.

Chapter 2

Making Sense of the Past in the Present – History and Culture of the British-Indian Community

British-Indians experience divorce within their particular context, shaped by their ethnicities, migration histories, and particular protective and risk features that are present in their environments. It is essential therefore, to understand the context for British-Indian children and obtain an insight into the development and practices of the British-Indian community. This is important to understand the environmental processes and practices, their rationale and how they influence children's development. This chapter also aims to present the British-Indian community within a larger socio-historical perspective to enable a culturally sensitive paradigm that does not pathologise the community. It is in fact only within this developmental context that the impact of divorce for British-Indian children can be understood. Indeed, Weaver (1999) indicates that for development of culturally sensitivity, four areas of knowledge are important: 1. Knowledge about diversity and difference within groups, 2. Knowledge about history, including histories of oppression, feelings about it, reactions to it, 3. Knowledge about culture that includes wider world views, values, practices, communication patterns and 4. Contemporary realities which indicate current issues, and concerns. This chapter aims to provide a background towards understanding some aspects of these four knowledge forms for the British-Indian community.

This chapter briefly explores the historical development of the British-Indian community, since immigration and the community's current economic, education and socio-cultural profiles. Some cultural, religious and social values that govern British-Indian lives and family organisations are also explored. Particular focus is placed on the cultural adaptation and contemporary family life practices of British-Indians. Subsequently, the implications of divorce in this context in terms of incidence, impact on families and coping is discussed.

British-Indians in the UK

Contemporary British society comprises people from different cultures and ethnicities that contribute to its population demographics. Most official statistics often use categories that combine Indians, Pakistanis, Bangladeshis and people from other South-Asian ethnicities under the larger sub heading of South-Asian. Though White British formed 88.2 per cent of the total population (59.1m), almost

11.8 per cent, that is 6.7m people, belonged to other minority ethnic[1] groups according to the 2001 census (ONS 2007b). South-Asians, as a group, constituted the largest minority ethnic group and form four per cent of the total population in the United Kingdom (UK). The Indian population within this group, constituted 1.8 per cent (1,053,000) of the total population in the UK in 2001(ONS 2006, ONS 2007b).

The Indian group, like other minority groups, has its their own distinct appearance, language, religion and culture, contributing to UK's religious and cultural diversity (ONS 2007b). Most of the Indian population comprises of immigrants originating from two communities in India namely Punjab and Gujarat. Most Gujaratis are Hindus while most Punjabis are Sikhs or Hindus (Hiro 1967, Helweg 1979). The 2001 census also indicated that Hindus (45 per cent) and Sikhs (29 per cent) together formed 74 per cent of the Indian population in Britain while Muslims formed 13 per cent and Christians formed five per cent (ONS 2006a). For this research, only Hindu and Sikh populations are considered as they form the majority of the Indian population and share similarities in their cultural practices (Singh 1998, Pinto and Sahu 2001).

In terms of demographic profile, Indians in the UK have a younger age structure than the majority White British but they are older than most other minority ethnic groups (ONS 2002). The 2001 census indicates that 67 per cent of the British-Indian population are between ages 16-64 while 22 per cent is under 16 years (ONS 2003). More than half of the Sikhs (56 per cent) and 37 per cent of Hindus in the UK were born here. Other Hindus and Sikhs present in the UK were born in India and Africa (ONS 2004c, 2006a).

Migration and post-migration processes have affected the establishment and profile of the different communities in the UK in terms of class, occupational status, age structure and other demographic features (Platt 2005, ONS 2007b). These processes have also shaped the social systems for British-Indians.

Immigration History

The immigrant journey is an important consideration as it marks the history of the British-Indian community. Furthermore, the experiences of these migrants have played a significant role in the organisation of the community.

---

1   In the UK, within most research studies and official statistics, diverse groups by way of ethnicity and race, other than White British are regarded as minority ethnic groups. Nonetheless, scholars such as Tuhiwai-Smith (1999) query western research in terms of their perspectives on knowing and naming indigenous groups and other communities. Some researchers such as Burman et al. (2004) in fact refer to these groups as 'minoritised groups'. In this book, 'minority ethnic' has been used, but, the book throughout acknowledges the racial and historical context, exclusion and discriminatory features within the larger context which minoritises these groups.

Immigration from India to the UK goes as far back as the 18th century. Prior to the First World War, early settlers included students, lascars and nannies of the East India Company. In the 19th century, Indians were free to enter UK as they were British subjects under colonial rule. Initial control of entry of Indians was first introduced in the 1920s to limit the entry of political activists with anti-British ideology from entering the UK. Restrictions to the entry of 'Indians of limited means' was introduced in 1930 after some lascars deserted ship and took up residence in Britain. In 1948, the British Nationality Act was introduced that granted free right to commonwealth citizens to enter Britain in 1947, which increased Indian immigration. Though there were some professional immigrants (mostly doctors), most of the immigrant workers were males from India, Pakistan and Bangladesh who filled the unskilled job positions in Britain (Desai 1963). The main communities that undertook this immigrant journey from the Indian sub continent included the Gujarati community originally hailing from Gujarat (India) and the Punjabi community hailing from Punjab (India) and the Mirpuris from Punjab (Pakistan) (Hiro 1967, Helweg 1979, Kathane 2000). Singh and Tatla (2006) note that political factors, agricultural and economic development patterns in Punjab, were push factors that have led Punjabis to emigrate; not just to the UK but also to other parts of the world. By 1961, over 100,000 Indian and Pakistani nationals were resident in UK. Labour shortages following Britain's post-war economic boom which lasted up to the 1970s prompted these job opportunities for South-Asians in Britain (Shukla 2001).

The 1950s and 1960s were periods of significant immigration, also called mass immigration, particularly from the Caribbean, India and Pakistan. Immigration at this phase indicated chain migration where early immigrants sponsored their family groups and village networks to emigrate (Desai 1963, Singh and Tatla 2006). Immigration control through passport restrictions in India for Indian immigrants was introduced in 1962 through the Commonwealth Immigration Act (Gish 1968, Desai 1963). This was followed by further restrictions in the Commonwealth Immigration Act of 1968 when the government passed legislation to control the entry to Kenyan-Asians (Solomos 2003). However, many African-Asians (Indians who had first emigrated to Africa) emigrated to the UK as refugees following the political upheaval in Africa in the 1970s. Additional controls to curtail immigration from the commonwealth was introduced in the Immigration Act of 1971 (Solomos 2003) and subsequently only family and kin of existing immigrants were allowed into Britain.

Immigration from South Asia is now restricted. Growth among the Asian population since the 1970s has mostly been due to the entry of dependent family members of immigrants in the UK and from the increase of second and third generation families of early immigrants in Britain. The growth of skilled immigrants from South-Asians was noted in the recent past. Of the total net migration to the UK, almost 21 per cent (121,000) migrated from the New Commonwealth countries. Nationals of Asia, specifically from Afghanistan, the Philippines, and India, formed almost half (83,700) of those granted permission to settle and remain in the UK in 2005 (ONS 2007b). The main reasons for settlement were asylum (38 per cent), employment (35 per cent) and reunification of spouses and dependents of British citizens or earlier grant holders (21 per cent) (ONS 2007b). However, it is expected that the current conservative government will introduce further caps on immigration, possibly banning unskilled non-EU workers from working in the UK.

Politics of Race

The history of immigration indicates increasing restrictions to the entry of Indians in the UK. Solomos (2003) highlights the discriminatory nature of these immigration Acts where selective clauses, administrative and legislative, were imposed to specifically control the entry of Asian and African immigrants. As a result of restrictive immigration laws, through the 1970s, it was mostly wives, children and dependent family members of the Indians in Britain that emigrated to the UK (Kannan 1978). Many immigrants, in the face of hostile environment, had initially intended to leave after accumulating some financial resources, but many remained and adapted to life in the UK (Hiro 1967, Helweg 1979, Kannan 1978). Wilson (1978) argues that immigration controls played a significant role in forcing these communities to remain in the UK and call for their families to join them, by reducing their options of entry and exit. This led to familial settlements and generational growth in the UK which affected the return plans of immigrants (Hill 1970).

The politics of immigration and increasing control of entry and exit of Indians through the 1960s and 1970s echoed the race related concerns of the British public. The perceived differences between Asian immigrants and the host society caused much alarm and concern within British society regarding the threat to Britain racial composition (Coleman 1987, Hill 1970). Variations in dress, religious practice, language, personal and food habits set South-Asians as distinct from the British population (Desai 1963, Hill 1970, Kannan 1978). For instance, Sikh men wore a steel bangle, a short sword, uncut hair tied in a turban, a comb in the hair and shorts as part of their religious observance and identity (Singh and Tatla 2006). Immigrants hailing from Punjab and Gujarat spoke Punjabi and Gujarati respectively. Hindu married women wore bindis (red dot on the forehead) and some communities wore specific ornaments to indicate marital status for women (Kannan 1978, Pinto and Sahu 2001). Most Punjabi women wore Salwar and Kameez (Kannan 1978).

South-Asians were subject to severe discrimination and hostility, particularly in the 1950s and 1960s, with violent attacks, politicisation of anti-immigration sentiments and seemingly racist immigration laws (Reitz 1988). Reitz also discusses the sentiment polls in May 1968 where 72 per cent people agreed that Britain should stop the entry of coloured immigrants. Subsequently, in response and in recognition of this discrimination, the Race Relations Act was introduced in 1965 (Solomos 2003). This Act has subsequently been amended to respond to the continued discrimination in 1967, 1968, 1976 and more recently in 2000. However, Joppke (1996) and Solomos (2003) argue that there is inherent conflict of ideology and practice on the government's part. While one the one hand, immigration controls are largely aimed at restricting immigration from the New Commonwealth countries through means that challenge human rights such as virginity tests, denying visa, and fingerprinting. On the other hand, there is a public commitment to promote racial equality with a concern to address discrimination and exclusion of these communities in the UK through Acts such as the Race Relations Act.

These intricate political, social and economic relationships have nonetheless shaped the policies of immigration in the UK as well as marked the beginning of race-relations in Britain (Solomos 2003, Gish 1968). Indian immigration to the UK thus shows different patterns and phases over the decades (Raj 2003). Experiences of hostility, racism and discrimination have also shaped the adaptation of Indians in the UK. This immigration history and adaptation has influenced British-Indian settlement, development of the community and their family.

Continuing Disadvantage

Contemporary studies continue to show disadvantage and discrimination for British-Indians. In spite of high educational achievement, Indians face ethnic penalties (Modood 1997b, Singh and Tatla 2006, Platt 2007). While, first generation immigrants were likely to face discrimination based on lack of education, equivalent experience and qualification, the second generation of immigrant family members, born and raised in the UK, to be disadvantaged as job opportunities available to them do not match their education and qualifications (Clark and Drinkwater 2007, Platt 2007).

Ethnic penalty refers to all sources of disadvantage that a community may face in view of their ethnicity compared to Whites in employment. This ethnic penalty is manifested in terms of employment opportunities offered, pay scales, matching qualification with jobs, and levels of jobs offered. It is associated with second generation Indians for whom barriers of foreign language, qualification and experience are not applicable and may be indicative of deep rooted, widespread and persistent discrimination in the labour market (Clark and Drinkwater 2007, Platt 2007).

Similarly, while Indian women seemed to show high participation in the labour market, they were disproportionally represented in manual and semi skilled work between 1982 and 1994 (Modood 1997b).

Modood et al. (1997) in their research on the extent and character of discrimination in employment found that Asians were likely to perceive discrimination against a job application based on their religion and race. Berthoud (1997) in the analysis of the fourth minority ethnic survey presented that low income Indian families outnumbered the high income Indian families. The survey data also suggest that Indian households were twice as likely as White households to fall below the half of the average income. Platt (2007) outlines the disadvantage Indians continue to suffer:

- Indians face poverty levels which are 10 per cent higher than White British people.
- Indians pensioners were poorer than white pensioners.
- Indians show average levels of deprivation but are overrepresented in the most and least deprived categories.
- Median poverty gaps are higher than average for Indians along with other minority groups.

Coping with Disadvantage

In spite of discrimination and disadvantage, British-Indians have shown great resilience and have achieved commendable successes. The economic outcomes for Indians over time have been positive. In 2005, Indian (36 per cent) men were the second largest group after Chinese (38 per cent) men to hold managerial or professional occupations compared to 27 per cent White men (ONS 2007b). British-Indian men had the highest rates of employment at 73 per cent, second only to White men who showed an employment rate of 81 per cent. British-Indian women showed 53 per cent employment rates; highest within the South-Asian group and third highest compared to all other minority ethnic women. In addition, unemployment for Indian men and women at 10 per cent and seven per cent respectively, was lower than for all other groups except Whites. Indians show high levels of upward mobility (Platt 2005) and differentials in income between Indian and Whites are low (Clark and Drinkwater 2007). Second generation Indians have higher chances of reaching a higher social class (Platt 2007). According to the 2001 census, Indians were more likely to own their property, have similar sources of income as the White British, and be less dependent on benefits and social security than other ethnic groups. Indians along with mixed and other groups are low users of state support and are the lowest users of income support benefits (Platt 2007). The fourth minority ethnic survey in 1994 also indicated that Indians were least likely to be occupants of council homes and only seven per cent said they were council tenants (Lakey 1997).

Indians show high levels of educational qualifications (Platt 2007, Bechar and Husain 2003). Indian men (32 per cent) are most likely to have a degree after the Chinese (34 per cent). Similarly, 23 per cent of Indian women have degrees with only the Chinese (35 per cent) and Irish (25 per cent) women outnumbering Indian women (ONS 2007b). Indian boys and girls are also more likely to achieve five or more GCSE pass grades (ONS 2002). Furthermore, for second and third generation Indians, the difference in education in terms of gender has also significantly reduced. Indian women were more likely to have a degree compared to any other women of their age (Modood 1997c). Participation in post-compulsory education was also higher for Indian men and women (Modood 1997c).

Some of the strategies used to counter disadvantage included building strong community links through the processes of chain migration and participating in the diaspora, selective adaptation which has helped them to maintain positive ethnic identities whilst also participating in the host community. The community links have offered strength and a means of resistance through steadfast adherence to traditional values and practices for British-Indians in a hostile environment of discrimination (Poulter 1987, Joppke 1996). Emphasis on close community ties, strong sense of family values and emphasis on education has also supported positive coping for the community.

Thus British-Indians have maintained positive ethnic identities but also selectively adapted in the UK. These strategies and the contemporary aspects of British-Indian community are considered in more detail.

Chain migration   The processes of chain migration, early settlers enabled others from their villages and families to migrate. Older and newer generations were more likely to live near each other and where job opportunities were present (Desai 1963, Lakey 1997). They were thus able to build close networks and build social capital and support. Putnam (2000) in his analysis of immigrant communities in the USA (German, Italian, Jewish, Polish and Black communities) also suggests that many immigrants use chain migration as a common strategy to conserve social capital as this helps to develop communities which can provide camaraderie, financial help, and political representation.

Housing patterns were also influenced as immigrants depended on their own familiar networks to find accommodation and housing, particularly due to discriminatory and exclusionary practices on the part of British White society i.e. unwillingness to rent and sell to Indians. This often led to overcrowding, bad housing and other social problems where minority groups resided (Hill 1970, Krausz 1971, Lakey 1997). Hill (1970) also notes that many Asians even bought their own house to counter these exclusionary practices. However, due to lack of information and support, many Asians suffered losses within the housing market and were unable to meet the financial liabilities of home ownership. Asians were thus likely to rent out to more fellow Asians to manage this financial liability at higher rates and this also contributed to overcrowding.

Most immigrants' settlement therefore indicate pockets of homogenisation in terms of ethnicity and place of origin. British-Indians are concentrated in different locales as compared to other South-Asians. Leicester and some areas of Greater London, West Midlands and the South East (Lakey 1997) hold greater proportions of Indians. Other South-Asian groups such as Pakistanis and Bangladeshis seem to have settled in other areas of greater London, West London, Humber, Yorkshire and the North West (Bechar and Husain 2003). According to the 2001 census, 52 per cent of Britain Hindu population was settled in London while the remaining were distributed across the East Midlands (12 per cent) and the West Midlands (10 per cent). The majority of the Sikhs, almost 31 per cent lived in the West Midlands and another 31 per cent lived in London (ONS 2004a).

In addition to support for housing, these networks provided community solidarity as well as opportunities for self-employment and a rise to internal economies within families such as grocery businesses (Desai 1963, Bechar and Husain 2003). Edwards et al. (2003) suggests that communities that are bonded through close ties can in fact compensate for material and cultural poverty and make social mobility for individuals possible. Sanders and Nee (1996) in their research on immigrant self-employment and the use of the family as a source of social capital showed that self-employed immigrant Indians in Los Angeles and New York may be encouraged to use familial resources to generate human capital and financial capital for investment. These contribute to low wage ethnic markets, which can be critical in the generation of an institutional environment that promotes ethnic enterprise, and provides ecological conditions for growth of larger firms.

Development of the diaspora   British-Indians continued to maintain close family links with their families in the home country as well as families settled in different parts of the world, thus becoming part of the Indian diaspora.

British-Indians maintain close emotional ties with the extended family structure globally through regular communication, letters, visits, telephones, and sharing social celebrations such as birthdays and weddings (Berthoud and Beishon 1997, Kathane 2000, Halpern 2005, Barn 2008b). Singh (2000) adds that the connectivity with India is also seen in religious and cultural organisations. For example, Sikh religious practices in Britain are very much linked to the religious politics in Punjab in India. Indians in Britain also regularly visit their country of origin. In the minority ethnic national survey, 47 per cent Indians had visited their country of origin within the last 5 years and 32 per cent had visited twice or more (Modood 1997a). This contradicts the idea that movements due to migration affect social capital by destroying intergenerational links (Putnam 2000, Edwards 2003, Halpern 2005). It may be likely that different communities and migratory processes have an impact on how and why social capital is maintained across international contexts. According to the Home Office Citizenship survey in 2001, Asian adults were more likely to keep in regular contact (through visits, letters, emails or telephones) with their extended relatives living elsewhere compared to White or Black families. Asian adults were also three times more likely than White adults to receive help from their extended family suggesting that Asian families may be more close knit (ONS 2004a).

This connectivity within the diaspora has helped British-Indians to maintain their links and connections with their homeland and preserve their cultural heritage and way of life in the UK. According to Shukla (2001), this diaspora embodies the disconnections between place, culture and identity and provides a place for the globalisation of culture. British-Indians can thus remain 'Indian' with regards to their cultural identity whilst also maintaining the practical membership of British citizenship. The diaspora also provides practical solutions and opportunities in terms of marriage, culture, politics and business through integrated global links for Indian immigrants (Singh and Tatla 2006). The diaspora thus serves as an important social network as well as a cultural resource.

Acculturation   British-Indians have adapted to the host UK culture in a manner that has enabled them to retain many cultural meanings and social practices from their home countries as well as respond to the social, economic and cultural forces in the host country (Foner 1997). This type of adaptation where both host and home country features are maintained simultaneously is termed as acculturation. This cultural adaptation is an ongoing process and involves a continuous negotiation for British-Indians in terms of their identities as British and as Indians (Ghuman 1999, Bhopal 2000, Raj 2003). For newer generations, more complex process of identity formation and culture construction may be expected (Bose 2000, Kathane 2000, Banhatti and Bhate 2002). British-Indians need and desire to adapt to host expectations in the UK, as well as retain their own cultural identities has also led to the reconstruction and reinvention of practices (Gans 1997). Thus for example, certain practices such as arranged-marriage have been retained though they have been modified to suit their new context. The acculturation of Asians in the UK has shaped this community that distinguishes it from their home culture as well as the host culture (Farver et al. 2007). British-Indian migrants and subsequent generations may thus be selectively adopting both traditional ways as well as western lifestyle choices in different contexts, and identify themselves in the spaces between the tradition and the western (Patel et al. 1996, Brown 2000, Kalsi 2003, Smart and Shipman 2004, Taylor et al. 2006).

British-Indians show adaptation to the host country in terms of clothing, participation of employment, language and skills (Modood 1997a, Kathane 2000). British-Indians attitudes and values about gender have also significantly changed from the traditional patriarchal conception in India. British-Indians no longer show a preference for sons over daughters (Dosanjh and Ghuman 1997). There have also been changes in gender roles as a result of increase in British-Indian women's employment and education in the UK (Singh 2000, Singh and Tatla 2006). British-Indian women more actively participate in economic activities and tend to be full time workers (Vaughan 1991). Barn et al. (2006) also suggests that Indian mothers are more likely to be in employment and least likely to be housewives. This is a departure from the early immigrant home context in India where the economic opportunities were curtailed for women due to a focus on their domestic and reproductive labour that was unpaid. More gender equality is also noted within British-Indian relations (Berthoud 1997). More Indians incorporate a British Identity. Almost 75 per cent of Indians in the UK identified themselves as British in the 2001 census (ONS 2006). According to the 2001 census, almost 79 per cent Sikhs and 69 per cent Hindus described their national identity as British, English, Welsh, or Scottish (ONS 2004b).

However, British-Indians maintain a great interest in preserving their religious, moral, sexual and social values and practices from their home cultures. Berthoud (2000) suggests that Asians in Britain are driven to preserve many of their culture patterns in Britain due to loyalty to their communities' histories and traditions as well as a means to retain solidarity. Most British-Indians are Hindus and Sikhs and this religious identity remains an important marker of ethnic identity for South-Asians (Kannan 1978, Barn et al. 2006). More than half of the Sikhs and Hindus living in England and Wales in 2001 said that religion was important to their self-identity (ONS 2006). Among the South-Asian population, Hindus and Sikhs are most likely to regard religion to be very important or important (Modood 1997a, Abbas 2003). Becher and Husain (2003), and Barn et al. (2006) comment on how South-Asian religious ideology underpins their individual and communal existence governing and influencing their individual, group, and social lives. However, other researchers indicate that Indians in Britain do not place too much emphasis on religion or to its strict adherence (Beishon et al. 1991, Abbas 2003). It may be that while religious identity and values are important, they are not necessarily expressed through strict adherence to particular religious activity. Religious spaces nonetheless serve as social spaces for the community, offering opportunities to network and build cultural capital and support (Desai 1963, Kathane 2000, Singh 2000).

There is a continued commitment to kinship systems of mutual dependence, extended obligations and family roles (Lau 2000). There is also continued emphasis on respect, sharing and high commitment to parenting and rearing of children (Lau 2000, Barn et al. 2006). British-Indian parents are keen to preserve their culture and transmit it to the following generation. British-Indian ethnicity and identity remains important and the main site through which this is maintained, is through the family and religion centred values such as family solidarity and loyalty (Modood 1997a). The following section provides a closer look at the family to understand the dynamics of the family and the ways in which it is a site for the socialisation and maintenance of these British-Indian values and cultural practices.

Family

Households and family relations For British-Indians, family life is highly valued and characterised by closeness, mutuality of interests, strong primary group controls, and mutual assistance in time of need (Medora et al. 2000). The traditional joint family systems wherein many generations and multiple-related families resided together resulting in large extended families no longer exist, partly due to the fragmentations of family clans as a consequence of migration (Wilson 1978, Kannan 1978, Singh and Tatla 2006). Thus, for some families, contact with grandparents and other members of the extended family can only be maintained across borders through means such as letters, telephones and visits (Berthoud 2000, Barn et al. 2006). However, for newer generations, it is likely that their extended families are also present in Britain. Around 14 per cent of Indian families are multigenerational (ONS 2007a) and 13 per cent of Indian families have children and their paternal grandmother resident with them (Berthoud 2000). In addition, almost 22 per cent of Asians in the fourth ethnic minority survey cared for their parents who were resident in Britain and Indians lived with their adult children in higher proportions than other groups except for Pakistani/Bangladeshi (Berthoud and Beishon 1997). British-Indian households are therefore slightly larger than the White majority at 3.3 persons per household (ONS 2007b).

Though the traditional family structures do not persist, many traditional values such as interdependence, and care of children and elderly are highly valued among British-Indians. In South-Asian families, the elderly are cared for within the family and until recently, it was unacceptable to send the elderly to nursing or care homes (Kathane 2000). This care ethic may also be reflected in the household composition. This may indicate a continued commitment to inter-dependence and mutual co-existence where possible.

Though there may be increasing opportunities for availability of extended family members in Britain itself, particularly for subsequent generations, it is unlikely that the traditional joint family model will be revived. Beishon et al. (1998) indicated that Indian families in Britain prefer for their children to live independently from them once they are married but to live close-by. This proximity seems to be a likely compromise to enjoy independent living whilst also providing opportunities to rely on the collective effort within extended family members to socialise and rear their children imbibing traditional values and norms through practice (Helweg 1979, Becher and Husain 2003).

Marriage   Marriage is a key institution for Indians and the commitment to marriage is highly valued. British-Indians' marriage rate was around 72 per cent while their divorce rates were low at three per cent according to the Households survey, presented in Berthoud and Beishon (1997). According to the fourth ethnic minority survey, 1997, Indian persons were mostly likely to be married and 72 per cent of all Indians in the sample indicated their status as married. Two thirds of Indian women in Britain were in a marriage partnership before the age of 25 years (Berthoud 2000). Indian women also show high fertility rates at 83 per cent compared to White women at 76 per cent. Cohabitation rates were less than four per cent in the Indian community, according to the 2001 census (ONS 2007c). However, Indian families in the UK are more likely to co-habit than any other Asian community and this was statistically significant for 25-39 years age group (Owen 1997). Family arrangements such as cohabitation and children born out of marriage are considered unstable and shameful among South-Asians (Beishon et al. 1998).

Hiro (1967) suggested that British-Indian family life in the UK bore great resemblance to the practices of family life in India and were congruent to the Indian cultural values associated to family and marriage. This is reflected in similarities in family practices such as arranged-marriages, living arrangements with the family of the groom and paternal grandparents, and patriarchal attitudes within married couple relationships where men retain authority over women and are prime decision makers (Beishon et al. 1998, Berthoud 2000). However, it is important to note that many of these practices have modified over time as explored in the previous section on cultural adaptation.

Among British-Indians, the process of arranged-marriages has been retained (Beishon et al. 1998, Ghuman 1999, Berthoud 2000, Raj 2003). Arranged-marriage is a process of arranging marital alliances between people through collective decision-making by family members (FCO 2008). This practice is believed to be a significant feature of continuation of Indian culture (Bhopal 2000). Arranged-marriages are a means by which ethnic identity and family cohesion is maintained (Modood et al. 1994). For many first generation migrants, arranged marriages were conceived across continents and through extended relations located within the diaspora (Kannan 1963, Singh and Tatla 2006). Harris (2000) suggests that these ties helped to promote self-efficacy, esteem and cultural identity for Indians in Britain. However, more recently, as the British-Indian population has grown and their children are increasingly British-born and socialised here, marriages are increasingly arranged and conducted between other Indians in the western context rather than with Indians in India (Harris 2000, Singh and Tatla 2006). However, this process of arranged-marriage has become less common and only 56 per cent of Sikhs and 36 per cent of Hindus, over 35 years of age, reported having had arranged-marriages where their parents chose their partners (Kathane 2000). Berthoud (2000) also suggests that Asians who were born here or arrived in Britain as young children were less likely to feel that their partner had been chosen by their families rather than by themselves. However, close involvement of parents and relatives in marriage decision continues (Kathane 2000). Beishon et al. (1998) and Harris (2000) point out that arranged-marriages in Britain among the Indian group follows a more negotiated process where young persons have a say in the matter. Brah (1999) comments that many young British Asians have faith in the arranged-marriage process and see it as a joint undertaking. This challenges the media portrayal of bullying Asian parents who force their children into arranged-marriage. It is also important to note that arranged-marriages are not the same as forced-marriages where consent of young people is not considered (FCO 2008).

Maintaining this ethnic identity and culture through marriage is important to many British-Indians. It is for this reason that Indians along with other South-Asians in the UK are least likely to enter an inter-ethnic marriage. Only six per cent of Indians, had married someone outside the South-Asian group. However, attitudes towards mixed marriages vary and in fact one in five British men of Indian/African Asian origin and one in ten British women of Indian/African Asian origin were married to Whites (Berthoud 2000, Beishon et al. 1998).

Parenting and socialisation of children   The family is also a central unit through which children are socialised. Parental authority is highly regarded in the South-Asian community (Modood et al. 1994). However, this parental authority does not necessarily represent an authoritarian style of parenting. Brah (1999) comments that Asians parents tend to be portrayed as authoritarian, and conservative which is not necessarily true and are mainly stereotypical assumptions. Barn et al. (2006)

comment that South-Asian parents are no more likely to use punitive methods to discipline their children than parents of other ethnicities. South-Asian parents use a variety of styles in combination and the use of physical punishment is only seen as a last resort (Barn et al. 2006). South-Asian immigrants, as parents, increasingly adapt a combination of parenting styles from their home and host cultures (Barn et al. 2006, Farver et al. 2007). British-Indian parents are, nonetheless, keen to instil cultural values of respect for parents and elders, teach them their ethnic language, promote positive behaviour and limit lies, theft and deceptive behaviour in their children (Helweg 1979, Modood 1997a, Barn et al. 2006). Second and third generation Indians in Britain are very likely to be bicultural and bilingual (Modood et al. 1997, Ghuman 1999, Singh and Tatla 2006). Parents are likely to refer to religious and moral themes to discipline and correct bad behaviour (Barn et al. 2006). These methods may also be a means of imparting cultural and religious education.

South-Asian parents do have concerns over the westernisation of their children in British society (Kannan 1978, Dwivedi 2002a, 200b, Singh and Tatla 2006, Barn et al. 2006). Children of immigrant families, especially girl children, may face more supervision and stricter parenting rules, meant to protect them from the influence of westernisation to preserve strongly held traditional cultural values (Kannan 1978, Handa 1997, Mohammad-Arif 2000).

Parenting of children is also supported by extended close relatives who provide assistance for child rearing and reduce maternal stress (Harris 2000). Harrison et al. (1990) also comment that minority ethnic families operate within extended family systems with role flexibility as it enables coping with stress and problem solving. Buchanan and Flouri's research has highlighted the positive association of involvement of extended family members, such as grand-parents with better outcomes for adolescents (Buchanan 2008). Barn et al. (2006) and Mohammed-Arif (2000) have noted that the involvement of grand-parents and other relatives in the parenting of children and in the transmission of cultural values to children, is valued by South-Asians. Indians, like other South-Asian groups are very protective of their children and prioritise their care and protection (Pettigrew 2003, Barn et al. 2006). They also exhibit a great degree of trust in extended family members in providing care and support for their children and are reluctant to leave the care of their children to people they do not know.

South-Asian parents also highly emphasise education for their children and prefer mainstream education is very much valued and preferred to religious education (Singh and Tatla 2006). Education is a high priority for South-Asians who see it as a means out of poverty and to combat racism, discrimination and exclusion (Kathane 2000). Parents are keen on high achievements for their children and there is often high pressure on their children to perform well in school (Beishon et al. 1998, Brah 1999, Mohammad-Arif 2000, McLyod at al. 2000, Abbas 2003, Barn et al. 2006). Barn et al. (2006) also suggest that Indian families are more likely to support their children's education through tuition and provision of study aid materials than other South-Asian, Black or White ethnicities.

The family is thus a central aspect of British-Indian community and plays a key role in preserving the values that are held dear in the community. Adherence to these values by community members in many ways defines and shapes the community. As a result of the high commitment to marriage, socialisation of children, inter-dependence and close knit family structures, divorce in Indian families is frowned upon. Divorce may be seen as a threat that can jeopardise this way of life, and the realisation of familial principles and values that are highly regarded. However, divorce, though rare, does occur in the British-Indian context and may present particular implications for divorced families in the community. Divorce is not an acceptable family form in the community as it challenges the married family norm. Divorce and its implication are now considered in the community to highlight the difficulties that persons who divorce in this community face.

Divorce in the British-Indian Family

Incidence   According to the 2001 census, divorce in British-Indian communities was lowest at 10 per cent (ONS 2006). This married-family structure is striking in the mainstream context of UK where family structures have been changing with increasing cohabitation, divorced families, step-families and lone-parenthood (ONS 2007b). Divorce rates (in the UK) stood in the order of 11.9 per thousand marriages in 2007 (ONS 2008b). Around 45 per cent of marriages in the UK are expected to end in divorce (ONS 2008a).

According to the 2001 census, the incidence of lone-parenthood was also the lowest for Indian families: only 10 per cent of Indian families were lone-parent families (ONS 2006, ONS 2002). Other Black and Black Caribbean families recorded highest rates of lone-parenthood at 55 per cent and 45 per cent respectively. Only nine per cent of children in British-Indian families were from lone-parent families (ONS 2003).

Cultural and societal norms reflected in collective values, familial organisation of the British-Indian family, high value attached to marriage, importance of parenting roles, as discussed, may play a role in making divorce unacceptable and difficult in the British-Indian family (Chandrasekhar 1954). However, as Younge (2000) noted, though divorce is not preferred among Asians in the UK, there are Asian couples who do divorce to improve their lives. Singh and Tatla (2006) also comment that divorce is becoming more accepted in the British-Sikh society. In the British-Indian context, where divorce is rare and largely unacceptable, the reasons and consequences of divorce can present different risks and protective factors.

The context and consequences of divorce in the British-Indian community   While, the consequences of divorce, as suggested by other researchers are applicable to British-Indian families, their location as a minority ethnic group in the UK, their acculturation patterns and their migrations histories, present particular issues for British-Indian divorced families.

As illustrated, marriage remains a central institution for British-Indian and family forms that deviate from this are rare and largely unacceptable. Divorce leads to significant stigma, loss of honour in British-Indian families and implies a failure on the part of individuals resulting in the end of marriage (Helweg 1979). While, stigmatisation of divorce, disapproving attitudes by society and disadvantages of lone-parent families have been studied in other western contexts as well (Popay et al. 1983, Ahrons and Rodgers 1987, Gerstel 1987, McKendrick 1998, Fawcett 1999). The nature and experience of this stigma in the British-Indian community may differ from that of other western communities due to concepts of family honour, social structures and relations as well as emphasis on certain cultural values.

Divorce in Indian communities can result in strong stigmatisation and marginalisation of individuals or family members from the divorced family, especially for women (Amato 1994, Helweg 1979). Singh's (1998) is one of the few studies that explored lone-motherhood in South-Asian families and illustrated the extreme effect of stigma of divorce and of lone-parenthood. The divorced status in the British-Indian community is severely looked down upon, and the effects of stigmatisation is significant resulting in feelings of guilt and shame, loss of identity and social opportunities for divorced people (Amato 1994, Singh 1998). Other researchers have also reported on the pervasive nature of this stigma on divorce which often results in condemnation of the divorcing couples by their parental family and siblings (Ranga Rao and Sekhar 2002, Goel 2005). Goel (2005) adds that this stigma, particularly affects women and extends beyond the divorcee to her parents, siblings, and children, as supposed negative traits of the divorcee as ascribed to siblings and children, making every member of the divorced family less desirable. People may gossip that the parents did not raise their daughter correctly, and this is why the divorce occurred. Like their British counterparts, British-Indian divorced women were more likely to be lone-parents than men. There were only seven per cent of Indian children in lone-mother households and one per cent of Indian children in lone-father households in the UK in 2001 (Box et al. 2001).

Divorced families along with other family forms such as cohabitation are considered to be unstable for children in the British-Indian community (Bieshon et al. 1998, Goel 2005). This sentiment is also shared by British people in general. According to the 2006 British attitudes survey, 29 per cent adults in the survey thought that married couples made better parents and 49 per cent thought marriage was more financially secure than other forms of partnerships. However, the British Attitude Survey also reflects that 66 per cent adults surveyed felt that there is little social difference in living together and being married. It is unlikely that British-Indians share a similar opinion due to the high sanctity of marriage in the community.

National studies have indicated the likelihood of poverty among divorced families. For British-Indian families, their minority status, fragmentation of family structures due to migration and issues of racism may impose additional vulnerabilities for single-parent families in this community. Researchers note the vulnerability of Asian women in a patriarchal community combined with the racist society creates a uniquely difficult set of circumstances for immigrant women (Roy 1995, Menjivar and Salcido 2002, Ahmad et al. 2004). Immigrant South-Asian women may suffer due to loss of familiar support systems, language and culture differences and access to resources (Wilson 1978). Singh (1998) noted that most women (62 out of 73 divorced/separated Asian lone-mothers) did not receive any maintenance from their husbands as they did not know of it and had lost contact with their husbands. Wilson (1978) notes how the immigration process fragments the familiar systems that women are used to in their home countries and exposes them to new systems which they are not familiar with. Singh's (1998) study also highlights the vulnerability of Asian women within the family. Singh recorded the reasons of separation and divorce to include violence, alcoholism by husband, neglect by husband, infidelity and abuse by in-laws. Violence was reported by 44 out of 73 divorced/separated women. Some mothers in Singh's (1998) study believed that domestic violence was part of the Asian culture and hence put up with it while others remarked that divorce and domestic violence are likely to be hidden and blame is generally attributed to women's actions or inactions within the Asian community. Lone-mothers also reported mental and emotional problems ranging from loneliness, stress, depression, feeling unable to cope, guilt and even suicidal (Singh 1998). Goel (2005) suggests that South-Asian immigrant women may get trapped in the phenomenon of 'culture freeze' where they idealise Indian values of the era in which they left India. They may perceive changes in modern India as an unfortunate result of westernisation and subsequently fight harder to resist the western culture and preserve traditions and rituals as they did in their home country.

For Asian lone-mothers, lone-parenthood and divorce also result in an experience of confusion and culture conflict (Singh 1998). Asian lone-mothers often have to negotiate their lives across two cultural contexts and many are able to selectively adapt the values of both home and host cultures (Singh 1998, Guru 2009).

Thus while much of the context of divorce such as poverty, stigma as well as attitudes towards marriage are shared between British-Indians and the larger British society, there are also differences in structures and approaches that can impact on the nature of the experience of divorce. For British-Indians, divorce is highly resisted and consequences of divorce are severe which can be exaggerated due to particular issues of access, availability of social support systems and institutional frameworks and discrimination.

The context of divorce is different for British-Indians in terms of the risks that are present in such family transition. As a result, divorce is highly resisted in the community. Nonetheless, some divorces do occur among British-Indians. It is likely that divorce in this community may be prompted by high conflict scenarios (Helweg 1979, Ranga Rao and Sekhar 2002). Gohm et al. (1998) suggests that in collectivist cultures of anti-divorce sentiments and pro-marriage norms; and where divorce rates are low, children benefit as divorce in such contexts occurs in high conflict scenarios and more support may be available in collectivist cultures. It may be the case that the collectivism of South-Asian families may lessen the impact on children due to presence of extended support networks and adults (Medora et al. 2000).

The collectivism among British-Indians has indeed been a source of resources and strength for migrant families. It has helped build businesses, promote ethnic identity and provided emotional support as well as practical support (Medora et al. 2000, Srinivasan 1995). It is clear that British-Indian families and community show high regard for collective values, interdependence in the family and emphasise parenting and education. These features indicate high cultural and economic resources that contribute to greater social capital and may underpin the development of the British-Indian community (Lareau 1987, Portes 2000, Edwards et al. 2003). Such support systems and high social capital may perhaps provide resources and support for divorced British-Indian families. Some studies have reported on the support that Asian divorced and lone-mothers are able to generate resources within their family in the UK and in India (Singh 1998, Ranga Rao and Sekhar 2002).

Social capital, however, largely relies on establishment of social networks in an environment of trust, use of effective norms and sanctions (Coleman 1988). These norms and sanctions within a collectivist society reinforce action in the interest of the collectivity through status, honour, social support and other rewards that strengthen families (Coleman 1988). It can be argued that strong trust and networks are generated and maintained within the British-Indian community through their particular cultural and religious identity. Single-parent families in the British-Indian community may be perceived as having acted against the norms of the community by divorcing. These divorced families in the community therefore suffer loss of status, honour and stigma and their access to resources and capital may become limited. Thus, in Singh's (1998) study on Asian lone-mothers, while most mothers were likely to receive support from family and friends, the association of blame and stigma with divorce also lead to extended family and relatives feeling angry, hostile and unsympathetic towards divorced women.

On the other hand, social capital can be manifested in different forms and through relations that are formed through different mechanisms (Halpern 2005). For British-Indian single-parent families, if networks within the British-Indian community are compromised due to divorce, networks outside of the community within larger macro environment (Halpern 2005) can be developed to generate support and resources. Indeed, for some South-Asian divorced women, the larger context also provides them with opportunities for growth and presents some positive aspects (Singh 1998, Guru 2009).

In the face of current research and literature, it can be suggested that the British-Indian incidence and experience of divorce may differ from that of mainstream divorce communities. This can be attributed to the particular context of British-Indians which has been shaped by historical processes and continues to be influenced by ongoing cultural processes of adaptation. Against this background, this book aims to inform on divorce as a family transition in the British-Indian community, through the narratives of adult children of divorce. It aims to consider the particular risks and protective factors that are available for children.

The findings also have implications to inform culturally competent policies and practices that regards the specificity of the contexts in which minority ethnic lives are organised. In addition, locating particular risks and protective factors within communities can help to understand the dynamics within communities and support them. This can be particularly significant in understanding how cultures is negotiated by minority groups. Finally, the findings of this study may further inform strategies to support divorced British-Indian families and children, particularly as divorce rates are predicted to rise in this community (Singh and Tatla 2006).

This book, however, does not claim to exhaustively represent all experiences of divorce in British-Indian communities. However, the findings do indicate the diversity of experiences of divorce, the larger cultural and normative attitudes and frameworks towards divorce and how these are informed by historical religious and structures.

Summary

This chapter outlined the historical, socio-economic, religious and cultural profiles of the British-Indian community to provide a context within which the experiences of divorce in the Indian family can be understood. It is clear that the British-Indian community is shaped by the experiences of immigration, presence of racism and discrimination in the UK as well as their adaption to it through close community networks, their selective and bi-cultural adaptation.

The British-Indian immigrant journey was explored and the difficulties and discrimination they experienced were highlighted. Hostility and racism have promoted solidarity among British-Indians to resist discrimination and organise themselves. This solidarity has helped them to develop economies in the early stages of their arrival and influenced their settlement patterns. Their close community links in the home countries have also helped them to develop diasporic links. This has helped in the creation of a community and a space which have enabled British-Indians to retain and maintain their cultural ways and practices.

Though British-Indians are keen to preserve their language, religious and cultural values and many family life practices, they have also adapted and accultured to the British context. They have negotiated and modified many of their practices to suit their lives in the UK including dress, language, participation of women in labour, and modification of practices such as arranged-marriages. The family, however, remains an important site of cultural, social and developmental activity for this community. Strong family ties and collective family values are core constructs of the community. While this community provides support, it also demands adherence to cultural norms and values. Incidences of divorce within the British-Indian context are rare and add another set of complex dynamics and inter-relations in their families and community. Divorce is highly resisted and stigmatised in the community and divorced people face the risk of social exclusion and marginalisation at different levels. Divorced families, however, also receive support from the larger family structures to cope with divorce and consequent family changes.

Within the larger British context, in spite of positive development of the British-Indian community, there is polarity in the development of this community. For British-Indians, as ethnic minorities, there are specific risks, disadvantages and opportunities present in their micro and macro contexts within which these communities are situated. It is clear that migration and structural issues of racism and discrimination have significantly shaped the development and practices within the community. The difficulties of lone-parenthood and child poverty can get exacerbated for British-Indians, and indeed, other minority ethnic families, due to the specific structural and contextual issues.

Though divorced families in ethnic minority communities can indeed feel additionally disadvantaged, collective attitudes within their communities may also be supportive. There are however no studies that have considered risks and protective factors for children of divorce in this community. The study presented in this book addresses this gap. It seeks to analyse the context of divorce, impact, and coping of adult British-Indian children to identify risks and protective factors.

PART II
The Method of Investigation

Chapter 3
The Study and the Challenges

Some researchers have reported that studies with minority ethnic populations are often challenging in terms of gaining access to the population and obtaining their participation. This is exacerbated if the topic or method of study is sensitive to the population. This chapter explores some of the challenges in recruiting participants for this study, particularly since divorce is a sensitive and personal topic.

In addition, details of the study in terms of from whom and how the stories of British-Indians who experienced parental divorce were collected, and analysed are outlined. Socio-demographics of the participants are also provided in terms of their ages, gender, education backgrounds, and professional engagement.

The Research Plan

A qualitative methodology was used to address three primary questions from the perspective of British-Indian adult children of divorce, namely:

- Understanding the context of divorce and exploring their experiences of family life both prior to and after parental divorce, and gain insight into their personal views of marriage and divorce.
- Exploring the perceptions of the impact of parental divorce on physical, social, emotional, financial and educational/career aspects of their lives.
- Exploring narratives of their own coping with the process of parental divorce by identifying coping strategies, resources, support systems as well as difficulties and challenges to coping.

The study was informed by interviews with British-Indian adult children of divorce who volunteered and consented to participate. The data was then analysed to identify significant and recurring themes.

However, due to the sensitive and personal nature of the subject of study, some particular ethical issues were considered in great detail prior to the study.

Ethics

Protecting the identities, anonymity and confidentiality of adult British-Indian children of divorce who participated in the study was a key concern because of the low rates of divorce and the stigmatisation of divorce in the community. All data and contact with participants was therefore conducted in the strictest of confidence. Participant details only remained with the researcher. All data collected from participants were anonymised to remove any identifying features such as names, dates and locations. Pseudonyms have used instead of participant names throughout the book.

Participation was voluntarily sought from the community. Interested persons who fit the criteria were requested to directly contact the researcher to participate in the study. All those who volunteered were details about the study in terms of the expectations and purpose of the study, risks and benefits involved, as well as assurance of anonymity and confidentiality. Data was collected from participants only after they gave their informed consent. Participants were also told that they were able to withdraw at any point if they no longer felt comfortable or had changed their mind.

Selection Criteria

Particular criteria were used to select participants for the study. This was important to define the parameters of the study. The criteria included:

- Individuals who were children of divorced parents and above 18 years of age at the time of the interview.
- Individuals who identified themselves to be of Indian ethnicity.
- Individuals who identified themselves as belonging or identifying with Sikh/Hindu community.

The first criteria of only inviting adults to participate was to minimise psychological distress that may be overwhelming for children. The decision to not interview children was thus made to protect children from any risks and psychological issues that may arise by asking them for their narratives. Mitchell (1985) also believed that interviewing children close to the divorce period may be traumatic and distressful for children and that interviewing at a later stage may, in fact, enable a more balanced view of the divorce, its impact and processes. Many researchers have used adult narratives or narratives of older children and observed that the time lapse between the divorce event and the interviews did not hamper memories and many respondents did remember vivid details of the experience (Wallerstein and Kelly 1980, Mitchell 1985, Wallerstein et al. 2000, Moxnes 2003, Abbey and Dallos 2004).

The second and third criteria were based on the constructionist notions that religion and ethnicity are key elements of identity and socialisation of children (Berger and Luckmann 1966). Furthermore, the literature on British-Indians outlined the importance of ethnic identity and religion in economic participation and social life practices (Abbas 2003, Platt 2005, Platt 2007). The context of ethnicity and religion were therefore considered important. This prompted a focus on British-Indian ethnicity and Hindu and Sikh religious identities. Muslim, Christian and other groups, who also form part of the British-Indian population have been excluded in this study to control ethnicity and religious factors. Hindu and Sikh groups have been combined in this study, not for purposes of comparison

Table 3.1   Recruited participants: Venues of access

Venues of access	No. of participants
Adverts (posters/college webpages, internet blogs)	5
Newspaper	1
Counsellors	2
Personal networks, snowballing, community contacts	13
Total	21

but because they share many cultural and family life aspects. Modood et al. (1994) in their research on exploring ethnic identities with 74 people of South-Asian and Caribbean origin also found that Sikhs and Hindus were more likely to say that they shared similarities with each other than other Asians. Beishon et al. (1998) in their qualitative study, using 68 minority ethnic families, also used a singular category for these two groups for this reason.

Only Indians were considered for this research since many studies have noted differences between South-Asian groups. In the fourth ethnic minority survey (Berthoud and Beishon 1997) as well as Barn et al.'s (2006) study on parenting practices, Indians were distinguished as group from Bangladeshi and Pakistani groups.

Recruiting Participants

Locating participants for the study presented considerable challenges. As outlined earlier, divorce among British-Indians is relatively rare. Furthermore, potential participants could not be easily identified due to the retrospective and sensitive nature of study.

The study was advertised in a variety of venues. These included twelve colleges/universities in London, local Hindu and Sikh Temples (gurdwaras) in London as well as Leicester, emails to Hindu, Sikh, Asian, and Indian societies within student bodies, career centres and university online forums. Adverts were also placed on websites which cater to South-Asian populations, such as www. vivastreet.co.uk, www.clickwalla.com as well as other online pages such as www. gumtree.com. In addition, participation was requested through an advertisement in one popular Asian newspaper (*Eastern Eye*) and two radio interviews (BBC Asian Network, and Club Asia radio) which catered to Asian populations.

Various individuals, community members, college administrative staff, community organisers, Asians community workers, counsellors, priests and management personnel of temples were also approached for assistance in spreading the word about the project and invite participation. This combination of strategies and venues of access yielded results and a total of 21 individuals agreeing to take part in this study.

Approaching community members and establishing personal rapport and contact seemed the best way to establish links and reach potential participants for the research. Establishing these links also made potential participants more likely to consider participating in the research. This may be because in close knit and collectivist societies there is a social expectation to build connections and relationships in order to gain access.

Building these connections also enabled community members to scrutinise the ethical and cultural sensitive practices. When approaching community members, temple officials and others, most had strong opinions on the issues of marriage and divorce. People in the community were very keen to discuss this at a social level and share their ideas on divorce, and what should be studied.[1] These discussions were very important to build rapport and seek support from gatekeepers. The topic of divorce in most cases invoked interest and discussion from individuals in the community and many freely shared their own ideas and thoughts on this.

Some individuals shared concerns about the shifting gender roles and its impact on courtship, marriage and traditional family norms. One community member commented on the changed socialisation and the separation of marriage from intimate relationships.

> Divorce is more common now because children now have access to more sex because of which the novelty of sex after marriage is lost sex.

Indeed, marriage as the only means to form intimate relations and take on parenthood roles has changed. In today's contemporary British society, many family forms outside of marriage exist, for example: cohabitation, single parent families, same sex families and unmarried families. These alternative family forms are not encouraged in the British-Indian context and this comment couches concerns of the westernisation of children and the changing values and commitment to marriage in subsequent British-Indian generations.

Other members also questioned the subject of the study and raised concerns that the study may not be able to incorporate enough diversity of experiences.

> You should study parents of divorce and get the picture from both sides because both parties have to be at fault. You are seeking children's views which is not right because most children live with their mothers and hence take their mothers side. I know a lot of cases where the woman is at fault too …

It is likely that studies have focussed on women's perspectives than men. Indeed, there is limited literature on divorced male British-Indians.

---

1   Please note that community reactions and comments are recalled from researcher's notes during the research process. These comments were not recorded or received as part of the study.

However, many 'gatekeepers' were also resistant to the subject of this research and its negative consequences on potential participants. These gatekeepers often resisted giving their consent on behalf of the participants and refused to promote the research. Community gatekeepers thus introduced dimensions of power in terms of access and knowledge (Grant et al. 1987).

> I know a lot of people and I come across various scenarios. But I don't think they should come to you and you go and reopen their wounds all over again and I will then have to fix it later on. Some people from Channel 4 also contacted me for a programme on divorced couples and I think it is very unfair to exploit their experiences for research.

Many individual gatekeepers did not want the posters inviting for participation to be displayed and did not always provide an explanation for this. In one instance, one member of a temple committee said she would help me with the research but did not let me display a poster seeking research participants in the temple premises as she did not think it would be appropriate.

Some community members also felt that seeking participation would be difficult due to the private nature of the subject and stigmatised notion of divorce in the community.

One Indian shop owner whose business was situated in an area where Indians were highly visible commented

> I know a lot of people who are divorced ... but they won't talk to you. They will say 'it's none of your business – it's their private life' It's very difficult to find people to talk.

Many individuals commented that it was hard to present the topic to families and individuals due to the sensitive nature of the subject. Many gatekeepers nonetheless offered support and assistance.

> It is a sensitive topic. I don't know how to approach the families but I will try.

Thus, in engaging with the community, the researcher was exposed to different degrees of scrutiny about the research project and support was gained after successfully responding to their concerns. Obtaining contact through community members may have also assured participants of the research process and the research person.

In fact, eleven participants responded that that they participated because they were requested to do so by a close or respected member of the community.

> Interviewer: Why did you participate in this study?

> Payal: He's a very dear friend of mine and he said that he'd met you and you
> wanted to carry out some survey and whether I'd like to help out with the survey
> …

In addition, dialogue with community members also provided a wider context to understand divorce in the community, such as contemporary issues surrounding divorce and diverse perspectives on divorce within the community.

Reasons for Participation

Because recruiting participants had been a challenging exercise, participants were asked what had motivated them to participate in the research. One of the most recurring themes for participation was to help the researcher – fourteen participants said that they participated to help the researcher.

> Vikram: I felt a bit sorry for you … because I thought it was quite an admirable
> endeavour and it would be very difficult to find people who would help you
> out.

Some participants indicated that they were motivated to participate to raise awareness and advocate for services for children in the community who become marginalised on account of parental divorce. Seven participants thought it was an important study.

> Divij: … because it could be valuable research and if I could do something that
> could help come out with some new knowledge or something, then that's good.

Though many researchers have highlighted difficulties in accessing participants in minority ethnic communities, researchers such as Culley et al. (2007) and Eide and Allen (2005) have also commented on how community rapport can aid access to participants and subsequent data collection. This research suggests that minority community members do participate and are interested in the outcomes of research for policy, practice and advocacy. However, it is important to generate trust in the community context and work in partnership.

Data Collection and Analysis

Rich qualitative data was collected from the participants through interviews. They were asked to talk about their family story, starting from what they knew about their parental marriage, conflict, if any, the divorce, events preceding and subsequent to the divorce as well as the various impacts that parental divorce had on them. Responses to impact in terms of financial, educational, social, emotional and physical states were sought. They were also asked about how they coped, what helped them to cope and what presented difficulties. The accounts were thus not

Table 3.2   Outcomes of interview plan

	Primary interview	Second interview	Total
Personal interview	5	10	15
Telephone interview	16	4	20
Total	21	14	35

linear responses and events, feelings, contexts were intertwined and grounded in specific family histories of each individual. Individual narratives were analysed to identify the contexts of divorce (nature of conflict, the process and progression of conflict to divorce, resistances and support for divorce, type of family structure prior to divorce, significant events), impact of divorce, their coping, involvement in the divorce and other family matters, and so on. These were then compared across all participants to identify recurring themes. These themes have been presented as findings in the following chapters. Specific contexts which revealed alternative processes or a shift from these themes have also been presented.

Due to the sensitive nature of the study, interviews were conducted over the phone or in person, depending on what each participant felt comfortable with. All the interviews were tape recorded after obtaining consent from the participants, transcribed and thematically analysed to identify key themes. All twenty one participants were interviewed and major findings from this data were complied in a preliminary report. This report was shared with fourteen participants in another additional interview. This second interview thus enabled participants to engage with the analysed data, understand what kind of findings had emerged as well as how they would be presented. Some researchers point out that these practices may not be adequate as participants may not be able engage with theory or the research process to check their validity (Glaser 2002, Silverman 2000). However, other researchers have suggested that participants do worry about being mis-represented (Knapik 2006). Participants in this study were informed that their feedback and particularly any disagreements that they have with the analysis or data would be recorded and presented in the findings. None of the participants, however, indicated any such disagreements. While it can be argued that seeking this validation has remained a tokenistic exercise, it has, nevertheless, also been a process of re-engaging with participants with outcomes and findings of the study. In total, 35 interviews were conducted across twenty one adult children. Summary of the interview methods are outlined in Table 3.2.

Profile of Participants

Of the twenty one participants, eleven were Hindu and ten were Sikh. Seven participants were male and fourteen were female (as shown in Table 3.3).

Table 3.3   Gender and religious distribution of participants

	Male	Female
Hindu	5	8
Sikh	2	6
Total	7	14

All participants were either both in the United Kingdom or had been UK residents since they were children and had British nationality. All identified as being of Indian ethnicity.

The average age of the participants was 25.5 years. This ranged from 18-35 years.

An analysis of participants' occupation showed that sixteen held professional roles or were engaged in business and another four were at University. Only one had not completed a degree or seeking one.

Only 20 out of the 42 of the participants' parents had degrees. Other parents did not have a degree and/or had engaged in vocational training in the UK, and had been educated elsewhere. Participants showed a distinct upward mobility in terms of professional roles that they occupied as compared to their parents. While most participants were employed in skilled or specialised professions such as medicine, auditing/ analysis related jobs; their parents had mostly been engaged in unskilled or semi-skilled work or small businesses. It is possible that many of the parents may have skills or experience that were not recognised in the UK due to their migration, forcing them to experience a downward class migration. Platt (2005) reports that many skilled Indians did experience downward class migration on their arrival in the UK and that while three quarters of Indians had working class backgrounds on their arrival to UK, second generation Indians show higher mobility to professional classes. Platt (2005) also suggests that pooling of resources for second generation, social capital and relative geographic concentration to provide for cultural resources may all have played a role in determining these outcomes for second generation Indians The socio-economic profile of the participants seems to reflect this advantage over the previous generations who had undertaken the migration journey. All the participants interviewed were born and raised in the UK and hence may be more attuned and able to benefit from acculturation and citizen status (Platt 2007). Table 3.4 presents a comparative outline of participants and their parents' occupations.

Reflections

Research can be valid only if the researcher familiarises himself/herself with the real world, engages with it and accordingly is ready to change perspectives based on findings and involvement (Blumer 1969, Pyett 2003). My engagement with the topic of study, as the researcher, has had a substantial impact on the way in which

Table 3.4   Representing occupation of participants, their mothers and their fathers

Occupation	Participants	Participants' mothers	Participants' fathers
Graduate professionals	14	9	11
Business	2	3	1
Student	4	–	–
Housewife	1	2	–
Manual/ Unskilled	–	7	8
With degree	20	10	11
Total	21	21	21

information from participants has been obtained as well as the type of information that has been received. My own position also has a substantial impact on the interpretation and analysis of the findings. Some of the key issues that I believe are significant include my ethnicity, gender and language.

Language   I had decided to collect the data in English as I believed most second generation British-Indians would be fluent in English. Apart from English, Hindi was likely to be the only other common language between myself and the participants. While designing the research, I recognised that the sensitivity and stigmatisation of divorce may be linguistically organised and emotive. It is difficult to translate certain Hindi words such as 'shame' and 'honour', while also incorporating the cultural meaning of these words. Bhardwaj (2001) in her research on suicide among South-Asian women also experienced this cultural force behind language and believed that terms such as 'izzat' and 'sharam' (which translate as honour and shame respectively in English) transcend linguistic interpretation and embody enormously powerful cultural judgements that have the power to exclude and ostracise. My experience with interviewing adult British-Indian children also indicated that certain cultural assumptions are embedded in language. Some interviewees indeed used these Hindi words to communicate meaning and experience, even though the interviews were conducted in English.

Sharing some aspects of language and understanding their meaning had also helped me to relate more meaningfully with the community in my efforts to advertise my study and invite participation.

Gender and ethnicity   My own Indian ethnicity enabled me to better contextualise participants' responses and react in ways that would be culturally appropriate and sensitive. I was able to share some aspects of Indian culture, norms and traditions, particularly with regards meeting expectations of appropriate behaviour. These are conveyed through different behaviours and actions such as decent dress, appropriate respectful manners and behaviour and are aligned in terms of gender and age. These were particularly important in my engagement with the community and I believe indicated cultural sensitivity on my behalf. The community also responded positively to this by supporting me in the recruitment process.

This gender component also had an effect in my interviews with participants. I was more comfortable in the interviews with female participants. I was also more aware of my gender with male participants and more careful in my interactions with them. However, this may not necessarily be something that is culturally significant for British-Indians. As outlined, British-Indian culture is constantly being shaped through acculturation processes and hybridised. As an Indian from India, I am as much as an outsider to the British-Indian context, community and culture even though I may share aspects of culture, language and history with British-Indians.

I believe my gender and ethnicity did have an impact on the way interviews were conducted, some positive and some not so positive. Nonetheless, a reflection worth noting that my engagement with the community was critical is preparing me to understand the British-Indian context and became more culturally sensitive to the use of language and meanings expressed in participant narratives.

Interview methods   It is also pertinent to note the impact that the use of two different forms of interviews (personal face to face and telephone) may have had on the information obtained. I asked fourteen of the participants who had experienced both forms of interview to comment on their experiences and preference.

Ten expressed a clear preference for the personal interview although they did not mind the telephone interview.

> Interviewer: Did you feel differently about the personal and telephone interview?

> Ipshita: yeah … definitely … I definitely prefer this (personal interview). It's something about seeing someone, being able to see reaction, body language, see if the other person is comfortable.

It can be argued that a face to face interviews allows a better understanding of the other person and provides additional cues through posture, tone and body language (Berger and Luckmann 1966, Schwartz and Jacob 1979). Personal interviews are also preferable for sensitive topics and understanding complex issues (Walker 1985, Mathers et al. 1998).

However, the other four participants did not have a preference and did not think that the physical absence of the interviewer made a difference. Though the telephone interviews eliminated visual cues, they were an extremely accessible option to manage spatial distances between researcher and participants and minimise costs (Mathers et al. 1998).

> Interviewer: Ok. Did you feel differently about the personal and telephone interview?

Harpreet: Umm … I'm not sure … well … I don't mind either.

While two methods of interviewing were available according to the preference of participants, most participants still felt that personal interviews were more responsive. However, telephone interviews may be a valuable tool for some participants and allow more possibilities in certain circumstances, particularly if large distances are involved between the locations of the researcher and the researched.

Limitations

This study recruited participants voluntarily and in most cases directly from the community. The call for participants for the research was advertised at various locations (agencies, community centres) as described previously in this chapter. Participants were expected to self identify themselves and approach the researcher to participate. This method was adopted to ensure that participants volunteered of their free will and no participant was identified specifically for the study unless they expressed interest. This self selection of participants may have resulted in a biased sample. It is likely that only the participants who felt they had mostly positive outcomes, or participants of a certain personality type who may have valued research, or participants for whom this subject was less sensitive may have volunteered for the research.

The venues and strategies for advertising may also have targeted particular types of respondents such as students, internet savvy persons, individuals who were seeking counselling or individuals whose family members were undergoing counselling. It can be argued that these methods of snowballing and voluntary participation may have led to a select sample of individuals (Mani 2006). The participants may not necessarily represent the experiences of all British-Indian adult children of divorce as a general population.

The study was a qualitative one and themes have been identified from 21 participants. This participation can meaningfully inform qualitative studies and indeed analysis has been conducted at micro and macro levels. This study has therefore sought to shed light on processes and some outcomes of divorce and does not claim to generalise these findings across all cases of divorce in the British-Indian community.

Much research on the effects of divorce on children proposes there are gender differences in the experience, impact and coping for children of divorce (Pett et al. 1992, Evans and Bloom 1996, Simons et al. 1999, Wallerstein et al. 2000, Lang and Zagorsky 2001). However, in this study, an analysis of narratives according to participants' gender was not conducted due to the uneven gender distribution among participants. However, gender themes that were found across all participants' narratives such as victimisation of their mothers through domestic violence, mothers as single parents who had custody of participants and stigmatisation for participants in single mother households have been discussed in the findings. Finally, it is important to note that the phenomenon of divorce is constantly changing. Participants indicated in this study have highlighted processes of divorce that occurred in the 1970s and 1980s. It is very likely that these processes, divorce and marital contexts have shifted and changed. Thus while this study presents some insights into divorce processes, their contribution to understand this phenomenon for recent divorces should be carefully considered.

Summary

The study aimed to explore the context, impact and experiences of divorce of British-Indian (Hindu and Sikh) adult children. Voluntary participation was sought from the community for the study. Narratives from participants were collected through interviews. These were conducted over the phone or through face to face personal interviews in accordance to participant preference. The data was thematically analysed to inform the objectives of the study.

Recruiting participants was a considerable challenge due to the very personal and sensitive nature of the topic of study. A variety of access strategies were used to invite participation from persons in the British-Indian community. Though many researchers have identified issues of recruitment with minority ethnic communities, incorporating appropriate strategies for recruitment within the research design that are culturally sensitive can help to invite participation. Engaging with the community and establishing personal contacts was the most successful method of recruitment. Personal engagement with community members also provided an opportunity for the researcher to understand the views and opinions of people within the community.

Twenty one British-Indian adult children expressed interested and participated in the study. Participants were keen to help the researcher and interested to participate as they believed it could inform and help others understand the subject better. The study sought to understand their experiences through individual interviews that were focussed on understanding the divorce from their perspective. Participants were also given an opportunity to consider the major themes that emerged from the study through a preliminary report that was shared with them. This report was shared with 14 participants. In total, 35 interviews were conducted, 15 face to face and twenty over the telephone.

The majority of those who participated were female. All except one of the participants were professionals and indicated upward economic mobility compared to their parents.

The adopted methodology for the study provided particular insights for engagement with minority ethnic communities and seldom heard participants. In addition, the different methods of data collection such as telephone interviews and face to face interviews also provided scope for reflection. The research process along with particular researcher characteristics, such as age, gender and ethnicity, influenced the research outcomes and have been briefly discussed.

PART III
Participants and their Stories

Chapter 4
Context of Parental Divorce

Introduction

While divorce as a family transition implicates multiple significant changes, there is also diversity in the experiences of divorce. The context in which divorce occurs and its management plays a role on the subsequent impact and coping of divorce for family members. For example, as explored, the impact of divorce on children in high conflict marriages may in fact be a positive development. Similarly, contexts may also be able to support children appropriately and foster their resilience to help better manage the family transition without negative outcomes. This context, impact and coping may differ for British-Indians due to the particular socio-cultural, historical and structural spaces that they occupy in the UK. Thus while the experiences of divorce may be similar to the experiences of the impact of divorce recorded in mainstream western communities, the context within which divorce as a family transformation occurs in the British-Indian community is different. This is not to indicate that divorce events and processes are unique to British-Indians, but rather that these occur within particular ethnic context shaped by their histories of immigration, acculturation and continuation of tradition, survival, identity and adaptation in a larger host society.

This part is divided into four chapters. The first three chapters present the direct accounts of British-Indian adult children who participated in the study. They are henceforth referred to as participants. The context of divorce, impact of divorce and coping from the perspectives of participants are systematically explored in these chapters.

Chapter 4 presents participants' narratives of context, Chapter 5 presents participants' perceived impact of divorce and Chapter 6 presents participants' reported strategies of coping and support. Chapter 7 combines the understanding of risk and resilience across the first three sections and discusses them.

Context of Divorce

Most families and married partners do not take the decision to divorce easily. Divorce decisions are followed through after much deliberation and often involve repeated efforts at reconciliation between married partners. The decision to divorce is often a resolution to end a marriage where conflict or marital unhappiness is significant and when all other possible means to continue the marriage for an amicable life have been exhausted. For many families, this conflict precedes divorce for a considerable period and frames the context for divorce. The dynamics of this conflict and context is important as it plays a role in the unfolding of divorce as a family transition and has an impact on all members of the family and also affects other extended family members and friends.

For participants in this study, the context of conflict and its beginnings could be traced back to conditions under which their parents immigrated to the UK. Participants' narratives of conflict emerged from context of parental marriage and how immigration had shaped their marital arrangements. This immigration is briefly explored as it provides a contextual understanding of participants' parents' marital context and conflict.

Origins and Migration of Parents

Some participants reported that their parents had migrated to the UK as children or were born in the UK. However, for other participants, their parents had directly migrated from India. Thus participants' parents were either first or second generation migrants in the UK.

Some of the participants' parents had met and married in the UK itself, while for others, marital alliances were made across the border between British-Indians and Indians. In some instances, both parents were of Indian nationality and had migrated after marriage or migrated for work reasons and got married.

> Dia: Well … they (mother and father), both of them were born in India. But they moved here (UK) when they were very young.

> Aryan: My dad and my mother originally came here (UK) at the same time … to take advantage of the boom in UK and took up banking jobs. They met here in the UK and married here.

> Sonia: My father was from here (UK). My mum came here when she was 18 when she was going get married to my dad.

For most of the families, the connections with relatives and communities in India continued. Larger extended families and community connections along with many traditions remained prominent in their lives. It is within this environment that marriages of parents were established. Twelve participants reported that their parents had an arranged marriage where the marriage had been arranged by family elders or extended family members. Four participants commented that their parents had been socially forced or coerced into marriage. Five participants reported that their parents had married by choice with a partner they fell in love with.

Marital Context

It should be noted that marriages of parents had occurred between 1960s and 1980s. Arranged marriages among Indians during this period were highly common and the norm. Marriages by choice, referred to as love marriages, however, were likely to be considered deviant. Some participants believed that their parents had been coerced into an arranged marriage by elders or relatives through social or emotional pressure. These have been referred to as forced-arranged marriages. These marriages – arranged, forced arranged and marriage by choice presented particular issues for families in the immigrant context. These are selectively discussed.

Arranged marriages　　Arranged marriage has been a traditional form of finding suitable marital alliances and involves other family members in the marital decision making process.

Priyanka talked about how her parents had an arranged marriage in India.

> Priyanka: Both my parents were from India and had an arranged marriage. Obviously back in those days, they got married at a very young age. My dad came to the UK first on his own and then, only when my mother was about 21 she came home and then came here in 1967. My father came here (UK) first and then a couple of months later, mother came.

However, not all arranged marriages were well conceived and some participants reported how their parents were coerced, forced or deceived into arranged marriages that had implications for their future married lives together.

Many participants perceived their parents to have little say in the matter of their marriages. Ravi describes a more traditional process where elders make decisions regarding the marital alliance with little opportunity for his parents to have any input in the decision making process.

> Ravi: You got to think that the marriage to my father ... She (mother) met him like a week before they got married, I think. It happened in those days. It was common for a guy to make a call and through the guardians, they exchanged photos and the decision for marriage was made by the elders.

Ravi further explained that because the marriages were organised across contexts, there were differences in cultures and expectations. He outlined how his mother who was socialised in the UK had different expectations

> Ravi: She (mother) did not want to marry my dad because basically first they (relatives and family members) made out that my dad was a doctor but I think he had studied a PhD ... there was a miscommunication. My mum had a quite western point of view in that sense that she came to this country when she was around 11. So all her schooling from the ages of 11 to 16 was here. She obviously had quite an open view to life ... ummm ... with my dad, because he came from (India) ... not a rich background but a relaxed background and in those days they came from small communities. Basically, he was from a well educated family

and maybe he had big expectations from this country (UK) and in those days there was this big stereotype – you know, you go there (UK), you know you'd be chilling …

Marital alliances arranged across contexts provided lower opportunities to meet and understand the potential spouse across long distances. In addition, the manner in which arranged marriages were pursued across continents presented opportunities for misunderstanding, miscommunication and even deceit.

Ipshita: My father told lots of lies when he went back to India to marry my mother. He showed that he had lots of property and land in India. When my mother actually went to the UK, she realised that he actually had a lot of debt and in fact her entire dowry was used to pay off these debts.

In some cases, participants reported that their parents were emotionally and socially coerced to marry the person that had been chosen by the family.

Nadia: … well she (mother) went on holiday to India … my dad's dad was like a big colonel in the army. In the Sikh army and my dad's side are from the royal family … like the 6th generation, so when the proposal came from my mum, they said that they couldn't refuse such an offer from such a big family. So she was literally forced. She did like somebody else in England but she was locked in a room till she agreed to marry my dad.

Participants felt very strongly about this coercion that elders imposed on their parents and thought that their parents' marriage may even have been forced to ensure that they did not get married against the wishes of the family.

Pooja: It was a forced-marriage. Forced in the sense that my older maasa (maternal uncle), he knew that she (mother) had a childhood sweetheart back in India, he then forced her to marry this other guy.

Arranged marriages were most common and parents of twelve participants had this type of marital beginnings. According to four participants' narratives, their parents had a marriage that was arranged and forced on their parents.

Marriages by choice (Love marriage)   Five participants reported that their parents fell in love and chose to marry each other. Marriage by choice or by falling in love is not a traditional practice among Indians and in the past has been associated with loss of honour and fidelity of the part of individuals and their family. Thus the decision to marry by choice on part of young individuals, particularly if they did not involve consultation of elders may be considered deviant and defiant. Such marriages by choice are often disapproved and do not enjoy support by other family members.

> Aryan: Because they had this love-marriage situation, basically both sets of parents did not approve of the marriage and warned that they would not get support from the families if things didn't work out. So for some time, my parents kind of kept to themselves…

Thus, while love marriages enabled individual choices and decision making of the young person to be married, it did not provide opportunities for collective decision making and could be badly regarded by others in the family and community resulting in isolation from the community and lack of support for the newly married couple.

Conflict

Conflict is perhaps the most common theme of divorce. Though conflict may exist as a precursor to divorce, the nature of this conflict and its severity may differ. In participants' responses, often more than one reasons was proposed for conflict. The reasons for conflict indicated were incompatibility (n=6), conflict with in-laws which affected the marriage (n=6), infidelity (n=7), and marital stress due to particular life events (n=5). Nineteen participants had memories of their parents together and the conflict between them. Two participants did not remember the conflict as they were very young at the time of divorce but offered what they perceived the reasons of conflict and divorce to have been.

Incompatibility In forced-arranged marriages, issues of incompatibility and mistrust were present form the beginning. However, these issues of incompatibility were also present in arranged marriages and marriages of choice or love marriages. While lack of opportunities to communicate and coercion were reasons for incompatibility in forced marriages, for arranged as well as love marriages, clash of personalities and values were also offered as reasons for incompatibility.

Dia believed that her parents were incompatible, even though they had a love-marriage.

> Dia: From the age that I remember which was a very young age, she (mother) was very different, personality-wise from him (father) … ummm he's very western and she is western but sort of holds on to a lot more traditional values than I guess my dad did and although, the marriage came about as a result of their attraction and they fell in love or whatever, they basically wanted completely different things out of the marriage.

Thus while a clash of expectations and ideals existed between their parents who were raised in different contexts, such as one parent raised in India and the other in Britain was noted, it was also present if these contexts did not differ. For example, Dia suggested that value conflicts were also present between her parents, both of whom were raised in the UK. These may be indicative of differences between individuals within a particular community and reflect the diversity of attitudes and practices within individuals. In the British-Indian context, different types and processes of acculturation and bi-acculturation in individuals could contribute to such conflicts. Differences in families and socialisation as well as individual orientations may also account for these incompatibilities.

Arjun presented a similar story of incompatibility between his parents who were both from India and had an arranged marriage in India.

> Arjun: Basically, they were constantly arguing and they were a complete clash of personalities. And this was the case since they had an arranged marriage some years ago. They got married in India in the 60s and had an arranged marriage. My dad is extremely introvert and my mum is an extrovert so the combination wasn't good. She wanted to do things all the time and my dad was the opposite … so she would be in a party mode and he was extremely strict and the opposite and there was a lot of friction so it didn't really work that well.

These incompatibilities often led to disagreements and difficulties in relationships which led to divorce.

Conflict due to in-laws   Other reasons for conflict in the family was attributed to particular cultural living arrangements after marriage. Among many Indian families, it is often common practice for the bride to move in with the husband's family. Such extended family and joint living arrangements caused friction between different members of the family.

> Payal: My mum and dad, they used to live next to mum's in-laws and stuff. But my father was influenced by his mother quite a bit and she didn't want us to move. My mum wanted to live away and this caused a bit of friction.

Difficult relationships with in-laws and their interference and involvement in family matters was a cause of distress and conflict. This also led to in-law's sometimes taking particular sides in the spousal conflict and further fuelling tensions and stress.

Infidelity   Six participants reported that they were aware of infidelity in their parents' marriage but only four indicated this to be the reason for divorce. Amar said that while there were stressors in the marriage after the birth of the first child and difficult relationships with in-laws, it was infidelity on his father's part that led to divorce.

> Amar: The reason they got divorced in the first place is because he cheated on her with this other like … lady.

While five participants reported infidelity on part of their father, for one participant, it was their mother who had had an affair with another man.

Marital stress   Five participants also indicated particular situations that created marital stress that their parents were unable to cope with, leading to divorce. For three participants this stress resulted from new births or changes in family structures. One participant believes that financial stresses had a devastating impact on parental marriage and for another participant, it was ongoing unreasonable behaviour on part of one parent that led to stress and incompatibility.

In Sonia's family, the familial stress at the death of her brother lead to blame in addition to troubled family histories that lead to the divorce.

> Sonia: My brother had passed away a few years before and that caused a lot of friction within the family between my parents and it was like my dad blaming my mother's affair as one of the reasons for his death.

For most participants, multiple reasons operated for causing incompatibility and stress. While for some, the reasons for divorce was a build up of previous conflicts, for others it was specific precipitating events that eventually led to the divorce.

Conflict and Violence

Nineteen participants reported an understanding of the conflict between their parents and had directly heard arguments and fights between them. Twelve participants also witnessed scenes of domestic violence, often on a recurring basis.

The domestic violence presented difficult scenes of conflict which participants were witness to. Meghna described the intensity of this violence.

> Meghna: … we could hear it and we could hear both of them screaming… knowing that someone is getting hurt. You'd come down and see glass and blood everywhere.

Participants' mothers were mostly the victims of such abuse. For seven participants, this violence was also associated with drink. Dia believed that her father's drinking habits were the cause of most of the trouble and violence in her family.

> Dia: when I was young and when he (father) was a young man, he used to drink excessively. In fact, that was normally the main instigator for trouble.

Madhuri offered a different reasoning and believes that the violence instigated by her father in her family may have been due to his exposure to domestic violence as a child.

> Madhuri … in the years later, I found out that actually he (father) witnessed his father (grandfather) beating up his mother (grandmother).

The impact of domestic violence and inter-parental conflict on participants was significant and participants reported being fearful for their parents. They also recalled becoming involved in the violence. Domestic violence thus presented emotional and physical consequences for participants.

Involvement of Children

All participants, except two, knew and were aware of the conflict between their parents.

> Urmila: No, no one told me anything … not really … I just used to hear everything. I used to hear them fighting and arguing. They were arguing all the time and then it got too much …

As outlined, some participants were also witness to scenes of domestic violence and some even gave accounts of getting involved in the conflict and getting hurt as they tried to intervene.

Meghna sketched an episode of domestic violence and her involvement.

> Meghna: … we've (Meghna and her siblings) all seen it (domestic violence) and it was best to not get involved … because it was between them (parents) … When I was older, that's when I started to intervene and start to get hit.

Some older participants were nonetheless able to protect their mothers from the violence through their intervention.

> Arjun: When the friction got to the maximum point and I couldn't take it anymore and basically I was acting as a domestic policeman really … he (father) had to accept that I could handle things by then and he was a bit more terrified cause at the age of 15-16, I was probably stronger than my dad and that probably scared him and he realised that actually he couldn't fight anymore and couldn't win this.

Participants also highlighted their fears associated with such conflict. Fear for themselves and their parents' welfare.

> Joti: I was scared for me and my mum… I was worried that one day I would come back home from school and my mum would no longer be there anymore.

Reactions to Domestic Violence

The private nature of domestic violence can isolate women further from seeking help. The cultural secrecy and shame associated with domestic violence often discourages women from seeking help and limits the role that support systems can play.

Ipshita illustrated the isolation, the privacy and the public knowledge of domestic violence in her family.

> Ipshita: Also, there is this element that this is a family private matter … she would never call the police for this reason, I never mentioned it to anyone. I think people knew and they were aware and my mum must have talked to her friend, but they also knew the need to keep it contained and not say anything – that it was my mum's decision…

For mothers, as minority ethnic women, being able to access help may have also been an issue.

> Ipshita: I don't think my mum knew how to get them (any kind of services) involved.

This, however, does not suggest that women do not have agencies and are passive. In fact, women often strategise and plan resistances against domestic violence.

Madhuri reported that her mother had made several attempts to leave her partner.

> Madhuri: My mum once left him (Madhuri's father) when I was about 13. After that, he pleaded and promised to change. My mum did go back to him. The violence then stopped for a few years but then it started up again.

Women often leave marriages when contexts change and they are more able to exert their agency to leave violent marriages. Many factors can and do impede women's decisions to leave violent marriages. These factors need to be understood to enable a more wholesome understanding of their situation, their agencies and their decision making capacities.

Some participants reported on the involvement of extended family members to help resolve the situation. Their intervention seemed to be geared towards providing opportunities to discuss issues, present solutions, encourage use of professional services, spiritual resources, if needed, and so on.

> Heer: Lots of family members got involved to help with the marital state but nothing ever really helped… mother's sisters and sometimes my grandparents, they would really try to sort my father out, they tried on various occasions to make him see sense and their husbands, they all would try to talk to him about his behaviour and he did seek help … and tried to get into some meditation classes and things like that. The extended family, cousins tried to keep my parents together most of their married life and they would have religious people

who said that divorce is wrong without reason. My parents were actually referred the spiritual advisor to help my parent's marriage.

However, participants were often excluded from decision making or conflict resolution processes led by extended family members.

In Dia's family, there was a lot of involvement of family and friends to resolve the conflict and domestic violence between her parents. However, she was not involved in any of these discussions.

> Dia: They had people, sort of friends, family friends, members of the family who used to come down and sort of sit them down and talk about all their problems and everything and this would happen regularly, at least once every couple of months. And when these sort of decisions were being made, my sisters and myself were always locked in the room when these discussions would take place. At this age I was probably about 12 or 13 years old.

For some participants, their extended families may not have known how to intervene to address the violence and there was great resistance to suggest divorce as an option for women to leave violent marriages. Vikram seemed to suggest an acceptance of this violence by his relatives and extended family members and a lack of support for his mother.

> Vikram: Basically, both sets of grandparents were ... and my uncle and aunts, I think knew that there was ... you know, that my dad could get quite violent and stuff. But even then, it was still, you know, divorce within the Asian communities is very frowned upon ... you know there was more of a 'just put up with it' and 'shut up already', So, no, there was not really any overt support for my mum.

Resisting Divorce

In spite of incompatibilities and incidents of violence in most of the families, eleven participants reported that there was resistance to divorce. Mothers were perceived to be more resistant to divorce as they felt it was against their culture. In addition, there was little support for divorce in the community and finally mothers were particularly worried about the future care of their children. Some participants also believed that their parents continued in the marriage in the hope that things would improve.

Cultural reasons and stigma   When explaining their parents' resistance to divorce, half of the participants felt that social stigma surrounding divorce was a crucial aspect. Though participants felt that their mothers were more prone to stigmatisation effects of a possible divorce, fathers were not immune to community judgements. A few participants highlighted the pressure that fathers faced in the community and their interests in continuing in the marriage. Fathers were afraid of being blamed for the failure of the marriage which was likely to affect their reputation and status in the community.

> Madhuri: My dad would never (divorce) because that would be ruining his public image completely. It would be the ultimate humiliation for him to go through a divorce and lose his status, lose his family, lose the big house that he lives in … lose the car. He would've never even contemplated it and he always maintained that he did love my mum.

Priyanka described the social exclusion that her father experienced from his family because the divorce was perceived to be his fault.

> Priyanka: Yeah … because, my dad's mother and father, they supported us. They didn't support my father. They didn't support their son for what he did. What he did was very bad, so they disowned him … and nobody kept in touch with him for years …

Blame for divorce seemed a key aspect of stigma. Though in Priyanka's narrative, her father was blamed for the divorce, more participants noted that it was their mothers who were more keen to avoid the stigma of divorce.

Sonia reported how her mother did not want to be blamed for the divorce and refused to sign divorce papers even when her father had filed for it.

> Sonia: My mum refused to sign anything and by not wanting to sign she was showing her family that she was not happy to end the marriage. So by her not signing anything or fighting for anything, it looked like she was the innocent party and my dad wanted the divorce.

Preeti also remarked why her mother did not want to divorce her father even though her mother portrayed her father as abusive, violent and unfaithful.

> Preeti: My mum's really into religion and stuff and she's like there is no divorce in our religion … She didn't leave him because, in India, she comes from a society where it really matters what other people think of you and if you are like a divorced person, it's like you are not seen as a good person sort of thing so it is like ideal for you to be married.

Many participants also reported how their mothers were reluctant to defy society and their families, to take the decision to divorce. Heer stated that support of family members was significant for her mother and that her mother resisted divorce due to their disapproval of divorce in spite of the high conflict and violence in the marriage.

> Heer: There were lots of reasons why my mum didn't divorce … She didn't want
> to bring shame to her family as her parents were very very set in their ways and
> still are to an extent. That was a very very large factor …

The community and other family members' disapproval and reluctance to support divorce as a strategy to leave a violent marriage also affected decisions to divorce. Heer indicates this shame that her mother would bring on her family if she decided to divorce.

Hope   Some of the participants' mothers did not want to fail in their marriages and believed that if they worked at the marriage, it would succeed over a period of time. It is this hope that many mothers held on to.

> Ipshita: My mother thought that things would change, things would be different
> if she just kept plugging on at the marriage and if she wasn't doing anything
> wrong…

As outlined, many relatives offered support and often there seemed to be engagement with services and improvement in the marital context, offering hope and a possibility of a better marriage.

> Heer: All my relatives would try to talk to my dad about his behaviour and he did
> seek help and tried to get into some meditation classes and things like that.

It is perhaps this hope that their marriages could improve and divorce could be avoided that participants' mothers clung to and resisted divorce for longer. Temporary improvements on account of interventions by relatives may have also prompted mothers to keep trying and working at the marriage.

Presence of children   Six participants reported that their mothers were concerned about the welfare of their children and financial provisions due to their economic dependence on their husbands that prevented them from seeking divorce.

Participants outlined their own presence as very young children to have limited their mother's decision of divorce.

> Arjun: I think my mum was (resisting divorce because of stigma) and that's why
> she probably wouldn't have done it earlier and also because we were very young.

> Vikram: She (mother) couldn't really do anything about the situation for the sake
> of the children – she wouldn't want to put us through this hassle.

This is also consistent with British-Indian family values that place high importance on child care and their beliefs that marriage provides the most stable environment for their care.

Table 4.1   Parent filing for divorce

Parent filing for granted divorce	No. of participant families
Mother	14
Father	4
Mutual	1
Divorce granted by absentee	1
Unknown	1
Total	21

Participants also seemed to be indicating that their mothers probably did not leave the marriage earlier to protect the children and ensure their safety and that their needs were met. Mothers, however, did make this decision when circumstances changed.

Filing for Divorce

The decision to divorce in the face of these contextual barriers – cultural, social, emotional; was difficult. For 14 participants, the decision to divorce was made by their mothers. The decision to divorce was made after considerable deliberation (minimum of two years; on average participants' parents' marriage lasted for thirteen years). Please refer to Table 4.1.

As previously explored, participants provided a number of reasons for divorce, based on their family history of conflict, as explored. Reasons for divorce included long history of incompatibility and domestic violence, conflict with in-laws, marital stress and infidelity.

However, the decision to divorce was not easy and participants reported a number of concerns that their parents had that prevented them from making this decision sooner, particularly in families where violence was a defining feature of the conflict. Participants reported that they believed their parents resisted divorce to avoid stigma, concerns over the welfare of their children and for hope that their marriage will improve. Participants' reported that their mothers made the decision to divorce when circumstances changed and when participants were older.

For some participants' mothers, the support of their older children was vital to encourage them to seek divorce and leave the marriage. Older children who were socialised in the UK, were a great source of support to their mothers as they were able to align themselves with their mother's concern and also understood the social services systems in the UK, how to access them and seek appropriate help and support. Five participants indicated how their support and involvement had helped their mothers to divorce.

Meghna reported how she was instrumental in getting help for her mother to initiate divorce proceedings.

> Meghna: We were being basically attacked by him and we just couldn't take it anymore. I thought of telling somebody at school, and umm … I took advice and they were like this is what you can do, they gave me options, to get in touch with social services, the police … me and my mum worked through it and then I kinda talked to her and we decided that what we have to do is to get rid of our father basically and if he's not leaving then we'll have to leave.

Vikram talked about the role that he and his sibling played in helping their mother make the decision to divorce.

> Vikram: We weren't willing to put up with the physical and mental abuse we were receiving from our father and she (mother) knew that we were able to handle it so.

Custody

Almost half of the participants were above 14 years of age when the divorce decree was obtained. For participants of 14 years of age or under, nine were under the custody of their mothers, one participant was under father custody and two participants were under joint custody arrangements.

The eight participants under 14 who were under the custody of their mothers reported little conflict with regards to their custody. In most cases, the mother seemed to have got custody by default.

Preeti did not have a choice and remained with her mother as her father left the house and did not return.

> Preeti: My mum was not aware that he was going to leave or anything like that at all … he just like packed his bags and stuff and he told me that he was going to leave but he said that he'll come back and get me later or something like that … he took our money and some of the things in the house and he left.

The other nine older participants were more likely to remain with their mothers and completely supported their mother at the divorce.

Arjun's parents divorced when he was 15 years old and he sympathised with his mother. Arjun explained that his parents were in conflict for a long time and he believed his dad was responsible for much of the problems that had ensued in the family and the marriage.

> Arjun: Because it was really his over-caution and his obsession with where everyone was and what everyone was doing that was causing part of the problem and he was more likely to lose his temper and basically my mother had been suffering for quite some time.

Contact

Participants had little contact with their fathers after the divorce. Eight of the twenty one participants reported that they did not have any contact with their fathers, seven had only superficial contact with their fathers and only six reported meaningful contact with their fathers.

A number of factors seemed to affect these contact arrangements and negotiations. Some participants reported apathy and a lack of interest on their father's part at maintaining contact which in turn affected their own motivation to engage with their fathers.

No contact   For some participants, the highly conflicted pre-divorce context made subsequent post-divorce relationships difficult. Twelve participants' exclusively supported their mothers, particularly since it was mostly fathers who were perceived as perpetrators of violence.

After years of conflict, when Ipshita's parents divorced, she did not have any contact with her father and did not want to have any contact either. Ipshita never had a positive relationship with her father but after the divorce, she didn't even want to be related to him in any way.

> Ipshita: I have had no contact with my dad at all after he left. I've seen him once
> or twice locally but he acts like he doesn't know us. I hated him. I didn't want
> to declare his name at the Indian embassy when I went to get a Visa for India. I
> felt like I'm not his daughter.

Among the eight participants, below 14 years of age under mother custody, four participants reported some contact arrangements with their non-custodial parent. However, none of these arrangements had been continuously sustained either due to the objections by the custodial parent or due to lack of interest on their fathers' part to maintain contact and relationship with them.

Nadia's father lost interest and she lost contact with him shortly after the divorce.

> Nadia: He was living about half an hour away from us so we'd go and see him
> sometime … my mum was always like happy to take us there and they were
> quite mature with each other after a while. But then my sister was ill at the
> hospital and he didn't come to see her … I felt … that he didn't care about us …
> it was almost as if he'd died because he completely disappeared.

For Manish, his mother did not support ongoing contact and eventually this affected his contact with his father.

> Manish: He (father) was living literally right off the road to my house so I did
> see him here and there but then slowly slowly that drifted away cause my mother

started shouting at me and saying don't know why you're talking to him. And as a child, you can't understand, you don't know what's right and wrong. So I just listened to my mother and stopped talking to my father I just had to listen.

For Payal, her father had just left and they had had little opportunities for contact.

> Payal: We didn't have a choice really. We didn't have an option. He just kind of left us.

Thus while some participants deliberately did not want contact with their fathers due to previous violence, others had little choice and had lost contact with their non-custodial parent when they were younger. For some participants, the lack of support from the custodial parent also affected opportunities for participants' contact with their fathers.

Superficial contact   For a few participants who did have some contact with their fathers, this was very superficial either because they did no longer felt they knew him or because they could not forget and forgive their parent for the impact that their behaviour had had on them.

Meghna talked about how her relationship with her dad was superficial as he was unable to understand the past from her perspective and she was therefore unable to communicate with him to have a meaningful relationship.

> Meghna: I realised that he was numb to everything that he put us through. He doesn't realise how it affect us and the millions of things that we had to go through, not just the violence but the emotions we felt and the hell that we went through. It dawned on me that he didn't realise the extent to which he had impacted us and that really upset me – the fact that he didn't want to know. That to him is the past and he's moved on.

Close contact   Only six participants reported close contact with their non-custodial parents. For one participant this was due to joint custody arrangements, for two participants it was a result of contact maintained by both parents after the divorce and for three participants, it was a result of their own agency and interest in establishing contact and rebuilding a relationship with them.

Urmila was one of the few participants who retained contact with her dad even though she lived with her mother.

> Urmila: My relationship with my dad has been the same. I'm just closer to my dad.

Aryan did not have contact with his dad for 15 years after he left the family. However, Aryan did re-establish a relationship with him when his father finally contacted the family, after he was diagnosed with cancer.

> Aryan: We had no contact with my dad for over a decade and then he got in touch with me. He said he wanted us to forgive him. He was also severely ill and I had a chance to stick it out with him till he died. He was my dad after all and if I did not, I would've regretted it. I felt sorry for him and I felt that after all he was my dad and I should be with him at this stage and I had missed him.

All participants, except for two, knew the whereabouts of their parents even if they had no contact with them. For some participants, this information about their non-custodial parent was obtained from the diasporic connections they had with other larger extended family members. This knowledge and information was useful to initiate or change relationships if and when participants felt ready. In fact, over time, contact and relationships with non-residential parents did change due to changes in circumstances as well as the increased agency of participants themselves. This has been further considered in the Chapter 6.

Parental Remarriage and Re-partnering

Most divorced families go through additional family transitions through the re-partnering and re-marriage of their divorced parents. This re-partnering of parents presents changes that children of divorce have to adjust to and engage in re-negotiation of relationships with their parents, step-parents or parents' new partners and any step-siblings or half-siblings that these relationships may introduce.

Participants indicated the presence of step-families but these families were mostly due to their father's remarriage. Ten of the fathers had remarried while only three mothers remarried. Three mothers had also re-partnered at some point after the divorce. However, only two mothers had remained in any partnership at the time of the interviews with participants. Thus, thirteen participants had step-families, only four had ever lived in a step-family. Many also had step- and half-siblings.

Participants' narratives offered some insights for the lower rates of remarriage for their mothers. Mothers seemed to experience high resistance from society to remarry. They were more likely to be bound by traditional norms, values, stigma, honour and shame. Cultural and social mechanisms that operated to control the choices of these women in difficult marriages continued to operate even after divorce and continued to restrict their choices and lifestyles.

Meghna thought that her mother may like to re-partner but felt that her mother's extended family in Canada were influencing her to reject such a consideration.

> Meghna: Her mum (grandmother) has actually said to her (mother) 'don't you ever remarry, I can't live with it' ... Their (grandmother) mentality is very narrow-minded in that sense. They would not want her to remarry. I don't know why ... they don't see her as 'Oh she'll be happy!', they see it as a...'oh! It's a bit of a, you know, shame in the family for her to remarry'.

Many mothers were themselves resistant to remarriage due to cultural notions and traditional beliefs. Vikram and Pooja would like his mother to re-partner but his mother did not believe this was culturally acceptable.

> Vikram: Well … the values that my culture holds dear which is kind of like you know the family unit, you know, the women, if the woman's husband dies when she's young, then she shouldn't get married again that kind of stuff.

> Pooja: Once you've married in the Asian culture, you can't remarry again because you've been with a man. Even my mum feels that way, that she can't remarry and I would like her to

Remarriage provides many single mothers opportunities and routes to escape poverty and return to pre-divorce financial states. For participants' mothers, lack of support for remarriage could have restricted these opportunities.

Nonetheless, three mothers had remarried but only two mothers had remained in the partnership. Ravi felt that his mother was prompted to remarry to provide him with a father figure.

> Ravi: She basically thought I needed a father figure, that I needed someone to depend on.

However, remarriage can also introduce changes and instability that can be present difficulties for children. All four participants who had lived in a step-family after their custodial parents' remarriage recalled the adjustment demands and instability this arrangement had introduced. Harpreet commented on the difficulties she and her sibling had as children due to the subsequent moves after her mother's remarriage.

> Harpreet: It was hard in the beginning because we were all going through a lot of changes. Mum's partner used to work here in this country and then when they got married, he moved to Canada and we were supposed to go there and we actually moved there for two months and I was upset that we had to move all the way there. I had my whole life here and my dad as well … but then we moved back to England and I started getting along with him and then as I grew up, my brother was beginning to get difficult and it was hard to set boundaries. My brother might turn around and say you're not my dad and problems like that.

Ten participants however reported that they knew their fathers had remarried, six participants reported that their father had not remarried while six participants did not know. It is likely that lower contact and engagement of fathers in the post-divorce family context may have prompted fathers to start afresh, whereas, lack of support for remarriage as well as responsibilities and concern over children may make women more cautious of remarriage.

Many participants, however, were embarrassed and upset by their father's remarriage which their perceived as a betrayal.

> Priyanka: I felt ashamed. Ashamed that my father was in his 40s – an old man and going out and marrying. I think the biggest shame was when he started having kids – that was the most shameful part.

Step-families

In spite of twelve participants indicating that they were aware of having step-families, only six participants were in contact with them and only four had lived in a step-family. All twelve of these participants, except one, refused to accept their step-parent as family. Three among of the four participants who lived with their step-parent also did not accept them as family members and had strong feelings against them.

The six participants who had contact were clear that their step-parent did not and would not share the same status as their real parent. Their use of language also reflected this resistance. Meghna commented that she would like her mother to remarry but would not call or consider this person as a father. Similarly, Nadia makes it clear that she refers to her step-father as 'uncle' and would refuse to call him 'father'. Divij confessed that he did not want to call his step-mother 'mum' but felt pressured to do so because of the expectations of his father.

> Divij: My step-sister used to call my dad 'dad' and I used to call her (step-mother) 'mum' … that's been the expected thing … my dad wanted me to call her that straightaway.

Nadia also reacted strongly to any suggestion of accepting her step-father or his family as part of her own family. Nadia's stated that she 'hates' her step-father for the control that he tries to exert when trying to parent her and her sister. She added that her step-father seemed to have more old fashioned traditional ideas regarding the upbringing of girls that he tried to enforce on her.

> Nadia: My mum, my sisters, my half brother … they are my main family. Obviously and my mum's immediate family and also my real dad as well to an extent and his family are brilliant. I love my real dad's family. I completely hate my step-dad. I really and completely hate his family.

For Neha, her step-mum is in no way connected to her family.

> Neha: I would never say step-mum … I just call her by her name. She's really nice. I like her but I wouldn't say family.

However, these six participants were more amenable and accepting of step-sisters and half brothers and more accepting of them as part of their family.

Although Ravi cannot accept his step-father as part of his family, he included his half-brother as part of his family.

> Ravi: I can't walk away from my mother and my brother (half-brother). That's because he's younger and everything. Don't get me wrong, it's not my problem but if he needs me, I'll be there for him sure.

Step-siblings on the other hand were not dismissed as step-parents were, but were located along the status of extended family members.

> Neha: With (step-sister) … just because she's little and she's the same as any other little cousin I have.

Neha's definition seemed to give her step-sister this part token membership and acknowledgment as a family member. Participants, however, indicated a deeper emphasis on biological relatedness and were more likely to consider half-siblings as family, than step-siblings. Step-siblings were considered more benign but did not indicate more positive or close relationships.

Participant narratives indicated ambivalence towards step-family relationships. While step-sibling and half-siblings were accepted as family, step-parents were not. Step-parents also seemed to affect the relationship of children with their parents.

Remarriage seemed to lower the support and availability of the remarried parent and introduced complex relationship dynamics which sometimes isolated participants.

Ravi had no contact with his father and his relationship with his step-dad was difficult. This also had an impact on his relationship with his mother.

> Ravi: The fact is, if I need some emotional support, I can't even turn around and say mum I've got this problem … my mother knows this and she agrees, she admits that the years after marriage with my step-dad, she'd shrugged me away and I also think that it hurts her now.

Thus even though remarriage could lead to financial gains for divorced parents which may serve as a protective factor for families, remarriage could also introduce relationship dynamics which can present risks for children by isolating them. For participants in this study, lower rates of remarriage for their mothers may have eliminated these risks.

Discussion

The narratives and analysis of context reveals a complex picture of family histories, relationship dynamics as well as cultural influences that shaped participants' lives. While participants' stories indicate great diversity, there are also common themes that many experienced. These common themes enable understanding of certain factors within the British-Indian context which serve as risks or protective factors for children of divorce.

Participants reported how the ways in which their parents married had a bearing on their parents' married life. Forced marriages introduced difficult situations where some parents felt they had little agency and decision making capacity in this important life event and also felt deceived. Arranged marriages across international contexts also presented issues as parents did not have opportunities to better acquaint themselves with their to-be spouse. However, arranged marriages and love marriages also introduced issues of incompatibility which caused conflict in participants' family lives.

All participants indicated inter-parental conflict. The reasons for inter-parental conflict, were incompatibility, difficult relational dynamics with in-laws, infidelity, domestic violence and marital stress due to particular life events. For most participants, there were multiple reasons leading to divorce. In addition, many participants reported conflict associated with domestic violence.

It is worthwhile to consider the patriarchal structures and practices that introduce hierarchies of power that make young people vulnerable. Within patriarchal structures old men yield the most power, followed by young men and then older women and finally young women (Kandiyoti 1988). Thus within these structures, both young men and women have to obey the authority of elders in the family and it is through these hierarchies that marital decisions are made. These arrangements ensure that family interests across generations are maintained through alliances of young persons. In the early stages of British-Indian migration, there was great interest in preserving these links even across continents to ensure that family values were maintained and that subsequent British-Indian children did not become westernised. While practices of arranging marriages across continents has become less due to the expansion of the British-Indian community and availability of British-Indian for marital alliances, other customs have persisted.

Participants' mothers, as young women, were more likely to be forced into marriages due to their lower power status. In addition, due to the patrilocal and patriarchal structure, participants' mothers as brides are expected to move into their in-laws household. This presents sudden changes in family dynamics due to the new entry of the bride. Control over the new bride by the mother-in-law under the patriarchal hierarchy can be a cause of dissent and conflict in the household and has been reported as one of the reasons for divorce in India (Ranga Rao and Sekhar 2002). In patriarchal structures, male power is offset by older women and mothers who have sons exercise their power over new brides by virtue of their son's loyalty to them (Kandiyoti 1988). Similar dynamics were indicated in some of the participant families.

Domestic violence was often a common feature. The context of domestic violence where it was mothers who were victims is consistent with most research which identifies the gender dimensions of domestic violence with women as the victims (Sen 1998, Barnett and LaViolette 1993, Johnson and Ferraro 2000, Bhardwaj 2001, Fried 2003, Gill and Rehman 2004). Many researchers believe this male aggression to be a pattern of patriarchal expression of control over women and include emotional abuse (Wilson 1978, Kandiyoti 1988, Barnett and LaViolette 1993, Sen 1998, Johnsons and Ferraro 2000). In addition, acknowledgment of domestic violence is often shameful for Asian women and is considered a private matter which isolates women from accessing support (Johnson and Ferraro 2000).

Some participants indicated the association with alcohol, and one participant claimed that domestic violence may have been a consequence of childhood experiences and modelling behaviour. Barnet and LaViolette (1993) argue that women victims of domestic violence also often engage in self-blame or provide rationalisations such as the partner was under the influence of alcohol or was abused as a child. However, alcohol does not seem to have a causal relationship with violent behaviour and is more likely to be a consequence of abuse and few, not all, children who witness domestic violence exhibit abusive behaviour (Barnett and LaViolette 1993, Johnson and Ferraro 2000). Yount and Li (2009) in their research on justifications of domestic violence in Egypt found that women's resources and constraints in marriage were associated with their attitudes towards domestic violence. Yount and Li (2009) concluded that socially and economically dependent wives may be at highest risk for domestic violence. It may be likely that participants' mothers who were most likely to suffer domestic violence for the longest time may have been socially and economically dependent wives. This is partly supported by participants' reports of their mothers resistance to divorce due to stigma (social dependence) as well as worries about being able to care and provide for their children (economic dependence).

This domestic violence and inter-parental conflict present significant risks for children. Not only are children in such families more vulnerable to abuse, they often get directly involved by trying to interfere and protect their mothers and siblings. Kavemann (2004) explains how children are often secondary victims of domestic violence and abused women and children can both show emotional and physical symptoms of the stress and sometimes even Post Traumatic Stress Disorder (Kavemann 2004, Walker et al. 2004). Domestic violence can also diminish parent's capacity to parent and increases risks of aggression, delinquency, anxiety, depression and low self-esteem in children who witness domestic violence (Johnson and Ferraro 2000, Barnett and LaViolette 1993). Children suffer anxieties and conflicting feelings on account of this violence that has an impact on their happiness and psychological well-being (Smith 1999). Participants in this study also reported these impacts of domestic violence on them. Smith (1999) believes that it is important for children to be given opportunities to talk about this and to find positive strategies to cope. However, participants reported few such opportunities to discuss the family violence. In fact, as one participant noted, strategies to solve the conflict by family members often excluded children. Families may have restricted participants' involvement at younger ages to protect them. This may reflect the child care ethic in British-Indian families and the patriarchal hierarchies where children's opinions or involvement in family decision making processes are restricted. Participants' interference within the patriarchal context where elder hold power may even be interpreted as disrespectful to the authority of elders in the family.

Participants reported how family members in some cases did try to intervene or suggest strategies to resolve the conflict – this was always geared towards preserving the marriage. There was great resistance to suggest divorce. Thus while there is close community support to resolve conflicts which can be considered a protective factor to support families in conflict, the lack of support for divorce was particularly risky for children and women in cases of high domestic violence and where resolution of conflict by such means were not successful.

Some participants also indicated how other family members who were aware often ignored the violence. This may be due to patriarchal ideologies that legitimise aggression of men over women through cultural, religious devices and socialisation (Wilson 1978, Kandiyoti 1988, Barnett and LaViolette 1993).

Participants' families were also resistant to divorce due to the cultural values that sanctified marriage and stigmatised divorce within the cultural framework of 'izzat' (shame) and honour for British-Indian communities (Helweg 1979, Amato 1994, Range Rao and Sekhar 2002). Women may be particularly resistant to divorce as divorce is often perceived to be the woman's fault and a personal failure as she is considered to be responsible for keeping the family together (Barnett and LaViolette 1993, Amato 1994, Falk 2001, Range Rao and Sekhar 2002, Purkayastha et al. 2003). The stigma of divorce is also noted in western cultures where divorce signifies failure in marriage and shame about disclosure of inner family issues in public (Fawcett 1999). McKendrick's (1998) research also indicated lone-parents dissatisfaction with negative attitudes towards them. In addition, for many women, concerns about their children's identities, socialisation and futures in the UK, combined with other factors of stigma and poverty, served as a deterrent to divorce and prompt many women to continue in unhappy and violent marriages (Barnett and LaViolette 1993, Amato 1994, Goel 2005). Women are often socialised to believe that they are liable and responsible for their children's welfare, to sacrifice their needs and prioritise their families needs (Barnett and LaViolette 1993, Goel 2005, Wilson 2006).

For British-Indian women, resistance to divorce may be further heightened by their migrant and minority ethnic status in the UK. For some participants' mothers, their positions as migrant women may have affected their access to services due to lack of awareness and knowledge of the systems in the host country (Dwivedi 2002b, Chana 2005). Researchers have noted the multiple challenges that minority ethnic women face including racism, unfamiliarity of social and economic structures, poverty and lack of resources, cultural and language barriers, and lack of family and friendship support systems (Wilson 1978, Mama 1989, Barnett and LaViolette 1993, Roy 1995, Menjivar and Salcido 2002, Walker et al. 2004, Ahmad et al. 2004, Goel 2005, Chana 2005, Wilson 2006). Pettigrew (2003) also noted in his report for the government that minority ethnic lone-parents often lack information and awareness of support agencies, the welfare state and the associated services that could support them.

Participants' mothers were however not passive in their acceptance of the difficult marital context. It is clear that participants' mother faced multiple pressures to preserve the marriage and little support to divorce. Many mothers also hoped that their marriages would improve. One participant also noted how her mother even temporarily left the marriage in an effort to address the conflict and violence. Barnet and LaViolette (1993) also suggest how women may feel helpless and unable to leave violent marriages for a variety of reasons. However, they also note that women do make decisions to leave violent marriages after they have considered their situation and feel ready to make that change, based on their current need and available alternatives (Walker et al. 2004). Indeed, it was participants' mothers who mostly took the decision to divorce. This is consistent with national profiles and other studies that suggest that women file for divorce in larger numbers than men (Singh 1998, Simpson 1998, ONS 2007c). For British-Indian women, older children seem to be a key factor in changing the context and encouraging women to divorce. As one participant noted in her case, mothers as migrant women may not be familiar with the systems in the host country and how to seek help. Participants, who are born and socialised here be a protective factor and a resource for their mothers as they are more attuned to the host systems and hence more able to communicate and seek support and assistance. The presence and support of older children seems to be significant factor that enabled mothers to take the decision to divorce.

Most of the participants remained in the custody of their mothers and there was little conflict about this. This may be due to the acceptance of gender roles of the community by parents where care of children is considered a female role. Those participants who were older at the time of divorce also supported their mothers due to the histories of previous inter-parental conflict. The pre-divorce inter-parental conflict continued to have an effect on post-divorce processes and relationships, as reported by Cooney et al. (1995), Amato (1996) and Smith (1999). Older participants often refused to maintain contact with their fathers who they regarded as perpetrators of the domestic violence and conflict. Singh's (1998) study also reported that Asian lone-mothers in London indicated that their children did not want to retain contact with their fathers because of the violence and conflict they had witnessed between their parents. The previous conflict also affected inter-parental relationships and co-operation after the divorce. Subsequently, younger participants under mother custody were not supported or encouraged to maintain relationships with their non-custodial parents. For participants' families with high level inter-parental conflict, this lack of contact may have been positive. While some research indicates outcomes for children who maintain good quality relationship with both their parents (Shaw 1991), a good relationship with a part-time parent which had the blessings of the custodial parent led to the happiest outcome for children (Rowlands 1981, Sobolewski and King 2005). This co-operation and support between participants' parents after the divorce may also have been difficult in cases of high pre-divorce conflict. Participants who had little or no contact with their parents reported lack of support from custodial parents, lack of interest and unwillingness to acknowledge the impact of their behaviour by non-custodial parents as reasons for low or absent contact.

Participants, however, provided little insight into their father's perspectives as many did not have contact with them. Spillman et al. (2004) have reported various obstacles that fathers face in maintaining contact with their children. These include fear of rejection, fear of making mistakes, not wanting to confuse their children, job demands, long distances and older children. It is likely that participants' fathers also faced some obstacles that limited their efforts at maintaining contact and may have not known how to renegotiate their roles in this transformed family. Divorce in the families of participants suggested a transformation by which most non-resident parents (mostly fathers) became separate from the previous family unit and there were few interconnections or contacts of the custodial parent and children with the non-resident parent. This may also explain why Asian lone-parent families have little contact or expectation of financial or practical support from the non-resident parent (Pettigrew 2003).

Cultural values and patriarchal systems continued to have an impact on participants' mothers' life choices. They were less likely to remarry as it was considered as stigmatising for some families and was not supported. Thus stigma continued to have an effect in deterring life choices even after the divorce, particularly for women (Link and Phelan 2001). Father's were less restrained by this stigma and were more likely to remarry. However, this may present significant implications for participants' mothers as remarriage is a key route out of poverty (Goode 1993, Morrison and Ritualo 2000, Smart 2000), and re-partnering, especially for mothers, outweighs the benefits of entering the labour force (Jansen et al. 2009). Rands (1988) in her research on 40 divorced females and males in Massachusetts discusses that women may be more cautious to re-enter relationships after divorce or that they may possibly face more difficulties in terms of finding opportunities to re-partner. However, Smart (2004) believes that re-partnering also introduces a number of problems, particularly in relation to sharing property, inheritance, pension sharing and so on (Smart 2004). Thus women may be more cautious about worsening their situation if they should divorce again. However, in the British-Indian context, many participants highlighted that it was also cultural systems that prevented remarriage. On the other hand, fathers may have been more likely to marry as the stigma of remarriage may be less pronounced for them as males in the patriarchal context. The severance of contact with custodial parent or children may have also prompted participants' father to reclaim the role of husband and or father through remarriage.

However, the lack of mothers' remarriages also have benefitted participants as they may not have had to manage additional family transitions. While most mothers had not remarried, many father had and thus most participants had step-families. The findings indicated that while only four participants had ever lived in a step-family setting, all had difficulties in accepting their step-parent. According to Dunn and Deater-Deckard (2001), children seem to have weaker relationships with their step-parents than their birth parents and may have reservations about calling them dad or mum (Mitchell 1985, Smart et al. 2001). The presence of a step-parent also seemed to affect the relationship of children with their parent. Ferri's (1984) longitudinal research also suggests that step-families can introduce complex family dynamics which negatively affects the relationship that children have with their step-parents as well as their parents. None of the participants accepted their step-parents as their families but were more likely to grant some form of family membership to their step-siblings and half-siblings, if they were in contact with them. There is much ambiguity and complexity in sibling relationships in families with remarried parents and distinctions are often made between full and half siblings (Anderson 1999, Hetherington 1999). Cicireli (1994) suggested that in certain industrialised contexts all siblings may be accepted, however, in other cultures, step, half and adoptive siblings are carefully distinguished and given only part or token membership. Researchers have suggested that difficulties in interacting with step-families, inherent contradictions and role confusions may be due to the lack of the institutionalisation of the step-family form (Pink and Wampler 1985, Giles-Sims and Crosbie-Burnett 1989, Widmer 2006). This study suggests that it may not be industrialised contexts that determine the acceptance of all siblings as families but rather the normativeness and social institutionalisation of step-family forms. Due to low divorce rates in the British-Indian cultural context, step-families may not be institutionalised. Within British-Indian families, the stigmatisation of divorce may also focus more sharply on blame of spouses or occur in high conflict situations which may demand for children and family members to take sides making continuing relationships between divorced parents, children and non-custodial parents as well as children and step-families difficult.

Risk and Protective Factors

Contexts of patriarchy that make certain members in the community vulnerable can present risk factors. In the British-Indian context, it is young women who may be most powerless. Young mothers, under these structures may have lower agencies and support. Ideologies such as the value of marriage and welfare of children are operationalised in ways prevent women from leaving difficult marriages in spite of difficult circumstances. In addition, patriarchal ideologies and organisations often justify domestic violence. This emphasis on preservation of family and the high stigma for divorce is also a risk factor for families of high conflict when other strategies to resolve the conflict have been unsuccessful. Thus while support from the collective to resolve conflict can be regarded as a protective factor within the British-Indian community, their low support for divorce when it may be a welcome strategy to resolve the conflict can be considered a risk factor. Patriarchal contexts that limit women's agencies to leave difficult marriage are also risky for children since children's lives are often intricately tied with their parents, particularly mothers who are often their main carers.

For minority women, their migration may also limit their awareness and support systems. This could make them even more dependent for support. Many British-

Indian women may thus be dependent on the communities and accept patriarchal practices as it may protect them from racism as well as provide support (Kandiyoti 1988, Goel 2005). Thus patriarchy, racism and migrant histories may interact in ways that can impose barriers for women in exercising their agencies and have an impact on the choices they make (Wilson 2006). Older children's agencies under such contexts can be a great resource in supporting women to leave unhappy marriages and can be valuable protective factors for women.

Nonetheless, divorce decisions may take longer as families have to negotiate these various issues. For children of divorce in such contexts, the long sustained conflict may make post-divorce relationships difficult. While contact with non-custodial parents is recognised as a protective factor for children, this possibility may be difficult in the face of previous histories of prolonged and persistent conflict.

Cultural and patriarchal norms also limit women's remarriage in the community and may be regarded as a risk as women's remarriage often helps divorced single parent families to recover their financial status. The lower remarriages of women however may benefit children in mother custody families as they do not have to adjust to additional changes in their living environments. Step-families in the British-Indian context may also be particularly challenging and negatively affect the relationship with step-parent as well as biological parent because of the lack of familiarity and institutionalisation of the step-family form in the British-Indian community.

Chapter 5
Impact of Parental Divorce

Children's lives are intricately linked with their families and parents. Family transitions through divorce affect children directly and indirectly. Divorce impacts on multiple aspects of children's lives and it is the overwhelming extent of changes that can be most challenging for children to cope with. Some key themes of impact that children face include changes in financial contexts, physical movements, difficult emotional states of loss, changes in social life and roles, changes in education and career development.

However, parenting practices, family structures and norms differ in different ethnic and cultural groups. For example, while authoritative parenting provides best outcomes for White working class and White middle class families in the United States of America, a combination of authoritarian and permissive parenting is more conducive for positive and supportive development of Latino and African-American families (Avenevoli et al. 1999). Thus for children from different cultural and ethnic groups, management of divorce and its outcomes can also vary. For example, King et al. (2004) noted racial and ethnic differences for many aspects of father involvement after divorce and discusses these to be a result of non-structural influences, such as cultural values or practices. British-Indian divorced families may also vary from the mainstream White British families due to their familial, social and cultural context. This particular chapter considers the impact of divorce on participants as well as the processes by which these changes impact on children to identify risk and protective factors. Impact across five domains as indicated earlier namely financial, physical, emotional, social and educational and career impact is considered in this chapter.

Financial Impact

The financial impact of divorce often produces a ripple effect as it has an influence on all aspects of social life. Most divorced families experience a reduction in the familial financial circumstances and consequently a fall in their standard of living, immediately after the divorce. Loss of financial status as a consequence of the division of property between parents, loss of incomes (as parents incomes were separated and often some parents became earners for the first time), and dismissal of parental financial responsibility where non-custodial parents distanced themselves from the financial responsibility towards underage children can produce effects of poverty for children of divorce. Participants narratives also highlighted a range of these issues as well as an impact on their inter-generational resources.

Financial impact on living conditions   Fifteen participants in the study were extremely aware of the financial aspect of divorce and recognised how this financial vulnerability affected their daily life conditions and activities.

Arjun's narrative expressed the financial difficulty and the change in family living situation after the divorce.

> Arjun: … a lot of the money was frozen, due to the litigation and so forth. It was a bit dodgy. We had a roof over our heads … (but) It destroyed the whole atmosphere at home because we had to live in difficult financial circumstances … like everyone else was going for holidays and I couldn't as I didn't have any money.

The changed financial circumstances also had an impact on the parenting capacities and availability of the custodial parent. Vikram presented a scenario where he and his sister had to manage around the working hours of their mother, making them more independent.

> Vikram: My mum would do a lot of night work. She'd be back in the morning, take us to school, get a few hours sleep and then pick us up from school. So my mum did everything and worked … and so we would go to school, come back from school, you make yourself something to eat, do your homework, and then you know … your mum will be up or she'd be going to work or whatever but certainly you know, we were very independent.

Preeti also comments on how Asian children often do not have to worry about money and are provided for, which was not the case for her.

> Preeti: I just find that in some Asian families where the parents are still together and stuff, their children's life is quite comfortable, like their children are quite … I don't know, like just that they are comfortable, they don't really think or worry about their financial situation.

However, in a few cases, divorce also liberalised women's earnings and opportunities. Some participants outlined great entrepreneurships on part of their mothers and successful businesses after the divorce. Urmila indicated that their finances improved after the divorce as their father was dependent on her mother's income.

> Urmila: There was more money after my father was gone. My mum was still working and she used to earn most of it anyway. So basically, she was spending less because he wasn't there anymore.

This presents an alternative scenario where divorce improved the financial state of the family. While, for most families, the financial consequences of divorce are hard to overcome, this poverty consequent to divorce is not a final certainty. Families do recover and seven participants reported financial recovery and highlighted how their mothers had showed great agency, creativity and entrepreneurship towards rebuilding their financial assets and having successful careers.

> Nadia: It actually got better ... because my mum got into show business and became a singer and she made something of herself and she was quite famous.

Conflict over finances   Six participants also reported some conflict over legal proceedings of divorce.

Payal's account portrayed the conflict over property divisions between her parents but is unable to recall details.

> Payal: Oh yes ... there was conflict with regards who was going to get the house, the car...

One participant, even supported his mother in legal matters and to helped her to sort out the finances, which continued many years after the divorce.

> Arjun: I think I left university and I was still going to court on my mum's behalf. I was 24 and going to court and they were still missing money and they still had bank reserves which still hasn't been claimed ... there are tonnes of shares but we can't find the paperwork ... so there's money everywhere. It was a nightmare financially and so much loss, and money wasted on barristers.

This is also an interesting aspect of participants' resourcefulness to their parents. Parents also seemed to use financial circumstances and means to influence participants' loyalties.

Sonia's illustration shows how divorcing parents may use financial aspects to influence children to take sides with them against the other parent.

> Sonia: Even in terms of inheritance, because I took sides with my mum, according to my dad, I am not entitled to as much money as my sisters.

Impact on inter-generational resources   Division of assets between parents also presented implications for participants inheritance and nine participants felt that the financial loss had a substantial impact on their lives and their futures.

Meghna believed that the divorce had diminished the financial resource that may have been available to her if her parents if her parents had remained married.

> Meghna: ... my mum did support me in a little bit, which is helpful of course but that would've been a lot more if my parents were together and they were earning a bit more.

Divorce and parental remarriage also seemed to affect inheritance that participants expected to receive from their parents. Eight participants felt unsure of their inheritance either as a consequence of:

- division of property between parents, and where participants no longer had a relationship with their non-custodial parent. ‚
- remarriage of parents and introduction of step-families.

Dia believed that it would have been her right to receive property from her parents and the division of property between her parents has been unfair to her and her siblings who have been isolated in the process.

> Dia: It angers me in the sense that we are being cheated out of things that should be rightly ours. The way I see it and I've said it all along is that my mum has her own property, lives in this very big … you know, this big house that we all used to live in. She is financially secure. My dad is also financially secure. We … you know me and my sisters just manage to get by every month paying our rent, paying our student loans off and all the rest of it and we don't have any financial security … I've sent them letters saying that I would like whatever money they would've put aside for our weddings for example, or our inheritance.

Participants perceived the financial impact of divorce to extend into their adult lives as it diminished the financial resources available for support. They also felt that they were losing out on accumulated financial resources over generations which are normally transferred inter-generationally. It is also likely that the changes in the family constitution and introduction of step-families further divided and redistributed resources that may have been available to them.

Physical Impact

Some participants reported changes in their physical circumstances, family moves and changes in the constitution of their family due to the temporary or permanent addition of family members.

Changes in residence   Even though, almost all the participants continued living in their family homes after the divorce, seventeen participants spoke of post-divorce movements in terms of their living arrangements to accommodate the family changes and care arrangements.

Pooja's family had continued to stay at the marital home. However her mother initiated a house change to move closer to her business.

> Pooja: We did eventually … when I was around 7. We moved to … basically above my mum's shop.

Changes in carers and family constitutions　For many participants there were also changes in the family constitution that introduced dynamics, role changes, and conflicts which demanded adjustments from family members. Temporary addition of family members to assist with care arrangements and role changes were reported by some participants.

Divij, narrative indicated international moves when his father left him in India to live under his paternal grandparents care after the divorce.

> Divij: Yeah I was initially sent to India for about two years … and I think ever since then (when Divij was 6 months old) I've been with my dad's side of the family – my aunt and grandparents would've cared for me …

Payal's grandfather and cousin came to live with her family for a short period of time after the divorce to support her mother, changing the constitution of her family.

> Payal: … during my parents separation period, my granddad was working in Birmingham so he and my cousin were living with us for a while yeah … but then my grand-dad left and then my cousin stayed for maybe a year.

Six participants also reported addition family transitions as a result of their custodial parents re-partnering, breaking up, and due to the introduction of step and/or half-siblings into the family (introduction of step-families through non-residential parents has been previously considered under Chapter 4).

Harpreet's case illustrated this where her mother remarried after divorcing Harpreet's father but then underwent a second divorce.

> Harpreet: Yeah … she had one partner … they got married when I was 12 and it was difficult, because me and my brother were growing up at the time and he was not like our real father … umm … I think they got divorced when I was 15.

For participants, changes in their resident household composition after divorce involved movements of different extended family members. Movements were also recorded of family members and children across countries where different family members may be located. Thus, in terms of impact, the displacement and dislocation of children's locations and their households compositions may be severely unstable after the divorce and their adjustments may sometimes include entirely new country contexts.

Emotional Impact

Families are central to the development of children and are characterised by strong attachments formed among family members. Divorce signifies a change in the family form and relationships that is also associated with loss. Divorce not only signifies loss of a parent but also loss of a way of life and demands a reformation of meaning, identities and roles that family members previously held.

Emotional consequences of divorce   All participants reported feelings of loss, loss of childhood, loss of experiences, loss of parent, loss of opportunities, loss of possibilities and loss of freedom.

Amar described a feeling of overall sadness and feeling lost

> Amar: (Long pause) ... I guess I felt very sad ... and most definitely felt very lost...

Participants missed the other parent or the role that the other parent was meant to play.

Payal talked about missing out on a social life as she had to grow up quickly and take responsibility for her younger sibling.

> Payal: Yeah ... I think I missed out on sort of little things like... messing about and going out, that sort of stuff...

Arjun realised that his parents were not compatible and that they should not be together but he recognises the loss of a father figure in his life as a consequence.

> Arjun: From my mum, there wasn't that kind of guidance, my mum's view was quite a small view which is everyone is nice and everything is good and everything is very chirpy whereas my dad's view was 'you won't get through if you don't work hard', it was quite serious. You need both mum and dad's viewpoint to learn. All you have is ... so you end up growing up with friends, instead of getting advice from someone who loved you from the day you were born.

It is important to note that though children reported that they felt loss, this did not lead them to conclude that divorce was the wrong decision for their family.

Feelings towards parents   The environment of divorce also had an impact on participants' emotions towards their parents. Most gave a dynamic report of how they felt about their parents. These feelings were embedded in history and showed a continuity with past feelings about their parents and about specific incidents. These past references were important to participants and shaped how they felt about their parents and how they interpreted certain events.

Participants who remembered violent conflicts between their parents were more likely to have feelings of relief and support their mother. These participants were also likely to have negative feelings towards their fathers who they perceived as perpetrators of violence.

Ipshita expressed her support for her mum's divorce in unequivocal terms.

> Ipshita: … she (mother) kind of said that ultimately we (Ipshita, her sister, mother) had to make a decision as a threesome but we can't go on the way we have. And I was very relieved. I was like I'm with you 100 per cent of the way, I don't really care where we are going. Let's go.

Madhuri expressed strong negative emotions towards her dad, drawing from her past encounters with him.

> Madhuri: … the older I became the more aware I became of everything … every time I see my dad, even now, I can't stand the sight of him because of everything that's happened, everything that he's done.

Participants who did not have recollections of the conflict and who did not have contact, showed lesser support towards their mothers as custodial parents and lesser negative feelings towards their non-custodial parent.

Manish did not remember his father and has no contact with him. His emotions were more neutral.

> Manish: Because I'd be talking to a stranger. I don't have any negative feelings. None at all. No hate. No feeling.

Preeti also did not have contact with her dad and does not remember the parental conflict. She believed that her mother was an equally difficult person to live with.

Feelings towards parents ranged from anger, love, hatred, fear and pity. These were dependent on the pre-divorce and post-divorce relationships with their parents as well as their memories of them.

Worries   Six participants recalled being worried about their lives in the new context. Most of these worries were welfare concerns for their parents as well as future concerns regarding their care arrangements.

Nadia was constantly worried due to the uncertainty of the situation and was unsure of how her mother would cope – how all of them would cope.

> Nadia: I was also more concerned about my mum being alone … I tended to worry about everybody a lot. I was constantly worried about my mum, constantly worried about my sister.

Pooja worried about who will care for her mother, give her company and emotional support when she is no longer there.

> Pooja: For uni, I lived out… and my main concern was I don't know what my mum's going to do? Who is she going to talk to … I didn't know what to do…

she (mother) doesn't have many friends … and so that's why I took Sky (TV channel) on board at that point. But in the longer term … I do think like what's she going to do … once me and my sister went to the fun fair and when we came back my mother was sitting there on her own, no TV, no light … just sort of staring into space.

Loyalty conflicts   Seven participants, who continued to have contact with both their parents or with their extended families, had to deal with situations where their loyalties were constantly challenged.

Harpreet explained feeling divided between her mother and her father, after the divorce. She also illustrates how her parents sometimes complained about the other parents to her.

> Harpreet: I live with my dad … so whenever I go to see her, he goes like 'oh! You're going to see your mum'. Because my mum moves around a lot, my dad sometimes criticises her and I kind of stand up for her. Or sometimes, my mum might say something bad about my dad.

Loyalty issues were presented by other social groups, and not only parents. Participants experienced loyalty issues that were pitted against a variety of opposing parties such mother vs father, mother vs grandparents, mother vs other extended family members. They indicated feeling that their loyalties were divided and had to be negotiated in light of new family dynamics or politics after the divorce.

Manish explained his dilemma of having to socialise with his extended family members in secret so as to not upset his mother indicating a loyalty conflict between his mother and his extended relatives.

> Manish: I see her (maternal grandmother) behind her back (mother) because my mum doesn't get along with her. I don't like hiding behind my mum like that but because of the way she is – there are certain things that I have to keep behind her back.

Due to the close knit families and involvement of more family members through the parental conflict and divorce, British-Indian children may be more vulnerable to conflicts between different extended family members. Changes in family constitution as elaborated earlier, may further contribute to these divided loyalties.

Meghna talked about how it hurt her to see family dynamics that included her but excluded her mother.

> Meghna: She (paternal aunt) gave advice, she was very supportive … my relationship with my her has now changed though due to the family dynamics. She's gotten very close to my dad and she's got distanced with my mum and

that's been hurting me and the children. She still cares about us but there's a difference in the way she treats my mum and it's painful for us kids to see that.

Thus changes in family dynamics can also have implications of loyalty conflicts.

Dia narrated how she felt torn between her dad's family and her mother, having been close to both parties, prior to the divorce.

> Dia: And because they (dad's family) were very loving towards us, including my dad and my bua (paternal aunt), my dad's sister, It was kind of like we (she and her siblings) used to feel torn between them. I had my dad and his family on one side and then my mum on the other side.

Loyalty issues existed both pre-divorce and post-divorce and participants were likely to be caught up in it. This may be due to the high conflict situations in their families. This aspect of divided loyalties prior to divorce is rarely noted in research literature on divorce.

Mental health   The high emotional context of divorce can overwhelm children and lead to distress in children. Nine participants reported suffering some mental health issues such as depression, emotional breakdown and even thoughts of suicide.

Priyanka expressed that she was highly distressed following the divorce which led her to attempt suicide.

> Priyanka: I was very very distressed in many ways. I had a lot of counselling … talking about stuff. I tried to at that time commit suicide as well. Took a lot of painkillers and things like that when I was about 16.

Arjun explained how his parents' divorce affected his mental outlook.

> Arjun: I struggled a lot, I got depressed, I was very involved when they broke up and I realise that it affected me for the rest of my life and everyone else around me. It was a lot of responsibility.

For some participants, their familial context and divorce presented long term impacts on their mental and psychological well-being.

Madhuri talked about how the parental conflict and divorce continued to affect her for a long time after the divorce.

> Madhuri: I'm actually having counselling so I'm trying to work through it … but it has still been such a traumatic childhood and adult hood, so how could it not affect me still!

Social Impact

The social impact of divorce was also significant and affected various aspects of participants' social lives within their family as well as within the community. This includes changes in social lives, social roles, their relationships, as well as participation in the community.

Role changes   Eight participants experienced significant role changes which included taking care of and protecting their parent, their siblings as well as themselves.

Aryan's narrative illustrates how he served in the role of caring and supporting his mother.

> Aryan: She (mother) was really depressed at that time I think, and would just sit in the chair all the time … so I used to make something to eat for us (Aryan and his siblings) and talk to her.

Participants showed great solidarity with their custodial parents by supporting them, taking on responsibilities within the household and assisting their parents to cope and deal with everyday affairs.

Harpreet explained how she took on the role of caring for her brother as a consequence of divorce and unavailability of another parent to support them.

> Harpreet: Basically because at times when my mum was single and by herself, umm … she'd have to work on Saturday's sometimes and if she just didn't get someone to watch us. I think I was about 11 and he was 9, so she'd have to go to work and when he'd wake up, I'd look after him.

Dia believed that due to her parents' divorce, she has had to fulfil additional roles, as an elder sister, around maintaining family relationships which would have been easier if her parents were together as they would then mediate these relationships.

> Dia: Sometimes, it's just assumed that I'll take on the role of sort of making contact with people and instigating visits and I don't ever see my siblings getting involved in that … but I think generally you would expect your older siblings to do that but now that we're of a certain age and all grown up, I have to facilitate meetings with family members from abroad who visit. If my parents were together then they would mediate a lot of this.

Stigma and impact on socialisation   For almost all participants, familial divorce had a significant impact on their socialisation, how they were perceived in the community and by other children. Many felt cut off from their social and cultural milieu as a consequence of divorce.

Preeti explained how she felt her family did not fit into the pattern of regular Asian families, leading to further isolation.

> Preeti: … I didn't have anything to talk to them about. It was weird, they were always asking about like family and asking about all that kind of stuff and I didn't really want to talk about my family. So they'll just say 'oh! Diwali, what did you do for Diwali!' and I was like I didn't do anything and they would go like 'oh!' … they were really close with their family and family mattered to them and so when they talked about their family so I wouldn't have nothing to say so I didn't really like hanging around them that much so even though they were my friends, I wouldn't really go out with them a lot.

Experience of social stigma severely affected participants and stigma was imposed socially by relatives and extended family members and by the community at large. Mechanism of employing stigma included rejection by the community, lack of support after divorce, comments and distancing by community and other family members.

Ravi spoke of how he felt that his extended family perceived them as burden.

> Ravi: Yeah … there was contact but we were like a burden on them. It was like … 'Oh! divorced family!'

Madhuri mentioned how some of her relatives treated her family as cursed after the divorce.

> Madhuri: … other people in the family actually live fairly away from us such as one of my mum's sisters who thinks we are cursed or something and she doesn't really see us anymore.

Ravi's and Madhuri's narratives also highlights how stigma of the divorce family is contained within the close family support networks itself. Relatives and community members exercised social and economic powers over the stigmatised 'divorced' family.

Stigma of divorce also had an impact on the practice of arranged marriages for participants, affecting their life choices and future prospects in the community. Priyanka and Ipshita, both provided a description of how the stigma of her parents' divorce was passed on inter-generationally and the impact it had.

> Priyanka: Many people have said many bad things about our family … they were saying no, no, no … we can't go for this proposal (proposal for sister's marriage) because her father has left home, he has run away from home and all this nonsense.

> Ipshita: And I got introduced to all these guys. Most of them turned me down. That kind of made me feel quite worthless as well … there were actually different reasons but some of them actually came back and said that they didn't want to marry into a family that was divorced already and blah blah blah…

The emotional consequences of this social stigma were severe and many reported feeling ashamed and embarrassed of their families and themselves. Divorce had strong implications in terms of stigma and social isolation within the British-Indian community.

Payal described how her family limited social contact with the community to reduce stigma which resulted in loss of social and cultural learning opportunities for her.

> Payal: when I was younger, I was learning how to read Punjabi and go to the gurdwara and learning more about my culture and that … but after the divorce, it meant that we couldn't go to the like functions and stuff because my mum would have to put up with stares of other people like what the hell are you doing around here … my mum just completely shut off from the community after that happened so we didn't really mix that much.

However, for some participants, divorce also brought relief, liberty and opportunities to rebuild relationships. For Heer, her social life improved dramatically as she could bring friends over home, something she had earlier avoided due to fears of how her father might react or if a violent incident occured in the presence of her friends. Heer reported feeling relieved when her father left. Neha also elaborated on the positive difference the absence of her father made, on her social life.

> Neha: when he was in the house, we were always very scared of him … you know. He didn't let us do anything on top of that, with his drink and everything, but now when he's gone, I have had a lot of freedom. My mum understood … I did my work but I had more fun with my friends, going out, them coming around. But when he was there, it was totally different, he was too strict. We weren't allowed anything like that.

Thus, while stigma had a negative impact on the lives and socialisations of most participants, some also recalled having more positive opportunities and social lives due to the absence of continued conflict in their family

Social relationships   While divorce affected the relationships with non-custodial parents as outlined in the previous chapter in terms of the contact and availability of non-custodial parents, it also affected participants' relationships with their custodial parents and siblings. The divorce presented changed opportunities within which old relationships were renegotiated.

Some changes brought about by the divorce context enabled rebuilding of social and familial relationships, for others, the impact was not positive.

Ipshita talked about how relationships have changed with her mother since the divorce.

> Ipshita: I don't think I would've have refuelled if my mother didn't leave my father … I don't think I'd have the same close relationship with my mother … I mean our relationship is just emerging again now four year later. We're at that stage where we can have honest conversations about what happened …

Vikram explained how his parental divorce has made him even closer to his sister.

> Vikram: Very very strong relationship with my sister. Well … my close family were my mum and my sister and I think I am closer to them because of what happened.

The context of divorce however also changed social roles and had a negative impact on some relationships. Some participants indicated feeling let down by their custodial parent in the way they handled role changes following the divorce.

Amar did not like the role that his mother as they took on after the divorce.

> Amar: I think … as I was saying earlier, I was badly affected by my mum because she would place a lot of restrictions upon me.

In addition, the introduction of step-parents for some participants presented difficulties for their relationship with their custodial parent as well as their step-parent.

Ravi indicated the difficult relationship he had with his step-father.

> Ravi: It was a very abusive background. Like if I didn't behave the way they (mother and step-father) wanted me to, I had to go to my room, couldn't eat.

This also affected his relationship with his mother as he felt hurt that his mother did not stand up for him but also understands the gender politics of his mother's context.

> Ravi: I am hurt because she didn't stand up for me but then I also understand her situation. She is stuck in this scenario … The scenario of her husband threatening her that 'oh! I'll divorce you', the suppression thing.

Urmila also felt estranged from her mother when her mother re-partnered.

> Urmila: Me and my mum were like best friends. We were like sisters or whatever,
> I mean we were so close, I never used to go out when I was younger. I would
> want to stay with my mum on a weekend or something. I used to be with her
> 24 hours a day after school, weekends, every minute of the day, I would spend
> it with my mum, and until she met her boyfriend and that was it, she was off!

All the younger male participants under the age of 14, except one, under mother custody, seemed have difficulties in accepting the authority of mothers after the divorce. Five female participants also reported troubled relationships with their mothers after the divorce.

The pre and post-divorce arrangements and the context of parental conflict were important determinants of how participants' social lives were affected by the divorce. For some participants, divorce meant freedom from high conflict situations and an opportunity to build closer relationships. However, for some participants, this meant changes in social roles and relationships dynamics that had a negative impact on their lives and relationships.

Impact on Education and Career

The physical, social, emotional and financial impact also influenced participants' development in schools. While all participants, except one, showed positive school achievements and indicated higher educational achievements than their parents, they nevertheless identified issues that affected their involvement and achievement in school. For many, high stress, lack of rest, uncertainty, and fear of disclosure affected their emotional cognitive and social development and performance in schools. These provide some insights into the difficulties children of divorce face and the processes through which their achievements in education are compromised.

Participation in school   Ten participants reported an impact in their participation in school, experience of education, as well as available educational opportunities after the divorce. In addition, four participants also reported the impact of conflict prior to divorce had an impact on their school participation.

Priyanka was badly affected by the absence of her father and described how her emotional state limited her participation in school and her experience of education in school.

> Priyanka: … obviously when I was going through this time, I was missing a lot
> of school and I wasn't … sometimes, I never used to be a part of anything in
> any of the classes.

Due to the financial consequences of divorce, some participants felt that they may not get the same support and choices at education that they would have if their parents had not divorced.

Amar believed that financial constraints would affect further opportunities and experience of education.

> Amar: … I am still allowed to get an education which I would be happy to get but wouldn't be the one I would've chosen.

Inter-parental conflict can affect children's participation and capacity in the school setting.

Dia described struggling in school due to the lingering conflict at the home environment.

> Dia: Living in my family was a nightmare and I regularly used to get involved in arguments till late hours … 1, 2 in the morning and then had to get up and go to school – regularly … especially when I was doing my A levels and I remember really struggling at school – being tired, stressed and worried regularly … every week … without fail.

The school is also a public site and Vikram focussed much attention to minimise, and hide signs of abuse and domestic conflict at school, highlighting the social element of the school space as well as the associated physical stress.

> Vikram: … you get very good at hiding these things (abuse at home) … if there has been a row at home, you haven't slept … you don't go to work or to school like you haven't had any rest … you try and get on with it … minimise any outward signs as to what's going on.

Continuation at school   Four participants were unable to continue with their involvement in school due to the disturbed family situation at home.

Madhuri dropped out of university and did not complete her college degree. However, three years after dropping out of university, she gained other work-based training.

> Madhuri: I became very very very depressed (during parental conflict and divorce which I felt led to me dropping out of university during my second year … and I didn't continue so I don't have a degree.

The lack of continuity in school was temporary and a flexible and supportive system enabled all participants, except one to continue.

Arjun was also affected by the divorce and took a short break before re-starting his school programme.

> Arjun: Yeah … I sort of gave up education during the divorce and I did badly in school and had to re-sit some of the exams, and I realised that there is no future for me till I finish these exams so I lost about 6 months. I was a good student but

at A levels my friends did well and I didn't grade at all. So while everyone was at university, I basically had to retrain myself and give those exams again and managed to get University grades.

Impact on career   Education achievement and development has a direct link with career and employment opportunities. Though, participants reported positive educational achievements, many felt that their family life had an impact on their career. For five participants, this impact was negative.

Dia was already working during her parent's separation and divorce and she had moved to her grandparents' house along with her mother and sister. Dia explained the implications this had for her work.

> Dia: Work was affected … within a few months of starting my new job, we had to move and we were living at my grandparents and commuting was difficult … and obviously not having a secure roof … I had to tell my new job what was happening about the commuting and the divorce …

Ravi believed that parental divorce had affected his support systems and consequently required him to make difficult decisions and take a back-seat at certain points in his career.

> Ravi: My step-dad didn't like me spending so much time there (family home) … so I knew I had to move out of the house, so I bought this house but it needed a lot of work done to it … I was in a national position but I had to give that up and take a few steps back in my career so I could do up the house and have a place to stay.

Four participants however indicated that the divorce had influenced their careers, but not necessarily in a negative light. For Neha, the absence of a violent and strict parents enabled her to make her own career choices, while Heer diverted all her energies to her career to distract herself from the family environment which proved positive for her career.

Perspectives of Marriage and Divorce

Participants also expressed ways in which parental divorce had affected their own perceptions of marriage and divorce. Participants felt that the divorce had a severe impact on them and many emphasised the need to protect children from divorce. Some participants felt that if they had to face a divorce situation themselves, they would be more aware of the needs of children involved.

> Manish: I think if you have to (divorce), you have to. But when there's kids involved, it makes matters worse, I can definitely say that! If there are no

children involved and if you're not happy and you can't work it out in anyway, then fair enough … but if you have children they can get damaged … they get hurt, pain, lost, or no guidance.

Eleven participants felt very strongly about not going through a divorce themselves, however, nine participants thought that divorce may be necessary and desirable in some situations.

Neha's sentiments summed this up.

Neha: I'm not saying that it is not acceptable to get divorced. I think that is fine. I mean I can see people and their reasons as to why they got divorced and everything but I hope to god that I don't have to be one to get divorced.

Participants also commented that they would adopt a range of strategies to ensure that their marriage does not fail. These included choosing the right partner for marriage, working at the marriage consistently and taking one's time in making the decision to marry. Family and marriage, nonetheless remained an important institution for most participants. They believed that marriage was a strong commitment that was important, particularly for raising children.

Preeti: I think that if you are not married and can't commit to each other you can't commit to your children.

Pooja: … (marriage is) very important … fulfils life … I don't know why it's important … I just see it as part of life … everyone has to go through it.

Participants also offered diverse views on marital processes and practices, particularly arranged marriages, in their community.

Four participants did not regard the idea of arranged marriage as right for them and were more keen to choose their partners on the basis of love.

Neha: None of us (her and her sisters) would definitely have an arranged-marriage … I definitely want to be with someone I love because you would spend your whole life with them.

Others indicated how social pressures continued to work for participants to follow traditional forms of arranged marriages.

Priyanka did not want to have an arranged-marriage but felt great pressure to accept this.

Priyanka: No, I don't want to at all (arranged-marriage) but obviously because of the way the family is … she (her mother) wouldn't ever come to terms with me bringing anybody home from any other background, or culture or religion … I think it would tear her apart … you know she's got over this (the divorce) and her kids have grown up and they have done very well for themselves… she doesn't want her kids doing anything wrong now because she has gained all that respect and she has built it all over again …

However, four participants were not opposed to the idea of arranged-marriage.

Nadia: I wouldn't mind. In the past my mum suggested boys and introductions. They will be arranged and I will be willing to meet the guys but at the end of the day, it will be my choice, my decision.

Discussion

Participants' accounts of the impact of divorce across various dimensions enable further understanding of the multiple impacts as well as the processes and the pathways of these impacts.

Participants indicated the direct and indirect impact of changes in the financial conditions after the divorce of their parents. Participants highlighted the loss in family income and loss of opportunities. Indeed, studies have indicated that lone-parent families suffer substantial financial consequences and poverty, and take longer to recover from poverty (McKay and Rowlingson 1998, McKendrick 1998). Between 1991 and 2004, lone-parents with dependent children were also at highest risk of persistent poverty at 21 per cent. In 2004/05, 89 per cent of lone-parent families were receiving support and income related benefits from the state (ONS 2007b). More than half of all lone-parents with dependent children in Britain live in social sector housing at 52 per cent compared to 14 per cent of couples with dependent children in 2005 (ONS 2007b).

Most participants were living in single-mother households. This gendered dimension in which most lone-parents are female-headed is also seen in the wider context where almost 22 per cent of dependent children in Britain lived in lone-mother households in 2006 (ONS 2007a). Single-parent families suffer from poverty, as well as disadvantage and discrimination due to their child care commitments (Carbone 1996, Goode 1993). The dimensions of ethnicity may bring in additional contextual features. Though Indian women seem to show high rates of employment at 53 per cent (Equal Opportunities Commission 2002), they are more likely to be over-represented in low pay manual labour jobs (Modood 1997b). Singh (1998) also found that of the 73 Asian lone-mothers she interviewed in London, only 24 were employed of which 20 were engaged in manual or unskilled employment. Additional barriers and vulnerabilities of the Indian women in Britain as explored in the previous chapter may also have an impact of the economic, health and social capacities of British-Indian lone-mothers.

Findings also suggested the impact of additional demands on the custodial parent to provide an adequate income for the family resulting in lower availability and contact with their custodial parent. Poverty of single-parent families also results in custodial parents seeking part-time/full time employment, which in effect reduces time available for parenting and possibly the quality of parenting, often making children more independent (Weiss 1975, Wallerstein and Kelly 1980, Mitchell 1985, Robert 1996, Wallerstein et al. 2000).

The loss in income results in more negative and less positive effects for children (Moxnes 2003). However, However, for some families which were always reliant on mother incomes or when mothers were able to find appropriate jobs that could support them, the financial impact was minimised and in some cases reversed. Thus appropriate and meaningful opportunities for women that can flexibly support their child care needs and enable mother to provide for their families, is a protective factor.

Division of finances also introduce another theme for conflict between divorcing spouses. While there is little literature on the role children play in such conflicts, this study suggests that older children may be involved in helping their parents to resolve these issues and support their parents in the legal context. As British-Indian children may be better socialised here, they may participate more in processes to represent their parents in resolving financial matters, particularly if their custodial parent required such support. This support, as explored in the previous chapter may be particularly useful for migrant and minority women who may depend on their older children.

Another area that has received less attention is how division of financial resources between parents can have an impact on inter-generational resources for children. Participants indicated the loss of their financial inheritance as a consequence of their parental divorce which they believe has an impact on their futures and diminished opportunities and accumulated resources that may have been available for participants if parents had stayed together. British-Indian families may provide a great deal of support to their children and children may have higher expectations of such resources and support. Thus British-Indian children of divorce may feel the loss of this support in comparison to their British-Indian peers. This lack of support may also have an impact on parent-child relationships presenting implications for future support giving by children. Indeed studies suggest that adult children of divorce have poorer relationships with their parents and have less expectations of support from them (Amato and Booth 1996, Amato and Sobolewski 2001).

Many participants also talked about changes in their familial residence and the movement of extended family members to support the newly divorced family. This is consistent with other findings which indicate that though children of divorce often continue living in their family homes after the divorce, many experience post-divorce movements in their living arrangements (South et al. 1998, Moxnes 2003). South et al. (1998) indicates that such movements are often to poorer neighbourhoods on account of the financial impact and can present changes in schools and localities that children have to adapt to. This multiple changes can be regarded as a risk factor for children's adjustments. However, within the British-Indian context, changes in residence reflect a propensity to move closer to other extended family members. The close knit extended family structures and relationships within British-Indian families throughout the diaspora helps towards providing support in fulfilling care roles, respite and alternative care arrangements when children are involved (Medora et al. 2000, Barn et al. 2006). These close support networks and systems may hence prove to be a valuable resource for divorced families by providing flexible assistance and practical everyday support. These moves thus may, in fact, be protective factors for children in single parent families, particularly in the context of difficult financial circumstances that might implicate parents to spend lesser time at home.

The emotional impact of divorce is substantial for children and results in anxiety and stress (Walzack and Burns 1989, Wallerstein et al. 2000). Emery and Dillon (1994) note that feelings of loss and grief in divorce is in some ways harder because it is cyclical in nature since there are possibilities of reconciliation. The nature and type of support available, the nature of changes that follow as well as social and emotional reactions to bereavement and divorce are different and all of these could affect the experience of grief for children in a divorce process. Participants also indicated feelings of loss and grief. The divorce and pre-divorce circumstances also affected participants contact and their emotions towards their parents.

For participants who had contact with both their parents, loyalty conflicts were present. Parents can present loyalty conflicts even when they seem to co-operate, by deriding each other in front to their children, thus making children take sides which is both confusing and saddening for children (Emery and Dillon 1994). Landis (1960) also reported that 44 per cent adult university students who experienced parental divorce as children felt used by parents in the sense that their parents competed for their affections and as a tool for negotiation during divorce and for hurting the other parent. Though, there is literature that parents often pose these loyalties to their children indirectly (Emery and Dillon 1994, Landis 1960), there is little investigation into the loyalty conflicts that children experience not just between parents but also in terms of their relationships with extended families who may have taken particular sides in the parental conflict. Smart (2004) did note the loyalty conflicts that grand-parents can introduce when they take sides and try to influence children of the family. Within close knit communities, the attribution of blame and involvement of other family members may present additional loyalty issues for children of divorce and their relationships with different extended family members. Extended family members may have different opinions and take sides which present difficult dynamics for children of divorce when there continues to be contact across these relationships after the divorce. This may present complex social dynamics and emotional conflicts for children. Children may feel loyalty conflicts across different relatives depending on the competing agendas of relatives. This may affect the involvement and relationship of relatives with the divorced family and consequently the support they offer.

Divorce and consequent changes can present negative mental health implications for children. They are more vulnerable to mental health illnesses, and psychological distress (Popay et al. 1983, Amato and Booth 1996). They also show lowest well-being scored compared to both bereaved and intact families (Glen and Kramer 1985, Amato 1993). Cherlin et al. (1998) found that children of divorce showed more emotional problems even up to ages of 33 years and their life courses seemed to diverge considerably compared to adults whose parents did not divorce. Asian lone-mothers in London also report that their children showed difficult reactions to divorce. Asian mothers reported their children to be depressive, insomniac, showing aggressive behaviour and eating disorders (Singh 1998). Participant's direct narrative as children of divorce also highlighted high levels of distress that often continued years after the divorce, presenting mental health issues for some.

The social lives and social roles of participants were also significantly affected by divorce. Consistent with other studies, many tried to support their parents and took on roles of responsibility to support the transition through divorce in their family, often resulting in early maturation (Weiss 1975, Wallerstein and Kelly 1980, Mitchell 1985, Wallerstein et al. 2000). Children often recognise their parent's emotions and needs and try to help in various ways, either by taking care of themselves, or performing other supportive roles in the family (Brannen et al. 2000, Moxnes 2003). Participants also reported trying to help their parents in various ways by caring for their siblings and themselves as well as supporting their parent when they were able to. This involvement may have helped participants to build stronger and positive relationships in their families.

Participants also reported how changes in the roles of their custodial parent and introduction of step-parents had an impact on their social lives and relationships. It is likely that difficult relationship dynamics unravel within the context of step-families resulting in adjustment problems for children, parents and step-parents. King (2009) also reported that adolescents may be less receptive to their mother's remarriage or re-partnering if this weakens the mother-child bond. Participants did indicate how their parent's re-partnering or remarriage affected their relationships with their mothers. Step-parents may be regarded as intruders by children and any measures they may take to discipline them may be perceived negatively. These issues may be particularly difficult to deal with in communities that have little experience of understanding and supporting such relationships. Within the Indian context, low rates of divorce and remarriage may indicate that step-families and relations are not normalised thus making it harder for children and step-parents to accept each other and for others to support these relationships. Biological parents may also feel less able to support such relationships and may not know how to do so.

In addition, in Indian families, parenting roles may be highly gendered and are often characterised by 'Strict Father, Kind mother!' (Raoa et al. 2003). Child rearing is the role of the mother and the mother-son relationship is particularly dominant. More authoritative and disciplining roles are normally held by fathers. The divorce status forces a change in these roles which may have an impact on the previous parent-child relationships. The adoption of stricter roles by mothers in the absence of the father may cause upset and resentment among children in Indian families. Parental stress may also affect parent-child relationships negatively. Male participants may be more affected by the changes in mother's parenting role as it may introduce shifts in this dynamic of the mother-son relationship due to increasing disciplinary duties adopted by mother.

The stigma of divorce had a large impact on participants' social lives. This stigma is less explored in research. In the British-Indian context, the experience of divorce as outside of the norm is most visible in social and community spaces. Many participants suffered the direct and indirect effect of belonging to a divorced family, and face stigmatisation. Stigma was exercised through economic, social and political power and involved the separation of stigmatised identities from other groups in society (Link and Phelan 2001). Participants were socially excluded within socialisation processes with other British-Indian for whom their intact families were central to many of their conversations. In addition, the stigmatised identities were invoked at various occasions to marginalise participants as children of divorce. Participants also highlighted these processes of stigmatisation by extended relatives and community members. Previous literature has highlighted the close associations and ties that Asians have within in the diaspora (Barn 2008a, Barn 2008b, Shukla 2001). Kathane (2000) adds that these close relations are maintained through regular meetings and gatherings at weddings, festivals and cultural spaces such as temples. Divorce for children in the community stigmatises them and affects their participation at various cultural and family related gatherings. The issues of inter-generational stigma that researchers such as Goel (2005) and Ranga Rao and Sekhar (2002) have noted was also evident in the future marriage choices available for participants, in the community as they were considered less favourably for marital alliances. However, for a few participants, divorce enabled children to have more fulfilling social lives in the absence of conflict in the post-divorce situation.

The impact of divorce on educational achievements has also received much attention. Children of divorce often show lower educational achievements and completion of secondary school for children of divorce as a result of psychological damage, lack of support and financial hardship (Landis 1960, Evans et al. 2001). A similar picture is also portrayed in Britain where children in lone and step-parent families showed lower attendance in education. According to the 2001 census, 62.5 per cent of 17 year olds in two-parent families were in education while only 19.9 per cent of female and 3.9 per cent of male children in lone-parent families were in education. Only 7.7 per cent of children in step-families were in education (ONS 2007a). Cherlin et al. (1991) indicate that children whose parents eventually divorce do less well in school than their peers as problems in marriages which lead to divorce crop up much earlier than the actual divorce. Forehand at al. (1986) compared teacher reports and study grades and found that inter-parental conflict seem to have a negative effect on the social and cognitive capacities of adolescent children of divorce. Findings in this study suggest that even though many participants were exposed to high levels of pre-divorce and suffered multiple post-divorce consequences, most participants were upwardly mobile, particularly in comparison with their parents. This may be due to the history of immigration where participants, representing the second generation that migrated to the UK, may have better access and opportunities in the host country and thus show higher academic achievement compared to their parents (Platt 2005). Nonetheless, participants indicated difficulties in their participation in education and sometimes the continuation in their education. However, most participants were able to recover. It may be that participants were positively influenced by the high cultural value and expectations placed on education within their community and by their parents as many Indians see education as a means out of poverty and disadvantage (Abbas 2003, Barn et al. 2006). However, it may also be difficult to ascertain achievements of parents as many parents being first generation migrants may have faced downward mobility on migration (Platt. 2005). It is also likely that the access strategy selectively identified and encouraged people with higher academic achievements to participate.

Participants also indicated the effect of divorce on their working lives. For some participants, the tensions at home due to the divorce processes had an effect on their working lives. In addition, some participants indicated the loss of support and social capital to enable progress and growth in their careers. Indeed, social capital as well as financial inheritance may have an impact on accumulated resources across generations that participants may lose out on compared to their peers from intact families (Elder 2001). Nonetheless, the divorce also had indirect positive effects on the career's of some participants who focussed their attentions on their careers and for whom the calmer environment after the divorce was a positive development.

Participants also indicated the impact that parental divorce had on their own perceptions of marriage and divorce (Wallerstein and Kelly 1980). Participants' views suggest that while they are less opposed to divorce, they continued to highly regard and value the institution of marriage, particularly for raising children. This is consistent with the values of marriage in the community. These are interesting findings as expressed attitudes and perceptions suggest a high commitment to marriage. Other studies, on the contrary, have in fact suggested that children of divorce have more liberal views to divorce and show lower commitment and resistance to marriage (Greenberg and Nay 1982, Choudhary 1988, Duran-Aydintug 1997). Research evidence, nonetheless, indicates that children of divorce show higher rates of divorce in their own marriage (Amato and Sobolewski 2001; Amato and Keith 1991a). Studies have discussed that higher rates of divorce among adult children of divorce may reflect limited interpersonal skills to sustain a marriage as they have not had the opportunity to learn these skills by observing interactions between their parents (Amato 1996, Tallman et al. 2001). This study seems to support that it may be lack of inter-personal skills, rather than a pro-divorce attitude that may lead to high rates of divorce among children of divorce.

British-Indian children continued to value marriage. However, there was mixed indication towards their attitude to divorce. They felt strongly about divorce and did not want to get divorced themselves but also felt that divorce was a valid option in difficult and oppressive marriages. These attitudes and values reflect both a traditional stance with regards to the value of marriage as well as adaptive and transformative stance with regards to acceptance of divorce in some cases and the emphasis on managing divorce transitions.

Participants' accounts also gave an indication of the ways in which British-Indians were shaping their culture in contemporary contexts, particularly with regards to arranged marriages. Though participants acknowledged the problems associated with arranged marriages, particularly for their parents, this practices was not entirely rejected by them. Bradley (1983) comments that in spite of getting bad press, new generations do not seem to have a wish to abolish the practice as a whole but rather aim to modify the practice and indeed some participants expressed this view. Participants thus indicated a dynamic negotiation with past traditions and adapting them in more contemporary contexts. This is consistent with research on adaptation where newer contemporary generations may continue to feel pressure to comply and maintain traditional practices. These can be attributed to acculturative stress as newer generations find different ways to manage their identities between host and traditional cultures in families with migration histories (Foner 1997 Berry 2006). Second generation immigrant children may be selectively adopting both traditional ways as well as western lifestyle choices and identifying themselves in the spaces between the traditional and the western (Patel et al. 1996, Modood 1997a, Brown 2000, Kalsi 2003, Smart and Shipman 2004, Taylor et al. 2006).

Risk and Protective Factors

Risk factors for children included the loss of financial resources and capital that affected their daily lives, educational opportunities and may even indicate inter-generational loss of financial resources. This financial risk has particular implications for single mother families. However, skilled, flexible employment opportunities for mothers may be protective and help mothers to cope with these financial risks. Conflict over finances also often implicated older children. Thus, older participants continued to be a resource and protective factors for divorced women.

While multiple changes and moves can be risky for children, for British-Indian children and their families, these moves are more likely to be towards areas where they are able to enjoy more social capital and benefit from resources through relatives. Under difficult transition phases after divorce, extended family resources may be highly welcome resources for children and their families and can be a protective factor.

Divorce situations involve dealing with high degrees of emotional loss for children. For many children, negative emotions associated with the divorce context can lead to feelings of hopelessness and have implications for mental health for children, both in the short and long term. These feelings are also aggravated by worries for their parents as well as their own futures. British-Indian children may be particularly sensitive and worried about the difficulties their mothers faced particularly as they are stigmatised and isolated. In addition, for British-Indian families, the high level of close contact and involvement of extended family members presents additional loyalty conflicts between different relatives, even though loyalty conflicts between parents may be limited due to low contact of participants with non-custodial parents

The social stigma presents particular high risks for children in the community as it isolates, marginalises, excludes and stigmatises them in various social settings within the community. Many children may have to take additional responsibility which puts pressure on children and limit other activities. Finally, changes in the role that custodial parents play can mark a distinct shift from previous roles they undertook. Adjusting to these role changes has particular impact for children. Introduction of step-parents presents additional risk factors due to the difficulties that children may have in accepting the authority of step-parents but also because it affects the custodial parent and child relationship. However, for some participants, changes in their social life were positive as they had more freedom and relief in the absence of conflict post-divorce.

Finally, the stress of divorce and the emotional impact affects children's participation and continuation at school. Nonetheless, all participants, except one showed positive school achievements. This could be attributed to opportunities for schooling as well as high positive regard for education in the community as a means to overcoming poverty and discrimination. Such values and expectations of educational achievement may be a positive factor for children. However, for many children, divorce may also result in loss of social capital and resources and affect their careers.

Finally, participants indicated how their parents' divorce had affected them. While participants' continued to value marriage highly and were resistant to divorce, they were more accepting of divorce in difficult circumstances. Nonetheless, participants seemed to stress on the need to manage divorce appropriately, particularly in consideration of the impact on children. Participants' children's responses to family change and conceptualisation of divorce may be influenced by their own experiences as well as the dominant norms of the community.

Chapter 6
Coping with Parental Divorce

In the face of multiple changes that divorce brings, most children show great resilience and cope. Children are active agents and cope by using resources and support systems that are available to them to adapt to the new situation without the need for external or outside intervention (Smart and Wade 2002). However, whether the coping is positive or negative is always qualified within contexts and in terms of outcomes. Thus children meeting identified developmental needs, social expectations of behaviour and achieving positive goals in society may be regarded as positive coping. Similarly, coping that may result in negative behaviours such as low achievements in school, career, behavioural problems may be considered as maladjusted.

Participants in this study highlighted a range of coping mechanisms and resources they used to deal with the family transition. Their coping mechanisms were dependent on their socio-cultural context and the resources available to them. The strategies used by participants also indicated their agencies in showing understanding their family situation, taking active measures to address impact and minimise harm for themselves and their families. They did so in ways that they believed are culturally relevant and acceptable and by recognising and using resources available to them.

Mental Strategies

For most participants, strong mental convictions, clear vision of purpose and goals were important to cope. Participants indicated using mental/cognitive strategies and defence mechanisms to develop positive attitudes, to plan their lives and to gain control of their lives.

Mental attitudes and beliefs   Many participants used mental strategies such as creating a vision for their future, following certain role models and engaging with a positive belief system. These strategies seemed to focus on making sense of their own lives in a broader context as well as provide direction and hope for the future.

Preeti said that she began questioning the activities that she and her friends were engaged with and concluded that she aspired to different ambitions. She then focussed her energies towards achieving these goals.

> Preeti: … and one day, I think, I just stopped and went like, what is my life? I'm actually not going anywhere. And then I thought about my friends and they

were not going anywhere either … and I guess I just felt that I don't want to be like my mum one day, like hopeless and I don't want to rely on anybody else and to do that I have to study, to do that I have to get a job and get money and to do that I have to study and go to university.

Ravi's mental strategy was to follow the ideals of role models and figures from religion and history that he respected and used their examples to inspire him in his life and in the particular oppressive context he found himself in.

> Ravi: … I used to read about Hindu Warriors, they had a different battle in the sense that Hindus were very suppressed at that point in time and I could relate to that. I was like 'hang on!' I'm being suppressed. And I started to see, I began to understand the ideology that they had from the Gurus. And although I didn't have a Guru, I was like the Guru should be within me now, the guru should be in the book, so I started thinking that these warriors like Shivaji, Rana Pratap, Jhansi, they had these issues with the British and the Moghuls and I thought alright! You know I've got these sort of problems, they had those problems, different scenario. I realised I needed to make a strategy to fight this.

Both Ravi and Preeti indicated a process by which they were taking charge of their own lives indicating a high locus of control.

A positive belief system such as belief is god is often cited as a resilience factor for children. For fourteen participants this is an important factor that helped them and their families to make sense of the world and cope. Belief in god was useful and a source of strength as it inculcated hope and inspiration in their lives when they were unable to devise other options of ways of dealing with difficult situations.

Payal's ideas of spirituality helped her to strengthen her family. Spirituality enabled Payal to appreciate and care for herself.

> Payal: I'm really into like spiritually, the consciousness, like a holistic approach to love, then really looking into looking after myself and my heart. I think, you know you're just born spiritually. It's helped me to make my family stronger.

Priyanka's belief in god helped her and her mother to cope.

> Priyanka: In god, my mother kept faith. We started going to the temple a lot and we slowly slowly started finding solitude in that and that was a very big comfort for us. My first biggest source of strength for coping I would definitely say is my faith in god because … when you start going to the temple at a very late age … you don't really understand it. But if you've got that faith from a very young age and living with it every single day, it starts helping you. So when I used to go to pray or I used to do something and that prayer was answered I used to feel it working for me.

Thus while practices of religion seemed to help promote a sense of ritual, normality and connectedness, use of religious figures and stories also helped to provide supportive role models and a vision for a future.

Defence mechanisms Many participants felt overwhelmed by the emotional context of divorce. Fifteen participants employed a range of psychological defence mechanisms to avoid or divert their attention from the familial issues. These defence mechanism included ignoring/avoidance of the situation by not thinking about it, letting go and moving on, distracting or diverting their attention to other issues and not getting bogged down with current problems.

Neha preferred to not think about things and just moved along without deliberating on issues and holding on to them.

> Neha: I prefer to just forget about it than to keep dwelling and keep getting upset over it. I just think if you want to move forward what's the point in thinking about it.

Heer immersed herself in her work so she did not have the time to think about her family. Her work thus served to distract her attention and help her cope.

> Heer: I try not to think about it, I focus on my job and my work as a means to not have to think about what's happening at my home.

Behavioural and Physical Strategies

A range of behavioural and physical strategies were also used to minimise impact. Sometimes these were combined with other mental strategies and at other times, employed as a reaction. These strategies were used to avoid, protect or attract attention for help.

Common behavioural strategies included confrontation, avoidance and physically removing oneself from the family scene, using drink/drugs as well as other risky behaviour such as stealing, drugs, and misbehaviour.

These strategies could present a constellation of physical and behavioural characteristics that are mostly categorised under impact of divorce. However, these behavioural strategies are discussed here are presented as coping behaviours because participants talked of these behaviours as coping strategies.

Distancing In addition to using psychological strategies to cope with the family situation, thirteen participants reported that they stayed away from their homes as much as possible or tried to leave home as soon as possible to escape the family situation. The reasons outlined for wanting to distance themselves included difficult relationships with their custodial parent, difficult relationships with their step-parent and dissatisfaction with their family lives.

Preeti coped with the family situation by distancing herself and spending as much time away from the family as she could.

> Preeti: I didn't want to be home. That's the main thing, because my mum was always talking about my dad non-stop, so I didn't really want to be in the house … I think I also wanted to go somewhere where I didn't have to think about those kind of problems in my life … so I used to call my friends quite a lot, umm … but basically going out a lot … I think some of the things I did were quite dangerous and extreme like drink excessive amounts. I think at one time I was in hospital because I was drinking so much and I had passed out.

For Preeti, this coping strategy of staying away also had an impact on the kind of social life and activities she engaged in. Other participants also reported similar strategies where staying away from home exposed them to situations which encouraged their engagement in dangerous or anti-social activities. This dissatisfaction with the home environment drove many children to leave home early.

Ravi left home because he did not feel welcome in his mother's home due to his step-father.

> Ravi: … I was away at university for 5 years and then I went back to my mum's house and lived there for a while but nothing had changed, he (step-father) was still the same, abusive and drinking, being rude … so I now live separately.

Aryan left home when he was 14 years old due to conflicted relations with his mother who was his custodial parent and his siblings.

> Aryan: I would not get along with my mother … she had become different and was always trying to control me. I got into a lot of fights with her. I stole her credit card once and she was very upset. I couldn't take it anymore so I left home to stay with some friends when I was 15 and then just basically lived a hippy life for the next 4 years.

Arjun seemed to be expressing a sense of disconnection from his family in his narrative and decided to leave home of his own agency.

> Arjun: … I kept in touch with no one … I cut everyone off at that point. I basically did a one way ticket. I wasn't sure what to do and I just wanted to try something else and I thought the best way of doing that was to just go…

Substance abuse and behavioural reactions   Ten participants reported engaging in behaviours that involved instances of acting out excessive alcohol consumption, drug taking, and stealing. For some, these behaviour were associated with staying away from home, having lower supervision and peer pressure.

Preeti reported drinking due to her staying away from home and influence of peers.

> Preeti: When I was 14-15, I used to go out a lot with my friends and go to like house parties and things like that and drink. We used to just go out and drink and all that kind of stuff.

Some commented on their use of substances such as alcohol and marijuana as a mechanism to cope. Amar said that coped with his parents divorce and the way he was feeling about it was to use marijuana.

> Amar: Umm … I guess, the best friend that I had was the marijuana … so if you don't know I'm a marijuana addict.

Arjun recalled a time during his college days when he got very depressed and drank excessively.

> Arjun: I was depressed and there was never a day when I went without (alcohol). You know how it is in college … available alcohol, no one to say anything to you.

Arjun alludes to the absence of someone to monitor and watch out for him. Dia mentioned a similar scenario where she engaged in drinking and smoking to calm herself but had to ensure that people from the British-Indian community did not spot her as such behaviours would be highly disapproved of by her family relatives and the community.

> Dia: When I was in my teens and I acted out very strongly against my parents and you know did all the things that you are not supposed to do, going out and drinking and smoking and all that rubbish … But my immediate vicinity was filled with all English people and as far as my family – the people that I would be worried about i.e. my grandparents, they didn't know because they live further away. So, although I was rebelling against my parents it wasn't commonly known. I think I probably would've looked at things differently if I was in colder contact with my community people … I probably would've been more vary of doing it.

It is important to note however, that though participants reported excessive use of alcohol or drugs at certain difficult phases in their life, none of them, except two, indicated continued dependence at the time of the interview.

Participants' Agencies

Participants also reported on their own agencies and selectively using resources and strategies to cope with particular situations. Participants renegotiated relationships

Table 6.1   Summary of re-negotiated relationships between British-Indian adult children and family members (rated positive or negative in terms of outcomes)

	Positive	Negative	Total
Father	8	3	11
Mother	4	–	4
Siblings	3	–	3
Extended family	–	6	6
Total	15	9	24

within their environments to promote their own well-being, used strategies to actively cope with stigma and situations of poverty.

Renegotiating social relationships   Social relationships and the social impact of divorce were significant and relationships subsequent to divorce seem more dynamic and open to change. While, younger participants had little control over these dynamics, older participants were more effective in using their agency and determining these relationships.

Twelve participants had attempted to re-establish and renegotiate relationships with their parents, siblings and relatives of their own agency. Table 6.1 presents a glimpse of the relationships that were re-negotiated either for positive or negative outcomes. Positive outcomes indicate a formation of stronger and more positive relationship while negative outcomes indicates a weakening or a trend towards a less positive or negative relationship.

Many of these relationships allowed participants to understand the divorce from different perspectives and to find closure. For some, these relationships promoted dialogue and communication which helped them to understand, while for others it enabled them to gain further insight into their parents behaviours and let go of unmet expectations and negative emotions such as anger, sorrow and loss.

Many participants, particularly those whose parents divorced when they were younger, realised that their absent parent's perspective on the divorce might be different from the version that they had heard from their custodial parent. While not all participants felt that they may have the opportunity or felt the need to learn more, some participants did want to know more about the divorce. One of the participants found out about his father and hopes to meet him one day. Another participant, Divij, had in fact, contacted his mother to find out about her point of view.

> Divij: … and some relatives now and then also asked if I knew where my mum is and that she must miss you a lot … my dad would suggest that that's not the case and she doesn't care but other people were telling me different. There are always some relatives that are interconnected … some relatives of hers may know some friends who are friends of my aunt and something like that. I think

she used to ask information about me through them so they were always asking
me questions every 6 months or whatever. So I got the number from them and I
contacted her and met her after 20 odd years.

Divij also indicated how the inter-connections and links in the community due to
the large extended and family networks helped him to locate his mother. Other
participants also reported that they knew whereabouts of their non-custodial parent
even if they did not have contact with them or even if they were no longer in the
UK through their networks in the diaspora. Older participants were also able to
consolidate previous difficult relationships with their non-custodial parents as well
as their custodial parents (in light of the relationship issues with father discussed in
Chapter 4 and the relationship issues with custodial parents in the Chapter 5). Thus
participants were able to re-establish relationships in positive or negative ways.

Dia was older when her parents got divorced. She had supported her mother
during the divorce but later got estranged from her. Dia reported that she was
trying to re-establish a relationship with her mother.

> Dia: I have tried to visit her (mother) several times, but she, she wasn't in. It was
> her birthday in February so I went to drop her a card but I think she was in but
> she didn't answer the door. But I am determined to keep trying.

Similarly Aryan had trouble accepting his mother's authority and had left home.
However, he has since re-connected with his family.

> Aryan: My relationship with my mother is definitely better. I call her like three
> times a week. Things with my sisters have also improved now and both sides
> understand what was going on and why they did the things they did.

Relationships with extended family members also changed for some participants
and were re-assessed by participants when they were older.

> Vikram: Since the last 6 months, we don't really speak to my dad's family
> anymore. They are a bit of a … they are kind of sly and not dependable … and
> my family does not want to be involved with them anymore and be part of the
> way they do things.

Aryan also refused any further contact with his extended family members.

> Aryan: I voluntarily do not keep relations with all the so-called relatives …
> they are all fair weather relatives and what's the point in that.

The agencies of older participants are a key factor in the establishment and
renegotiations of these social relationships. This also enabled participants to
challenge stigma by relatives and even restrain from contact with them if this

resulted in interference or negative impact on them as explored in Vikram and Aryan's case.

These negotiated relationships supported coping by contributing to further understanding, as well as generating additional resources for coping as well as limiting the impact of negative or harmful relationships. These relationships offered opportunities to take control, uncover new perspectives, new truths as well as to consolidate their feelings.

Dealing with Stigma Stigma was reported by almost all the participants as an impact of divorce and different ways of coping this stigma were indicated. Some confronted these attitudes of stigma while others isolated themselves from social settings where they would be likely to face such stigma. Some chose to ignore these stigmatised attitudes.

Neha dealt with issues of stigma by ignoring them and not focusing on them.

> Neha: We didn't let it get to us, no, I think … I don't even know whether they were talking about us or not, they probably were because you know they probably found out because the police used to come all the time. Police cars, loads of police and everything, you know. We were used to it because if anyone talked, you know, we didn't let it get to us, well I didn't anyway.

Nadia commented how she felt stigmatised by her boyfriend's comments and reacted aggressively.

> Nadia: A lot of people thought badly of my mum that 'oh! She's divorced!, there must be something wrong with her'. There was a huge stigma attached to it then. I must say that the guy that I was going out with when I was 17 … he always used to say, 'your family is messed up' and stuff … I used to get quite angry about it and I'd fight with him.

It is clear that stigma had a substantial impact on participants in terms of marginalising them from the community. Often times, coping mechanisms to avoid such situations led them to seek alternative contexts for socialisation.

For instance, Preeti talked about finding friends from other communities.

> Preeti: Some of my friends were Asians but they were the ones who used to study but I wasn't so close to them as they were always talking about family, I guess I didn't feel that I had anything to talk to them about. I was more close to my friends who were like black and white school friends …

Thus while, some participants felt isolated within the Indian community, they sought friendships from within the wider society where divorce experiences were more common and more accepted.

However, for some participants, the fear of stigma led them to self-censor their activities in an attempt to avoid stigmatisation.

> Ipshita: ... the comments from other people but also I think the worst thing about that stigma is that it really limited my life ... I became even more shy, even more introvert. Although I graduated, I went to university, I went to work and then I came back home. That was the cycle of my life. I wasn't allowing myself to have a social life, I didn't allow myself to have friends, I didn't allow myself to experience a lot of things in life.

Financial coping   The financial impact of divorce on participants considerably affected their lifestyles in terms of availability of parental care and limitations to educational, social and recreational opportunities.

Seven participants reported taking control of their expenses and income to support themselves and their families.

Preeti explained how she got a job very early on to help support her own expenses and made lifestyle changes to help manage finances better.

> Preeti: So when I was 14, I got a job as a part-time beginner hair dresser at Toni and Guy and so since then I have been working so my mum doesn't give me any money. I save up to buy my books and stuff. Sometimes, if it's like £20, I'll ask my mum and she'll give me money and I know she won't say 'no' because it's educational ... like food and stuff, I never, like, buy stuff from college, usually, I don't even carry any money on me so I always pack lunch from home. So I always pack lunch.

Other participants made compromises to help adjust to their parent's financial conditions and contained their needs and demands in light of this.

Payal mentioned how as a child she was very sensitive to her mother's financial difficulties and the compromises and decisions she made to assist her mother.

> Payal: Yeah ... I always felt bad about asking my mum for things because she couldn't afford things anyway ... she was looking after both of us and she was paying the bills and everything in the house. I always thought that I should compromise and earn my money and try to become independent financially as soon as possible.

Participants were very sensitive to their own needs as well as their families to cope. Participants also showed great agency to cope within their contexts.

Parents as Protective Factors and Resources

For six participants, their mothers, as custodial parents, were the most significant resource. Participants reported how their mothers provided support, encouragement, advice, solidarity and hope.

Ipshita talked about the high emphasis her mother placed on education as a means to escape the difficulties they were in.

> Ipshita: my mum would say that I need to get an education and she almost led me to believe that if I got an education I could get her out of that situation and we could…

Vikram also mentions the key role his mother played in his life as to help him cope.

> Vikram: my close family were my mum and my sister and they helped me to cope. Though friends also helped but i only talked about it (the divorce) with my close family because it was a private family thing.

Formal Support Systems and Resources for Coping

Participants used a variety of resources within their community and contexts. Many formal and informal systems of support were engaged in providing services to participants and their families. These were important resources and made a significant difference in determining outcomes.

Formal systems of support included those that were established by public policy and practice and hence were public service providers. Service providers within these systems were professionals and had expertise of some kind in providing support or assistance. Almost all participants reported use of some formal support system that addressed some of their family needs. The various supports that participants and their families used both prior to and after the divorce are represented in Table 6.2.

Benefits and financial support   Eight participants reported that they or their families received monetary support from the government as child benefit or job related allowances for single-parent families or support for education.

Nadia's mother had to go off work to care for Nadia's younger sister who was in hospital and the family had to get social security benefits to maintain themselves financially.

> Nadia: … my mum had to take a lot of time off work for that (sister's illness) and all that and we're obviously on social security.

Table 6.2   Summary of support from formal agencies, used by children and/or their parents and siblings

Formal agencies	No. of families
South-Asian agencies	4
NHS	3
Credits	4
Counselling	15
Social services	4
Police	9
Housing	1
Total	40

Vikram received means tested grants which supported him to study for a medicine degree.

> Vikram: ... fees hadn't been introduced when we were at university ... when I was at university ... there were means tested grants. So I did get like a £1500 a year from the council.

Social services and police   Eleven participants reported the involvement of police and/or social workers/services due to issues of domestic violence, and high vulnerability of children in their families.

Both Urmila and Pooja's case below highlighted the extreme circumstances of duress under which social services are referred.

> Urmila: I had a social worker when I went into care when I was 13 years old.

Pooja's family situation was indicative of the multiple difficulties that single parent families and their children encounter. As a single-parent, Pooja's mother had to work to support herself and her children, leaving Pooja and her sister alone in the home. This attracted concern from child protection agencies regarding the welfare of children in the family.

> Pooja: While she was working, my mum would leave us on our own and my sister would be looking after us. But then someone reported her to social services and they found that me and my sister were alone, so they went back to her work place with the police, in front of everyone. So my mum did say that she was a single-parent so they could either pay for the children or otherwise she would have to work. And she said that they were welcome to look after her children. I don't know how it blew off but it was ok after that.

Pooja's also indicated how single-parents find themselves financially vulnerable, forcing them to seek employment opportunities at the expense of their availability to care for their children.

Dia remembers several occasions when the police were called to restrain her father and the violence that he unleashed on her mother.

> Dia: police were involved in several times. My mum, herself called the police a couple of times. I remember them, there were several times when they were called.

However, for most children, the police presence was only a momentary dilution of the situation. As Ipshita comments, the involvement of the police did not amount to much except for warnings and temporary restraint of her father.

> Ipshita: The police came and gave my dad a warning and that was it.

Schools and therapeutic services   A high number of participants and their families indicated an involvement with counselling services. Nine participants used these services themselves and seven participants indicated that their families had used them. Referrals for therapeutic services were made by participants themselves or by social services such as the National Health Services or by other family members.

Nadia was referred to counselling due to health issues.

> Nadia: I went into a funny state mentally (because I had been so worried and stressed about my mum and sister after the divorce). Yeah ... I wasn't eating anything so they had to put me on the drip and then after that under psychiatric care for about ... 2 years but I improved after about 3-4 months... but they kept me under observations and I had regular sessions for 2 years with the ... clinical psychologists.

The school system also was involved in identifying four participants as vulnerable and referring them for counselling or other services. Priyanka was identified as having problems in school and was hence referred by her teacher.

> Priyanka: I started showing a lot of signs of distress and then one day, one of the teachers suggested that I speak to a counsellor and that's when I started speaking to a counsellor.

Counselling also seemed to be a commonly referred service to parents as well.

Preeti's mother was referred to an Asian women's centre for counselling by her lawyer.

> Preeti: I think it's like a help for Asian Women who divorce … so she used to go there for counselling and stuff.

However, the benefits of counselling services for children and their parents is unclear.

Priyanka and Neha did not think the counselling helped them much.

> Neha: We went to counselling as a family. I think my mum wanted all of us to talk about it and we did have a couple of sessions for each of us … umm … to be honest, I don't think it helped really, because I think if I wanted to talk about something, I would anyway.
>
> Priyanka: Counselling didn't help me at all. Because counsellors are there to listen to you and they are not there to advise you or anything.

There may be a gap in services and expectations from such services for some participants and their families. Cultural contexts can also feature in creating this gap. It is likely that collectivist communities like that of British-Indians may provide informal support systems to communicate, seek understanding and guidance and may not use counselling services. Counselling did not work for Priyanka as she expected guidance and Neha interpreted counselling as simply a process of talking and did not understand why it had to be a counsellor.

Preeti did not think her mother benefited from the counselling sessions either.

> Preeti: My mum … she didn't believe in getting help from people who are not family and stuff … so even though she used to go, she would not tell them everything and sort of … and there was an Asian counsellor as well so she worried about what they are thinking of her so she wouldn't really say the truth.

Cultural values such as family privacy, honour and stigma can intercept people's use and reception of formal services, as highlight by Preeti's mother who attempted to manipulate her counselling sessions as she was concerned that the truth would make the Asian counsellor think negatively of her.

However, for Madhuri who had recently started counselling felt that it was therapeutic and of benefit. She believed that counselling was helping her to come to terms with all the changes her family had been through.

> Madhuri: It's just coming to terms with everything that happened … takes a long time … how split my family has become and what it could've been … and I feel angry and wasted sometimes … I'm actually having counselling so I'm trying to work through it … I feel I'm getting a lot out of it, understanding why I feel the way I do about things and develop ways to cope.

There seems to be diversity in expectations from counselling as well as its perceived benefits. Older participants who approached counselling services voluntarily to address issues of their family life that continued to affect them may have been more clear about their expectations from counselling and see them as useful. Voluntary and involuntary participation with services also seemed to have an impact. This may be due to partnerships aspects of working together which may be easier to realise in voluntary access of services.

Informal Support Systems and Resources for Coping

All families had informal support systems that provided some help or resources directly to participants or to their families. These informal support systems included friends, family friends, relatives and other extended family members. Informal support systems were more organic and part of the social environment. They were also more continuous, more flexible and able to meet the needs of the family. These support systems provided various kinds of support which included emotional support, social support and material resources. Participants' extended families were the largest, most accessible and diverse resource of support. Sixteen participants reported support from extended family members. Eighteen participants indicated support from friends and other community members.

Communication and emotional support   Extended family members and friends were likely to be involved in participants' families right from the stage of marital conflict and provided social support and counsel to help remedy the conflict in their parents' marriage. Even after the divorce, these informal sources were involved in providing emotional support to parents and participants.

After the divorce, Aryan's mother was very depressed and it is only on the intervention and counselling from his uncle that his mother was motivated to restart her life with her children.

> Aryan: My mother was depressed, she wouldn't do anything the whole day, so at some point my mum's elder brother came over and told her to pick herself together for the sake of the three children. My mother then went and got a job at the council and did very well after that.

The emotional and social support from close relatives was also invaluable to help participants to express their feelings and to explain the situation to them

Meghna, for instance does not feel that she can speak to her immediate family but feels that her aunt has been a great source of support and someone she can talk to.

> Meghna: I can't talk to people who weren't directly involved to be honest. Like, I find it hard to speak, to talk to my mum and my grandma about certain things ...
> I can't say what's on my heart sometimes because I feel like it'll hurt them ... the most I rely on would probably have to be my aunty, my dad's sister, she's kind

of seen what's happened and she remains impartial … I can tell her everything. I
can rely on her to support me through everything.

For many participants, it was their extended relatives rather than their parents who
provided information and communication about the divorce.

Amar's uncle supported him and played the role of a father figure after the
divorce and he was the one who talked to Amar about the divorce.

> Amar: … my uncle was the one who kind of talked to us, whether we were ok and
> what you feel about what your dad said and like he would take us inside and you
> know … communicate to us about what had happened but he did it perfectly – he
> didn't say our dad was bad or anything, he just said that he had done a bad thing.

Friends, neighbours and community members also provided emotional support
to participants and their families to some extent. This was, however, limited due
to restricted sharing to private family matters with persons outside of the family
network.

Material support   Participants also received a variety of material and everyday
support such as provision of care and resources from extended family members and
friends.

Dia narrated how her extended family and her friends provide support for her
and her sister in terms of providing alternative places to stay.

> Dia: I lived with my grandparents for about 6 months after my mum left and after
> that I actually moved in with a friend for about a year. My aunt also helped us a lot
> … it wasn't financial help that we needed, it was more things like advice or when
> we were moving, helping us move house. You know helping us buy furniture,
> things like that!

Informal support from close family relatives also provided a great deal of support
in helping re-establish the daily lives, provide support for childcare for children and
their families.

Neighbours and friends also helped. Payal's neighbour helped her family by
taking her and her sibling to school.

> Payal: We got a lot of help from my neighbour. Yeah. He used to walk us to
> school and back.

Some participants also reported how their friends had even temporarily housed
them when they found it difficult to cope and stay at home.

Costs of informal support Extended families were also seen as sources of interference the lives of the divorced family and their involvement was often intrusive.

Meena explains how she felt issues in her family are never private but involved other extended family members. However, Meena believed that the support from her relatives was important for her mother due to lack of another partner and in exchange for this support, her mother was obliged to share news of her family with extended family members.

> Pooja: And that just makes it worse because then the whole family knows your business and sometimes you don't want that, you do want your privacy. But if she (mother) doesn't tell them (relatives) about what's happening … then later on they will say to her that you didn't tell us and it's your fault if things don't work out… Yeah … there is some sort of support coming from family. But if you can't get it from your partner then the family is the next best.

Payal also believed that there was too much interference in her family by her extended relatives.

> Payal: Oh yes! That (interference) was definitely there when I was younger but my mum would tolerate the interference.

Ravi also reflected a similar sentiment where he felt that the vulnerability of his family was exploited by other members and his family was used by other family members to promote a public image.

> Ravi:… because my mum had a house, it was just me and my mum so they didn't see us as having a family life so we were the house where everyone's kids were always dumped. It was usually the social place that people could use and basically we were always the people who would baby-sit when some of my aunts used to go to parties and stuff … they just took us for granted. Also my uncles had married into other families and he would take me with them to their families and say 'Oh! Look we are taking care of our sister's son' and I did find that was like a promotion gimmick like 'we look after our nephew!'

However, most divorced families did not disconnect from these networks and support systems due to their reliance on them.

Though friends also provided support and were less likely to interfere, their involvement was more limited. For instance, Meghna acknowledged the support that her friends gave her but she also did not want to burden her friends.

> Meghna: I did have a few friends, I did tell friends but it was with mixed feelings, sometimes it was just to get things off my chest but then it was also to justify certain things about my dad because I didn't want people to judge me but I didn't

expect any help back because they hadn't been in that situation and I felt I was burdening them with information that they may be uncomfortable with. But they were always there to listen, it didn't always feel right telling them though.

Discussion

The themes of coping strategies identified from participant narratives provide an understanding of the various ways in which participants coped as well as risks present in their environment that restricted their access to resources or support.

Many participants indicated the use of mental strategies that helped them to regain a sense of control over their lives and gain a sense of hope. A positive belief system and internal locus of control seem to promote resilience (Luther 1991, Daniel and Wassell 2002, Banyard and Canter 2004). In addition, participants also indicated the use of spiritual beliefs, rituals and religious practices. While Grotberg (1995) proposes that belief in god and morality fosters resilience, there is little on the role of religious and spiritual coping by children or families of divorce. Adaptive spiritual coping after divorce may in fact enable post traumatic growth for people by motivating people to manage the divorce peacefully and facilitate the control of negative emotions associated with divorce (Krumei et al. 2009). Spirituality and belief in god seems to bring in a sense of being cared for by a higher power and may foster self esteem. These mental and cognitive strategies supported participants to cope. Strong and positive religious identities of the British-Indian may have thus supported coping of participants (Abbas 2003, Becher and Husain 2003, and Barn et al. 2006). Belief systems that minority ethnic children can identify with provide them with role models and direction may be important for coping with divorce.

Participants' reports also highlighted strategies of distancing from the family to cope. Cherlin at al. (1995) study on British cohorts suggested that children of divorce are likely to leave home earlier due to conflict in their families and were more likely to cohabit. Children of divorce may be vulnerable due to the economic circumstances, conflict and disagreements at home and high life stress which may make them more prone to leave home, drop out of school and even marry early (Tasker and Richard 1994, Cherlin et al. 1995). Participants highlighted the various processes that led them to distance themselves from their families. Poor relationship with their step-parents as well as difficult relationship with their custodial parents seems to be key reasons for distancing. It is clear that such distancing presents risks for children, as it makes them overly rely on their peers, exposes them to negative influences outside the home and may encourage them to adopt ways of coping that may lead to negative impact on their future life choices. In addition, for British-Indian children's decisions to live away from their family may suggest a departure from the norms of the larger British-Indian community where families expect their unmarried children to live with them or to stay nearby (Beishon et al. 1998). Within Asian families, it is common for children to continue to live together with their families, especially for sons (Cain et al. 1979, Kandiyoti

1988, Range Rao and Sekhar 2002). Thus distancing from the family may also have an impact on their relationship with the community. British-Indian children may risk losing the support of the community or of exclusion from the community that may affect their coping resources.

Some studies indicate that there is a relationship between parental divorce and drinking, drug taking and anti-social or aggressive behaviour (Popay et al. 1983, Burgoyne et al. 1987, Needle et al. 1990, Grych et al. 1992, Hetherington et al. 1992, Hope et al. 1998). Participants indicated similar behaviours in this study as a means to cope, to suppress emotions or divert their attention. This may be associated with children's distancing from home and the lack of parental availability or attention to identify or control such behaviours. These may be maladaptive behaviours that can lead to further maladjustment and isolation. Barnett and LaViolette (1993) indicate that children can use such behaviours to cope due to a lack of learning more positive strategies. However, some participants also indicated that the close knit and vigilant community played a role in monitoring their activities and may have played a role in limiting such activities. A cohesive community thus may help to monitor children.

Participants also indicated using their own agencies to access resources, build relationships and address certain contexts of disadvantage (such as financial poverty as well as stigma). Researchers have often indicated the agencies of children to participate in their families and influence outcomes (Brannen et al. 2000, Smart at al. 2001). One of the key areas where participants showed their agency was in re-negotiating their relationships with their biological parents and extended family members. Biological relations are important to children and many children of divorce seek out and re-establish these relationships (Wallerstein et al. 2000, Smart et al. 2001). Many children exhibit a biological pull and a need to connect and identify their birth parents (Mitchell 1985, Smart et al. 2001). Welsh et al. (2004) survey of 2218 teenagers reported that 5 per cent out of 11 per cent of children in step-families considered their non-resident father as their main father figure even if these fathers were rated as being less involved with them. Older participants in this study also indicated similar intentions and sentiments. Abilities to make decisions and exert control over their own lives by engaging in relationships and changing them on their own terms are important to children and their coping (Smart et al. 2001). Thus, the agencies and opportunities of participants to obtain clarity and understanding as well as re-establishing relationships were positive factors for participants. The availability of information and connections within the diaspora to locate and reconnect with their absent parents were also a positive factor in the case of British-Indian children. While younger participants had little opportunities for this, older participants were able to use their agencies effectively for this purpose. This also enabled participants to redefine their relations with extended family members and address issues of loyalty and roles. Indeed, Smart (2004) comments on the individual choices that divorce family members make about which relationships to sustain and may be less willing to tolerate objectionable behaviour from kin.

Participants, as children in the family were deeply attuned to the financial constraints of the family and tried to support their family in the ways that they could. Other researchers within the sociology of childhood have also highlighted the agencies of children in participating in their own lives and families (Brannen et al. 2000, Maundeni 2000, Smart and Wade 2001). In terms of stigma, exposure to stigma presented risks for participants as it marginalised and excluded. However, participants' also indicated how they coped by challenging or ignoring stigmatised notions. The presence of the larger macro community and opportunities to interact within it were also useful to participants in providing them alternative spaces to socialise where they were not stigmatised. However, one participant also noted that she coped with stigma by further restricting herself. Children may need support and positive guidance to enable them to use their agencies in constructive ways that help them to cope positively.

In terms of coping resources, participants indicated that they and their families accessed a range of resources. Financial supports that are flexible can provide resources for coping. However, many participants reported the involvement of services such as police due to domestic violence and their unsatisfactory intervention or support. Gelles (1997) reports that domestic violence is a low priority for the police and is often treated with indifference, akin to the treatment that doctors give to the common cold. For minority ethnic women, statutory agencies especially police may lack knowledge and lack inappropriate services that could support women in their contexts. Researchers have commented on how police and social services can marginalise, discriminate, misunderstand and fail to support minority ethnic concerns (Wilson 1978, 2006, Chana 2005). Nain (1991) elaborates how white police may be hostile and have stereotypical impressions that shape the actions they take. Alternatively, police can also be overcautious and ambiguous over concerns of racial allegations and cultural insensitivity and thus refuse to take particular action. Thus race and cultural aspects can have an effect on services delivered, and on planned actions and interventions. This lack of cultural competence is another risk for children and families from minority ethnic groups.

Other intervention agencies such as schools and counselling agencies also offered support. While schools were most active in recognising distress, they mostly referred participants to counselling services. Some participants, however, did not find counselling useful. Trinder et al. (2002) in their study noted that children in their study were also reluctant to use counselling services and felt that counselling could not address the issues that they were facing. Furthermore, insistence of seeing counsellors and doctors forces a sense of vulnerability, powerlessness and incapacity on children which they may find oppressive (Mitchell 1985). Children also feel guarded about their private lives and are discrete in terms of the information they divulge regarding their family (Smart et al. 2001, Smart and Wade 2002). The issues of stigma may present further barriers for people to engage with counselling services (Mitchell 1985). Due to high stigma of divorce in the British-Indian community, persons from this community may be particularly resistant to use counselling services and may have heightened concerns of anonymity and confidentiality. Though some participants did find counselling useful, others did not feel that it addressed their needs and expectations. It may therefore be important to consider these barriers as well as the appropriateness of services for groups of people in terms of their expectations from these services. This supports Qureshi et al.'s (2000) understanding that it is not that South Asian families are averse to using support services but these services need to meet nuances and specificities of their cultures and expectations. Thus while schools were a positive factor in identifying distress in participants, services offered may not always be appropriate for them.

Informal support systems were the key resources for participants and their families. Informal support systems are more useful than formal systems. Single-mothers and subsequently their children may have lesser social networks compared to the general population (Gordon 2000, Brannen et al. 2000). The close knit family structures in the British-Indian community, does provide families single-parent with support. For some families this may be limited due to fragmentation of their family supports on account of their migration to the UK. Indeed, it has been noted that Asian lone-parents particularly relied on using family members for support with child care as well as for forms of financial support (Pettigrew 2003).

Participants reported the many ways in which extended relative supported multiple needs in a flexible and accessible manner. Many participants indicated that it was often their extended family members who they could freely communicate with and who supported them. Children often rely on grandparents, older siblings and friends for support and to express their views to attain coherent thinking about the divorce, rather than their parents as they did not want to further burden them (Mitchell 1985, Smart and Wade 2002, Trinder et al. 2002). Children of divorce value communication and opportunities to express themselves (Maundeni 2002) and for participants, extended family members provided this information and communication about the divorce. Unfortunately, communication about divorce with children is often found lacking in most families undergoing divorce in the UK (Dunn and Deater-Deckard 2001, Hawthorne et al. 2003). It is possible that under the difficult circumstances of divorce, parents feel less able to deal with and respond to children's questions and indeed children may be more reluctant to ask them. Under such conditions, the presence of close relatives who are able to perform these roles can be useful for children. Within the British-Indian context, the close collective nature of extended families may allow these opportunities and serve as a protective factor for children.

However, informal support systems also presented threats or inadequacies. Informal support systems largely included extended family members that could exploit the vulnerability of children's families or interfere with the private matters of the divorced family. Johnston and Roseby (1997) also note that often extended family members can become involved in the divorced family but their price for support is often obligations, demands and interferences. Smart (2004) however comments that the post-divorce, many families may not be prepared to tolerate objectionable behaviour and can make individualised choices of which relationships to sustain. However, these choices may only have been possible for participants' families when their vulnerabilities were lesser, that is, either when participants were themselves older and had more agency or when the perceived requirement of support from these extended relationships were lower. Nonetheless, for participants' mothers, as minority group members, the context in which they could have exercised these choices may be different and more difficult than for mainstream White communities in the UK. Some of these have been discussed in Chapter 4.

Furthermore, informal systems could also increase the vulnerability of certain members in the family such as members of the divorced family. Ranga Rao and Sekhar (2002), and Amato (1994) have commented on the pervasiveness of stigma on divorce which often results in lack of support, resentment among other family members and sibling rivalry, as divorce also affects their social status and life opportunities along with that of the divorcing family. Thus, while extended family and informal support systems provided a range of supports, they also stigmatised and interfered with the divorced family. Other informal support from friends in other communities was not associated with this stigma. However, the extent of material and financial help sought from friends were lower than that from the extended family system. Friends were recognised as providing important emotional support, however the extent to which friends could understand or intervene, particularly if they were from other ethnicities was limited.

Risk and Protective Factors

Children's coping responses were articulated in terms of the impact they were facing within their community. Some of the key protective factors that supported participants coping were positive belief system and mental strategies that helped them to have specific goals for the future and work towards them. Traditional histories and rituals were important as participants could relate to them and be comforted by them. Use of participants' own agencies in positive ways by renegotiating and re-establishing their relationships, coping with financial limitations and with issues such as stigma were also protective. These enabled participants to take control of their lives, and address stigma and poverty. The diasporic community was also supportive in making available information about their absent or non-custodial parents enabled participants to initiate contact. In addition, opportunities to interact and socialise with people from other communities where divorce was not stigmatised was also protective.

However, participants' could also use their agencies in ways that would present as risks. Thus participants who dealt with issues such as stigma by limiting their lives or participants who distancing themselves from the family and some by using substances to distract themselves may be considered as maladjusted coping and risks.

Poor relationships with their parents or step-parents with whom they were resident were also risks as this prompted coping in ways, such as distancing themselves and using substances, that marginalised or isolated them and had negative consequences on their futures. Nonetheless, for some participants, presence of a close knit community served as a deterrent and was a protective factor. Participants also reported how close relationships with their custodial parents was a positive factors and enabled positive strategies.

A range of formal and informal resources were used by participants. While financial services were flexible and appreciate by most families, police and social services seemed limited in their capacity to support participants' families. Schools were very active protective factors in recognising distress in participants and referring them to counselling services. However, counselling was of little help for some participants as they did not meet the expectations and needs of the participants Thus while systems that recognise children's needs are protective factors, there is also a need to provide relevant services to address these needs.

Finally, the extended family and close knit community also offered a range of informal support to participants. These were very valuable protective factors for participants. However, there were also costs associated with such support in that they stigmatised the family and excessively interfered with the divorced family.

Chapter 7
Risk and Protective Factors within the Ecological Context

The previous chapters highlighted the various contextual issues, and issues of impact that affected participants' lives and their coping. Chapter 4 highlighted the ecological context within which divorce is experienced remains an important framework to understand the impact of divorce. This context included the parental conflict, social relations, the diaspora, cultural and family values, as well as family dynamics and processes over time. Familial and individual factors such as the pre and post-divorce issues, post-divorce relationships, arrangements, availability and stability of care, all had an influence in determining the impact of divorce. Larger socio-cultural features such as particular familial and patriarchal arrangements, experiences in the community of family transitions, the socio-cultural notions of divorce, and positions of communities within the larger context also had an impact on the experience of post-divorce lives for participants.

Chapter 5 highlighted the multiple impacts of divorce. Divorce introduced multiple changes in the financial context, in the arrangements of care, relationships with their custodial, non-custodial, step-parents and relatives and expected adjustments and family expectations that had an impact on participants. Participants had to deal with the emotional contexts that the changes post-divorce introduced such as dealing with loss, re-negotiating relationships across their family networks, and dealing with uncertainty and worries. They also faced changes in their social lives, and in the social roles that they undertook. These multiple changes had an impact on their participation, involvement and completion of school and their future careers. While some research suggests that mental and emotional hardship can have a greater impact than financial impact (Rodgers and Pyror 1998); it is important to note that the impacts of divorce for participants were not isolated to one domain of physical, emotional, social or financial impact but these domains were interlinked with each other within the socio-cultural context. Thus, for example: the social impact of stigma was contextualised within socio-cultural norms of the community. This social impact thus stemmed from the context and has a social as well as emotional impact on children.

Chapter 6 considered participants' active agencies in coping with their family transitions. Though a wide variety of multiple impacts have been demonstrated, not all participants suffered from negative implications of divorce. Participants indicated coping with the family transitions in a variety of ways depending on the context of divorce. While for many participants divorce was a difficult process to adjust to, for some it meant an improvement in their familial environments.

Participants indicated using mental, behavioural and social strategies to cope. In addition, they actively used various resources available to them to support their coping.

The last three chapters indicated the risks and resilience features indicated in the narratives. This current section presents a summary view of the key risks and protective factors within the ecological framework.

Risks and Protective Factors in the Micro System

One of the primary risk factors for participants was the context of inter-parental conflict associated with domestic violence. This violence involved participants directly and indirectly. There is much literature dedicated to the negative effects of inter-parental conflict and domestic violence on children (Rodgers and Pyror 1998, Emery 2009). Participants reported their own involvement in the conflicts as well as the emotional concerns and fears it introduced. The conflict also affected participants' relationship with non-custodial parents and many lost contact with their fathers as fathers were unable to maintain contact or because participants themselves felt affected by the violence too much to be able to have meaningful contact with them. The findings also noted the exclusion of children from strategies that families engaged in trying to resolve this conflict. It is likely that strong hierarchical patriarchal structures, while they can protect young children, they can also infantilise them and reduce their power and agency from actively participating within their families.

The relationship with custodial parents was also difficult after the divorce due to changes in social roles which participants had difficulties adjusting to. In addition, the re-partnering of some custodial parents presented difficulties and most participants reported poor relationships with their step-parents. Remarriage or re-partnering also affected participants' relationships with their biological parents. Poor relationships with custodial parents was a significant risk factor as it isolated participants from their families and prompt them to use maladaptive coping strategies. These included participants' attempts at distancing themselves from their families or using substances to cope. However, close relationships with custodial parents was a high protective factor in protecting them and supporting their coping positively. Indeed child-parent relations and parenting behaviour serves a pivotal role in integrating different protective factors for children (Zaslow et al. 1999).

Participants reported the feelings of loss and worries following the divorce as they tried to cope and support their families. The emotional difficulties and worries following divorce were considerable as many indicated mental health issues. These are significant risk factors for children. Many participants also indicated how the difficult family environment affected their education participation and continuation. Loss of financial resources also implicated risks for participants in the short as well as long term. Loyalty conflicts due to poor relationships between parents and their other networks also affected participants coping and resources.

Finally the stigma of divorce was a risk factor for participants as it affected their future life choices in the community and their access to resources and friendship, and resulted in their stigmatisation.

Nonetheless, participants' narratives also highlighted protective features that helped them to cope. The divorce was positive for some participants and helped them to re-establish their lives in a safe environment, free from intimidation. Participants received great support from extended families and friends who provided care, financial, social and emotional support. It is important to note that the multiple links that participants had in the community and with the diaspora also supported them to be able to locate their non-custodial parents if they did not have contact with them.

Older participants were also able to use their own agencies effectively and positively to rebuild and renegotiate their relationships with non-custodial parents, parents and extended family relatives on their own terms. Older participants also used their own agencies to rebuild relationships and renegotiate their social resources that would benefit them. They participated positively in supporting their families and themselves financially. Providing encouragement and space for children to express themselves, take charge of their lives and participate meaningfully in their family lives can be protective factors as it enables children to take control of their lives. However, expectations from children need to be realistic and particularly younger need should be protected from becoming over burdened and taking on too much responsibility (Brannen et al. 2000). Participants also indicated how they used their agencies to cope with the financial circumstances and issues of stigma.

Participants own belief systems and faith helped them to cope. Many participants used positive coping strategies such as diverting their attention and committing themselves to education and their work as a means to escape the difficult familial context. Many participants actively coped with stigma by finding alternative sources for socialising or challenging the stigma they faced. Some participants even benefitted from support from school as well as therapeutic services that were made available. However, for others, therapeutic services such as counselling failed to meet their needs and expectations.

Chen and George (2005) indicate that protective factors for children of divorce include circumstances that can mitigate conflict, adequate parental support, extra-familial social support, open communication and the coping mechanisms that children themselves use. This is consistent with the protective factors identified for participants in this study.

Summary Key risk factors include high pre-divorce inter-parental conflict, continued conflict post-divorce and poor relationships with custodial parents. Stigma was also a significant risk factor for participants as it affected their social lives. Poor financial conditions, worries about parental coping and their abilities are also risk factors for children as these can overwhelm and have an impact on their emotional states, social relationships and education. Finally, use of negative coping strategies such as distancing from home or use of substances are also risky for children. This is also associated with poor parent-child relationships.

Protective factors included support from custodial parents, extended families and friends as well as services to develop positive strategies to cope and seek help. Some positive strategies include clear directions in the future, positive belief in the future, clear strategies such as education as a means to succeed. Participants' own agencies and opportunities to rebuilding social relationships, take control and participate in their family were also important for participants' positive coping. While access to appropriate services was useful for some participants, they were not for others. However, schools as systems to identify and be available to support children may be a protective factor.

Risk and Protective Factors in the Meso System

Primary risk factors that affected participants included poor inter-parental relationships after the divorce which had an impact on participants contact with their non-custodial parents. In addition, due to close networks and relationships with extended family members, difficult relationships between parents and different extended family relatives also presented a difficult environment for participants by introducing loyalty conflicts for them. In addition, the issues of stigma weakened parents' interactions in the community resulting in losses of opportunities and resources for participants.

The close knit community, however, did provide additional resources to monitor participants and provided supervision as participants reported their fears of being seen as engaging in behaviours that were not accepted by the community. Close interlinks between the custodial parent and extended family members provided a better environment of care for participants, particularly when custodial parents were dealing with the difficult adjustments of divorce. Parents and participants were thus highly supported by this network. The diaspora also retained and maintained inter-links over time which were accessible for participants and through which participants could re-establish social relationships with their absent parents or relatives.

Summary   The relationships in the meso system provide both risks and protective factors. The close knit links in the meso system between parents and extended families and communities present risks as they make relationships more difficult in conflict situations and introduce loyalty issues. However, these links also present opportunities that can help to monitor, provide care and supervise children. These links are also sustained over time which provided participants opportunities to re-engage with some relationships independently.

Risk and Protective Factors in the Exo System

Participants narratives highlighted how vulnerability of their parents, particularly mothers, affected the conflict situation as well as their agencies to leave the marriage. Many traditional practices such as arranged marriages and patriarchal features such as influence of in-laws in the family make women particularly vulnerable. Values such as high sanctity of marriage and stigma of divorce also make spouses resistant to divorce even in extremely difficult situations. Consequently, there was also less support for divorce even in adverse conditions. Participants' mothers may have been additionally vulnerable as migrants if they didn't know how to access services and lacked the knowledge to seek help. Finally, available services may not have been culturally sensitive or appropriate to support mothers in such domestic violence situations or through the particular barriers to divorce that they faced. Thus contexts in which patriarchy and racial issues combine to reduce women's agencies, particularly in violent families are extremely risky environments for children and families.

Reduced agency and dependence of women after divorce is also risky for children as it affects material, social and psychological conditions of women, who are often custodial parents and significant adults in children's lives. Participants' mothers continued to be isolated and vulnerable after the divorce and their life choices were limited. This was evident in the resistance to remarriage from the British-Indian community and mothers themselves. Participants' mothers may have been obliged to continue and follow the traditions to remain part of the community which did offer some protection, particularly in the larger social context which may be hostile to minority groups and immigrants. Thus, many women may continue to support patriarchal practices and adhere to practices and traditions due to a sense of ethnic identity and loyalty to their communities (Berthoud 2000, Goel 2005), and for the support they receive from the community. These multiple vulnerabilities may have made participants' mothers dependant on the British-Indian community for support even when this support implied addition scrutiny of their families, interference and a stigmatised identity. These can affect British-Indian mother's psychological states and ability to cope which also has an impact on their children's adjustments and parent-child relations (Rodgers and Pyror 1998).

Protective features in the exo system include support for women and children. were also present. The community provided resources and support for mothers in domestic violence situations and offered interventions. Extended family support was particularly helping for custodial parents providing alternative care, support and ideas to deal with the divorce. The extended family system and friends were vital in providing crucial emotional, social and financial resources.

Many participants' mothers were also able to financially recover and rebuild their resources after the divorce. Opportunities for custodial parents to regain their independence and re-establish their financial situations were also protective factors for participants and their families. These maternal resources, financial and social, also have a positive impact on children by decreasing the negative effect of divorce (Fischer 2007). The support of older participants was a significant protective factor which enabled mothers to leave marriages. Older children also provided support in the post-divorce context. Financial support from formal services was also a positive feature that helped to cope.

Summary Key risks in the exo system include the heightened vulnerability of women in the British-Indian community as they may be caught in multiple systems that marginalise them such as racism and patriarchy. These vulnerabilities systematically reduce the agency of women to protect themselves and their children by reducing support and choices. Nonetheless, the close community provides direct support to parents to cope with the multiple changes of divorce. Older children are also a support for migrant women in new contexts where they may lack knowledge of services. Finally, financial and flexible support from the formal services can also be protective in helping women in divorced families to cope. Custodial parents who are able to use opportunities to recover from financial constraints are also a protective factor.

Risk and Protective Factors in the Macro System

Some of the risks implicated in the macro environment were aspects of social services and police and their limited response in dealing with issues of domestic violence. In addition, services such as counselling may have been misunderstood and may have been culturally inappropriate in its scope and delivery. For some participants' mothers, the unfamiliarity and lack of accessibility to mainstream services also made them more vulnerable and dependent on their own community resources, even though services may have been available.

However, the larger macro context can be a positive support system and a protective factor by providing financial and flexible services to families in transition. In addition, the macro system also provides an environment for alternative socialisation that can helped participants to challenge stigmatised identities. However, participants also found themselves misunderstood and marginalised within this larger context.

Summary Key risks in the macro system may include the lack of culturally appropriate services and support and the lack of understanding of minority culture and their racialisation. However, the protective factors include the support and systems available for support as well as the opportunities within the larger macro environment to challenge stigma of divorce and engage in alternative socialisation processes that do not stigmatise divorced families.

Dynamic Risks and Protective Factors for British-Indian Children of Divorce

While various factors have been identified across systems that serve as risk or protective factors, it is important to note that these factors are multi-faceted. The narratives indicated the complexity of the divorce transitions and the variety of children's experiences, their interpretation of events and their coping. Cultural, historical and social processes underpin these experiences and interpretations.

The analysis also indicated the dynamic ways in which certain factors act as risks and as protective factors in different systems or even within the same system.

These various factors are inter-connected across the systems and dynamically interact with each other. These factors whether risky or protective for children were thus embedded within the context and not categorically defined. This interconnected and dynamics processes through which risks and protective factors were presented is further explored here.

Influence across systems　　Many themes such as inter-parental conflict, stigma and patriarchal attitudes had an influence across multiple systems. Inter-parental conflict had an impact in the exo system, in the meso system as well as in the micro system which affected participants' lives both directly and indirectly. Similarly stigma was also a key theme that had an over powering impact across systems. Stigma of divorce had an effect on mothers agencies in the exo system, it also had an impact in the relationships in the meso system and in the micro system where participants, were stigmatised and marginalised. Finally, stigma also indicated an impact over time as participants, as children of divorce, continued to be unfavourably regarded in community practices such as arranged marriage which limited their life choices in the community. Lack of financial welfare also affected participants lives and were intricately linked to lack of opportunities or vulnerabilities of mothers in the exo system.

The presence of such risk factors across systems can be overwhelming as they have they can affect multiple domains in a child's life and can set off multiple chains of impact. Thus while researchers have argued that it is the multiplicity of changes and impact that affect children of divorce (Buchanan et al. 1996, Amato and Zobolewski 2001), it is important to consider that a single risk factor that affects multiple systems of the child's development can also have a profound impact to affect children's development. Protective factors and risks can function cumulatively. Thus multiple risks can be detrimental for children's adjustments (Rodgers and Pyror 1998), however, multiple protective factors can also operate cumulatively and more protective factors can support positive development of children (Zaslow et al. 1999). The impact of key protective factors can also have a multiple impact. Therefore positive financial coping and opportunities for parents in the exo system can have a direct impact on welfare of children in the micro system.

Conflicting influences across systems　　Some situations introduced risk and protective factors differently across systems, for instance, some features introduced risks in one system and protective factors in another system. For example, resistances to remarriage may be regarded as a risk factor in the exo system as it limited participants' mother's life choices, particularly when remarriage may be one of the key routes to regain pre-divorce financial status for single mother families (Amato 1994, Goode 1993, Maundeni 2000, Morrison and Ritualo 2000, Smart 2000). These limited choices also affected participants in the micro system as they worried about their mothers' futures. Thus, limited remarriage introduced negative impact across systems. However, the lack of remarriage may also be interpreted as protective as it led to avoidance of negative stigma, as a consequence of remarriage, from the community in the micro, meso and exo system. Subsequently, the absence of step-parents may have benefited participants in the micro system as they did not have to adjust with further changes in the family constitution. This may have protected participants' relationships with their custodial parent which is a significant protective factor for children of divorce. Indeed, some participants indicated how remarriage had a negative impact on their relationships in the family and with their custodial parent. Remarriage may also be regarded as a risk factor in the British-Indian community due to the lack of institutionalisation of step-families make step-relationships complex and unclear.

Complex dynamics across systems   Many key features that presented risks or protective features were complex in their interaction with other factors in the participants' ecological system. They served as both risk and protective factors at the same time, through different processes and interactions. For example, cultural ideologies in the British-Indian community which prioritise marriages result in negative attitudes towards divorce which has a significant negative impact on British-Indian families that divorce resulting in their stigmatisation and isolation (Helweg 1979, Amato 1994, Falk 2001, Ranga Rao and Sekhar 2002, Purkayastha et al. 2003, Goel 2005). Participants reported how cultural and patriarchal ideologies reduced the agency of their mothers aggravating risks in high conflict families and where domestic violence is present. However, this cultural framework also presents a unifying force for the community and to form a collective community, which has been a source of strength for British-Indian communities in the UK through their history of migration, adaptation and discrimination in the UK (Poulter 1987, Joppke 1996, Modood et al. 1994, Farver et al. 1997, Putnam 2000). This strong cultural identity and history, practices and rituals of faith are treasured values among Indians and hence can be considered as protective factors which offer positive identities and positive coping strategies for children of divorce. For participants, faith, inspiration from historical and cultural figures and emphasis on education may be attributed to values within this cultural framework that are highly regarded.

Thus, while certain ideologies within the culture presented risks, others presented protective features. It is on account of these cultural ideologies that close community networks are available for British-Indians that support single parent families. Extended family relations and community members were available to provide informal sources of support and flexibly attempt to meet a range of needs for divorced families. These included participating in the care of children, providing material resources and emotional support. The large extended and connected British-Indian community also provided a range of diverse relationship opportunities and flexibilities. This enabled many participants to learn more about the divorce from different perspectives, to find their non-custodial parent if they did not have contact with them and so on.

Similarly, the macro system within which the lives of British-Indians and their communities are embedded also provide opportunities and risks for participants. The macro system provided alternative forms of socialisation and a social context where divorce is not stigmatised. For many participants, this is valuable as it does not limit the development of their identities within a social context where divorce is pathologised and stigmatised. However, these may not necessarily offer appreciation or understanding of the cultural contexts for British-Indian children and may not be able to provide appropriate support.

Other services available for divorced parents due to the acceptance of divorce as a normative family form also offer protective resources for families of divorce. Flexible services and services used voluntarily serve as protective factors. However, while various social services and systems offer support, failure to take account of cultural needs or deliver competent services can affect the efficacy of such services. Participants reported how some services failed to address their needs or take appropriate action. In addition, inability of services to meet needs appropriately along with aspects of racism and discrimination may drive British-Indians to form strong cohesive communities to defend against oppressive structural systems and seek support from each other. Thus British-Indian women may rely more on community support in spite of associated costs of stigmatisation and interference associated with such support.

Changes over time   Finally it is important to note that these risks and protective factors also changed over time. Not only did situations and characteristics of families change over time through remarriage, opportunities, maturation of children; the cultural landscape and the phenomenon of divorce has also changed. This has been noted in the histories and perspectives of divorce in White communities. It is likely that the incidences of divorce, its management and perceptions within the British-Indian community will show change in the near future (Singh and Tatla 2006). These will no doubt have an impact on the experience of divorce and in the risks and protective features that will be present in the lives of more recent divorcees and their children. These will be dependent on the acculturation processes and hybrid strategies that newer generations adopt in terms of conceptualising the family and realising the values that they consider as important.

Conclusion

The research presented an understanding of the context, impact and coping for British-Indian adult children. It systematically argued how ethnicity defines the ecological environment for children and has an impact across systems and determines protective factors and risks for children of divorce. To enable understanding of resilience for British-Indian children, risk and protective factors need to be understood as dynamic concepts within their socio-cultural context.

The various ecological systems are directly and indirectly linked and present risks and opportunities that constantly interact with each other. Risks and opportunities thus cannot be categorically identified but need to be considered within process and interactions of different factors. Thus, for example, while the British-Indian community presents risks by stigmatising divorced family members and limiting their support for divorce even in high risk conditions; they also present opportunities for growth and support by providing a range of flexible supports.

The narratives explored the context of British-Indian adult children of divorce holistically and highlighted the intricate and multiple ways in which outcomes of divorce for children need to be understood. For British-Indian children, their micro system includes their families and communities and interaction with school and children's experience and interaction across these systems drastically change as a consequence of marital conflict and divorce. Divorce also influences the meso system and the interlinks between different micro systems that children engage with. The larger British-Indian community frames the exo system for British-Indian children which shapes the experiences that parents have in the community and work place. These include their experiences with services, influences of community ideologies and religious practices and engagement with other community members. Ideological systems and services in the larger macro context such as the availability and impact of services, larger host culture, and discrimination also have an impact on the processes and developments that affect British-Indian children of divorce.

It is significant to note the temporal continuity of the experiences of children in their families. Divorce significantly affects the social, cultural and economic access to resources for children in the community. However, if and as divorce becomes more normative, these impacts of divorce may yet again show different dynamics and outcomes.

These various systems together form the ecological context for British-Indian children. It is within this larger framework that British-Indian children experience divorce. Their narratives show a link and continuity across the ecological systems that influenced their development and inform their context and their agencies for action and reaction.

While much of the impact of divorce reported for British-Indian children are common with research on impact that has been recorded for mainstream communities in Western contexts, the processes of impact, risks and opportunities present and the context through which impact is mediated are different. For example, though marital conflict affects all children, marital conflict and domestic violence within the British-Indian community may have additional dimensions of immigration, reduced informal support systems and cultural ideology that may limit the agency of women to leave violent marriages. Similarly, though all children of divorce face the risk of multiple family transitions and physical displacements, for British-Indian children physical displacements may involve movements closer to family members and may be supported by extended family members. In addition, the dynamics of remarriage and family transitions may present difficult adjustments in the British-Indian context where remarriages are resisted for women and where step-families are not normative in the culture. Other impact of divorce such as the emotional contexts of divorce for British-Indian children can also present loyalty conflicts between extended family relations due to the close knit family and community structure. The narratives of British-Indian children indicated difficulties in the school and their school performance which may provide an understanding of the processes through which children of divorce may suffer negative educational outcomes. However, inconsistent with other research (Amato and Booth 1996, Feng et al. 1999, Evans et al. 2001), British-Indian children continue to show significant and positive educational outcomes. The roles of ethnic value and parental emphasis on education have been indicated as one of the reasons for this. Finally, the social experiences of divorce are also significant for British-Indian children as they occupy a particularly stigmatised identity within the community.

The interactions of various systems that mediate the experiences of divorce are, however, not static, but show multiple facets. Thus risks and opportunities for British-Indian children present in their system are not linear and cannot be simply categorised. While some factors within particular systems present risks in certain contexts, they also present opportunities and serve as protective factors. It may be also important to note whether the divorce rates within the community change over time and how their increased incidence impacts.

PART IV
Implications and Conclusion

Chapter 8
Policy and Practice Implications

Family transitions, such as divorce have a profound impact on the life course for children and the subsequent opportunities available to them. Though impact of family transitions is common across many domains for children, there is also diversity within these experiences. For British-Indian children, as explored, these impacts are mediated by their ethnicity and specific ethnic contexts which present both risks and opportunities. Experiences of divorce and resources available to British-Indian children and families of divorce are dependent on the interactions across the various ecological systems within which their lives are intricately embedded. The interactions between systems are complex and risks and opportunities manifest in children's lives in dynamic ways.

For policy and practice to support British-Indian children of divorce, their ethnicities have to be considered central to their lives and in the ways that they experience divorce as a family transition. Children do not live their lives in isolation and hence outcomes and support for children has to take into account their micro, meso, exo and macro systems. There is need for practice and policy to address needs and issues of children in conjunction with their families, carers and their larger ecological context (Amato 1993, Ayoub et al. 1999, Smart and Neale 1999). Policy and practice issues to support these children need to be directed at minimising risks and bolstering protective factors for their contexts. Some suggestions for developing appropriate interventions for British-Indian families targeted at these identified risks and protective factors are considered.

Supporting Children

For many children and families, cultural and religious factors are important to promote cope and these should be reflected in the intervention and services available for children as they affect the experience of divorce (Hawthorn et al. 2003). Belief in god and religious practice seemed to boost some participants' mental strategies to cope. Furthermore, children and their families were more likely to rely on informal systems of support. In view of this, community informal networks, ethnic community organisations informal societies, temples, and gurdwaras (Sikh temples) may serve to provide valuable services to children and families in need. Most temples, gurdwaras and other ethnic community spaces do provide socialisation and cultural classes that impart religious education, ethnic language learning opportunities, dance classes, etc. (Singh 2000). The Department of Children, Schools and Families (DCSF) parenting fund of £16 million aimed to support projects from 2009 to 2011 could help support such developments (Family and Parenting Institute 2008).

Schools are key institution towards integrating services for children as they form an important micro system for children. Schools, therefore, are in a unique position to both identify children in need as well as provide support and advice. School is often the first agency or the only external agency within the child's micro system that the child could approach for assistance and schools can play an important role in protecting at-risk children. Teachers are often significant adults in children's lives and their influence can be helpful to children (Brannen et al. 2000). Training to teachers and counsellors to identify children's need and support them can be useful (Dowling and Barnes 2000). Further knowledge of the familial environment may assist teachers and school counsellors to support and deal with their family environments in addition to supporting children's educational needs. Though many researchers recognise schools are sources of help (Wallerstein and Kelly 1980, Walzack and Burns 1989, Amato 1993, Howard et al. 1999, Hetherington 2003), teachers are often not given information about the parental divorce to be able to help (Mitchell 1985, Smart and Wade 2002, Trinder et al. 2002). It may be important to foster closer links with teachers and families and strengthen the links within children's micro environments (Dowling and Barnes 2000). In line with the promotion of integrated services under *Every Child Matters* framework (DfES 2005), a further integration of school towards a site for identifying children in need and safeguarding children, may be a positive step. Rodgers and Pyrors (1998) in their review of divorce in the UK highlighted that integrating services for children through schools and doctors may be more appropriate and useful rather than specialist services.

In some schools, integrating social workers within the school environment has also been piloted to good effect in some schools. Social workers are able to effectively identify and intervene towards resolving issues that may have an impact on children's social, emotional, or educational development. Such measures are pro-active and support preventative work with children and families. Kroll (1994) also believe that social workers have a considerable role to play in helping children as individuals. They can also be a site to meet emotional needs for children as they are a natural context for children within which they can seek help and this approach is consistent with educational goals of schools. School based intervention programmes for children of divorce using group and individual work to encourage peer support and address issues of behaviour and academic problems may be useful to support children (Emery et al. 1999, Fawcett 1999, Smith 1999). These interventions with children need to also be accessible, and flexible whilst also respecting issues of confidentiality (Fawcett 1999).

However, schools may also result in service provision from an ethnocentric and deficit model perspective, particularly for British-Indian children whose appearance, language, culture, values, home communities and family structures do not match those of the dominant culture (Howard et al. 1999). Since cultural identity and esteem are important aspects of children's development, there is particular need to address gaps in services to address such needs.

For minority ethnic children and families, there is a need for such programmes to also understand cumulative risks and strengths within the ecological contexts towards developing interventions and support systems that are appropriate and relevant for children and families (Benson and Deal 1995, Ayoub et al. 1999, Gordon 2000). In the British-Indian context, it may be important for services to take account of particular cultural needs and incorporate an understanding of issues such as stigma. Some participants and their families did not find counselling or the relevant support offered to them as appropriate for them or their families. Recognising the diverse needs of families and children and providing flexible services accommodating different cultural and value frameworks may be more productive (Harris 2000, Lau 2002, Maitra and Miller 2002).

Supporting Parents with Family Transitions

One of the key risk factors for children of divorce is inter-parental conflict and inability for parents to co-operate in the aftermath of divorce. In addition, family transitions and changes in parental roles can also be challenging for children. Parents are critical sources of support for children and parent-child relationships are important to mitigate negative coping strategies and to help children to engage in positive coping strategies. However parents may need support for their parenting roles after divorce. One of the key ways of supporting parents is by informing them and helping them to prepare and manage family transitions after divorce (Mitchell 1985). However, even for mainstream families, there may be a need for more knowledge and access to support services (Johnston and Roseby 1997, Rodgers and Pyror 1998, Fawcett 1999). For British-Indians, skills to manage divorce and support them through the transition of divorce may be important due to the lower number of divorces in the community and lack of resources to understand or manage the process of transition. It may also be worthwhile to link and signpost divorcing parents to available support and advise on child-care, access to additional resources and services that lone-parents may benefit from. Pettigrew's (2003) report on lone-parents from minority ethnic families also highlighted the lack of awareness of different services such as the Child Support Agency or the New Deal for Lone Parents programme. For some minority ethnic families, particularly for non-English speakers, accessing and receiving support may be difficult and should be appropriately signposted. Other researchers have made valuable recommendations which have also been highlighted through the experiences and narratives analysed in this study. These include

- Supporting divorcing parents to cope by helping them to adjust to social life and activities post-divorce. Parents could also be aided in developing autonomy after divorce to be able to consider and deliver care for their children (Burman and Turk 1981). Parents may also need support to cope with the family transitions and the emotional effect of these transitions (Fawcett 1999).

- Setting up of clear boundaries within parent-child relationships as well as relationship between parents (Ahrons and Rodgers 1987, Brooks and Goldstein 2001).
- Need for discipline and structure through daily routines to help children adjust and pass through crisis phases (Walzack and Burns 1989, Furstenberg and Cherlin 1991, Emery and Dillon 1994).
- Responsible parenting without burdening children by expressing feelings to gain support (Wallerstein and Kelly 1980, Furstenberg and Cherlin 1991, Buchanan et al. 1996).
- Develop better communication skills to manage welfare in the best interests of the children involved (Ahrons and Rodgers 1987, Brooks and Goldstein 2001). Parents may need particular input on how to communicate to children about the divorce when they are themselves unable to think clearly as well as deal with the uncertainties and dilemmas that divorce introduces (Fawcett 1999).
- Incorporate children's wishes in the family arrangements that concern them (Dunn and Deater-Deckard 2001, Hawthorne et al. 2003).

Supporting Women

To support children and families, it is essential to recognise the unique position of women in ethnic communities and the pressures they face (Wilson 2006). It is important to empower mothers as they continue to be primary care givers for children of divorce. Vulnerabilities and lowered agency of women can be harmful for children as it reduces their capacity to protect themselves and their children. Indeed supporting women, protecting them from abuse and addressing issues such as domestic violence is crucial for supporting children's development (Smith 1999). Issues such as domestic violence, patriarchy and racism interact in complex ways for British-Indian women and for other minority ethnic women. It is useful for services to consider women's positions and work towards providing them realistic choices and support to express their agencies. British-Indian women may face multiple issues and need resources that are relevant and can appreciate their unique situation where the decisions they make has profound impact on their future lives as well as their children.

Service agencies and policy makers should consider victimisation and separation in an integrated manner (Walker et al. 2004). Agencies should help women to safeguard their safety and that of their children in different phases and to meet multiple needs (Walker et al. 2004). Police and statutory agencies should focus and address domestic violence with a serious attitude and without the ambiguity of categorising domestic violence as a private issue or presenting cultural defences for inaction when it occurs in minority ethnic families (Nain 1991, Gelles 1997). There is clearly a need for service agencies to act but this action needs to be culturally competent and provide support rather than victimise service users further. There is a need to further integrate understanding of discrimination and racism of policies and practices by listening to the direct account of minority ethnic women who have used these services or may need them (Mullender and Hague 2005). Finally the various reasons why women don't leave abusive marriages and the impact of separation on women and their children needs to be considered to provide appropriate support.

Financial support and opportunities to recover from divorce may be important protective features for British-Indian women. Providing appropriate financial and flexible support is also critical as this enables women's agencies to use resources as they best see fit for their families.

Though many services for divorced families and children are available in the mainstream context, however access to these services may be difficult for British-Indian women as members from a minority ethnic community. Lone minority ethnic women and families may not know about or be able to access communities like Gingerbread and One Parent Families which together represent 1.8 million lone-parent families in England and Wales (Gingerbread 2005). Furthermore, many may not trust these services and service providers due to experiences of structural racism and discrimination compounded by their unfamiliarity with the British context. Minority ethnic women may not find adequate support within such groups if there is little engagement of minority ethnic women in these groups. Furthermore, these services also need to understand, sensitively respond to and deal with issues that may be specific to some communities such as stigma of divorce and issues of honour for British-Indian women.

Encouraging the building of local women's groups or support groups taking into account their ethnic identities may help to build social capital and network systems. These groups and networks may help pool key resources such as child care and provide informal emotional and social support (Gordon 2000). For British-Indian women, this may be a useful strategy to find peer support and reduce dependence on community, particularly as divorce can be a very isolating and stigmatising experience. These strategies can also be incorporated within government plans towards providing more appropriate child care for families (ONS 2008a) and model the social network strategies of women in collectivist societies (Wilson 1978).

Research suggests that minority ethnic populations are often hesitant to approach statutory services as they both fear and mistrust them (Patel et al. 1998, Waites et al. 2004,). Minority ethnic community based voluntary organisations may be better able to penetrate minority ethnic communities and engage with them to provide a range of flexible services. This may be applicable to British-Indian single lone mother families as well. Better linking and integration of services that provide support within communities for vulnerable families may be a useful approach to reach single parent families without solely focussing on them which may further stigmatise divorced families in the British-Indian community.

Supporting Men

Children have best outcomes when fathers and mothers are both involved in their lives and care about their well being (Flouri and Buchanan 2003). However, conflict, violence and divorce results in difficult family environments which introduces complex and conflicting relationship issues. For many men, divorce introduces transitions which change and challenge the traditional role of men in families (Spillman et al. 2004). Men may also need support to negotiate new relationships in divorced family contexts and address barriers that limit their involvement in their children's lives such as work demands, distance and travel requirements (Dudley 1991, Swiss and Bourdais 2009). They may also need emotional support to deal with grief and loss.

No doubt, more research in this area, particularly on British-Indian men, and how they cope with family transitions will provide a deeper understanding on how to support them.

Supporting Communities

Community social work in building capacities of the British-Indian community to address marginalisation and exclusion of divorced families as well as developing community responses to address domestic violence may be important strategies to support women and single-parent families. The British-Indian community is an important protective factor as they protect and provide a range of supports. However, they also present risks. Working with the community and in partnership, addressing issues such as domestic violence and stigma of divorce may be useful to build their capacities to protect marginalised families and women in difficult contexts. This community work should focus on building support for marginalised families as well as addressing processes of exclusion. Such an approach respects the cultures of communities and presents opportunities to work in collaboration through engagement and co-operation to address difficulties. This partnerships between services and communities to devise solutions and generate resources can help towards addressing unique problems in specific communities (Lau and Bond 2000, Banhatti and Bhate 2002).

Wilson (2006) nonetheless warns that such working in partnership should not become collusive with aspects that need to be addressed in the community. It is important to note that cultural competent and cultural sensitive services should not colluding with unfair practices in the community but should incorporate negotiating stricter norms against violence and strategies for marriage dissolution if required. Building community awareness and knowledge of impact of parental conflict on children may be important to challenge views of protecting marriage for the sake of children, particularly in high conflict contexts. In addition, addressing issues of inter-generational impact of divorce and ideologies against remarriage could also be addressed.

Culturally Competent Services and Service Delivery

Cultural competence encompasses knowledge that incorporates awareness of diversity within particular groups, their histories, their cultures (general worldviews, communication patters, values), their contemporary realities and issues that affect them in the current climate; skills and attitudes that can promote engagements with them, willingness to learn, respect, non-judgemental attitude, and commitment to social justice (Weaver 1999).

Culturally competent services and service delivery should reflect these knowledge, attitudes and skills. They are important as they recognise the value and meanings of different cultures without pathologising them. This is particularly important for non-mainstream or minority groups and should be emphasised by service providers and policy initiatives. Practitioners and policy makers should be aware and sensitive to the ways in which interventions and services can have an impact on minority communities. Services need to be accessible and relevant to all groups and take into account the contextual factors that shape need and uptake of services. For practitioners directly working with minority ethnic groups, there is a need to appreciate the cultures and histories of different minority groups as well as appreciate the diverse perspectives within them. Risks and opportunities present in the environments of ethnic children are dynamic and an understanding of these various risks and resources is important to effectively intervene with children. This contextualising is important to design and deliver services in a manner that can be sensitive and appropriate. Cultural sensitivity however should be incorporated within policy and practice through an empowering model. Some suggestions include the introduction of appropriate services, appropriate training of social services and police, and working with communities in a critical manner. Banhatti and Bhate (2002), also suggest understanding and consideration of cultural tenets at various levels such as

- Primary level: sensitivity and diversity training.
- Secondary level: involvement of local community.
- Tertiary level: policy and practice frameworks that do not pathologise minority ways of life.

However, Fateh et al. (2002) notes NHS's reluctance to provide services towards addressing diversity by proposing that cultural differences like race, skin colour and ethnicity may have become vehicles for discrimination and power politics. Culture sensitivity can become a tool to justify and culturally defend practices that discriminate and oppress members within minority ethnic communities. It is therefore important to consider that policy and practice attitudes geared towards acknowledging diversity and diverse cultural practices are not misinterpreted but understood and negotiated through inter-cultural dialogue. In addition such criticisms of cultural sensitivity should not divert attention from structural and institutional issues that exclude and discriminate against some minority ethnic groups and their cultures. Helly et al. (2003) commented that the focus on change should be within institutional structures. This should be geared towards enabling communities to access, relevant support systems to form an inclusive society based on understanding the needs and issues instead of expecting high social responsibility and commitment from people.

Policies and practices need to recognise diversity within families and address the vulnerabilities and poverty within lone-parent families (Rodgers and Pyror 1998). There is scope for policy to address the feminisation of poverty within the context of lone-parent families adequately. The strategy to address this poverty in the UK has been to get lone-parents to work. Some positive ways forward is to provide realistic opportunities for lone-mothers to work through provisions of appropriate training, flexible working and providing child care facilities (Damme et al. 2008). For Asian lone mothers, good and supportive child care provisions is essential to encourage their employment as Asian mothers are reluctant to leave care of their children with unknown persons (Pettigrew 2003). Policy needs to consider flexible and diverse ways of acceptable child care provision if it seeks to encourage labour participation as a means to address poverty in such lone-parent families. Oppressive policies that force single parents to work to maintain life status equivalent to workless households need to be addressed (McKendrick 1998). There is a need for policy to address the larger gender inequality for women and the disproportionate ways in which budget cuts affect women. Reluctance to address these issues in an integrated manner will possibly result in victimising women that acutely affects marginalised women such as lone-parents or minority ethnic women.

Policy programmes need to acknowledge both the complex circumstances, needs and the diverse range of experiences of lone-parents as well as the cultural values and norms that guide parenting practices (Barlow et al. 2002, Evans et al. 2003). This book has outlined the various ways in which family transitions are shaped by cultural and structural aspects and has documented the variety of experiences of different children from the same ethnic groups.

Policy and Practice for a Multicultural Society

The macro context includes issues of deprivation and disadvantage, often structural due to the nature of immigration, hostilities or lack of acceptance in the host country, cultural issues and lack of social capital needs to be appropriately addressed (Box et al. 2001, Evandrou 2000a). Lack of accesses and acceptance often drive ethnic minorities to exist in enclaves where they can support each other, draw on cultural and social resources and protect themselves against discrimination (Platt 2005). These cultural and social resources are nonetheless important for minority ethnic children and families and can enable them to build positive links and identities in their community (Mossakowski 2003, Hepburn 2004, Shields and Behrman 2004). However, these enclaves of communities can be counter-productive where access to resources can become restrictive and risks get distributed rather than minimised

(Putnam 2000, Halpern 2005, Platt 2005, Heath and Cheung 2007). Thus for minority ethnic families and communities, disadvantages and deprivations often get multiplied that can have a negative impact on their employment, social capital, geographic concentration and access to resources (Clarke and Drinkwater 2007).

In addition, different communities may have different perceptions of parenting, expectations, patterns of socialisations, role structures in families, ideals and life transitions and may require different support systems in response to barriers of access that they face (Woehrer 1982, Hernandez 1997, McLyod et al. 2000, Dustman and Preston 2001, Anisef and Kilbride 2001, Hepburn 2004). Because all these cultural, and structural factors are inter-related, Reynolds (2002), comments that it is important to discuss the racial and cultural dimensions of family policy in terms of family structures and practices. Researchers have also emphasised the need to address the needs of people from different cultures and their families and address their exclusion (Barn 1993, Box et al. 2001, Barn et al. 2006). National services need to consider these various issues on providing services to minority ethnic groups. They need to support and build on the protective features of communities as well as mitigate negative risk factors.

It is important for policy and for practice to recognise the risk and protective factors within the environmental context for families. Structural and cultural factors play differently and show race and ethnic differences in parenting practices, marriage and divorce (Shaw et al. 1999, Bulanda and Brown 2004). For example, the risks for British-Indian women and children as lone-parent families may be structurally and culturally different. As migrant women, they may face language problems, isolation, uncertain status, opportunities and access in the host country. In addition, their vulnerabilities are further exacerbated by the superimposition of other systems of oppression, that is, class, race and ethnicity (Roy 1995, Menjivar and Salcido 2002, Ahmad et al. 2004). Policy needs to take into account these structural issues of discrimination as well as specific risks of gender exclusion, language barriers and access to services for minority ethnic families and children (Buchanan 2007). However, it remains critical that services do not essentialise the experiences of minority ethnic groups and couch diversities within groups. There remains a need for inter-cultural dialogue to develop communication processes that can enable negotiation of practices through working in partnership without essentialising but also recognising contextual features (Parekh 2006).

This contextual understanding and dialogue can be further developed to address issues of disadvantage through appropriate policy and practice. Policy and service provision should provide increased opportunities for such dialogue and allow families that use services to have more control of services and resources that they need (Buchanan 2007). However, service provision has rather approached the needs and family forms of minority ethnic families as pathological and this deficit model approach results in poor service provision since diverse cultural needs are not recognised or supported in policy and practice (Barn 1993, Barn et al. 2006). Minority ethnic families are overrepresented in welfare, under child protection and in care (Barn 2007), higher school exclusion rates, over-representation in the criminal system and unequal treatment in health and social care systems (Box et al. 2001). Evandrou (2000a) and Evandrou (2000b) comment on the existence of inequalities in services, access and resources in health, social and material resources and for minority ethnic communities. Targeted and culturally sensitive services are important to address these issues. A similar scenario can be presented for family and child services and the need for culturally sensitive practice. An evaluation of services available in 8 local authorities indicated that services were not strategically planned to be able to meet the needs of minority ethnic families (O'Neale 2000).

These institutional and structural issues need to be addressed through incorporating minority concerns and voices in delivery of services. There is much scope for development of dialogue and partnership working with minority ethnic groups in this regard. This is indeed compatible with anti-oppressive frameworks that underpin the practices of social workers, teachers and indeed other professionals in public services. However, to enable this, professionals need to approach the subject of inter-cultural dialogue with appropriate cultural competence that encompasses appropriate knowledge, skills and attitudes. Thus the development of culturally sensitive policy and practice has implications for all minority groups.

Within Britain's framework, under *Every Child Matters* (DfES 2005), the integration of services has been given particular emphasis. Integrating services with communities and micro systems that children engage with and applying a flexible approach that can incorporate partnerships with diverse groups and experiences can successfully address issues of access and provision of services. This integrated approach can also consider needs of families and women and address the links in the ecological system of children that have an impact on their welfare and development. Indeed, issues of poverty, disadvantage, lone-parenthood and ethnicity are linked. The context of deprivation, discrimination and isolation of minority communities are important features to consider at policy levels as well as to recognise and address children's needs within specific cultural contexts (Brewer and Gregg 2001, Platt 2007). After all, safe-guarding all children to enable them to be safe, healthy, enjoy and achieve in life, make a positive contribution, and achieve economic well-being, are key priorities of government (*Every Child Matters* 2003, DCSF 2008). Meeting these objectives requires an integrated understanding of how ecological systems link to children's development and consistently linking services across the system.

Conclusion

Divorce is a process that leads to significant transformation of the family. Over the past few decades, the conceptualisation of divorce, particularly in Western countries, has changed dramatically from one of deviance to a form of family change. Economic, social and cultural spheres have all played a role in influencing this. However, for the British-Indian community, divorce remains problematised.

Divorce threatens the traditional family form and thus challenges the family norms of the community around which many of the cultural values and practices that British-Indians emphasise are organised. These values have helped the community to retain close links and thus have represented a source of support for British-Indians, especially in the face of racism and discriminatory practices they have experienced in the UK. Divorce is thus highly resisted and stigmatised. Thus, for British-Indian children of divorce and their families, their experiences of divorce are situated within this particular context where their family form is not normative in the community. It is within this particular socio-ecological context that the experiences of children of divorce in this community have been explored. Other studies have indicated how particular ecological contexts matter for minority ethnic groups in terms of their parenting, acculturation and adaptation (Harrison et al. 1990, Ochieng 2003).

This book has highlighted the ways in which the experiences and processes of divorce in this community are similar to and different from mainstream communities. The findings of the study have also demonstrated diversity within the experiences of individuals and families in the community. They have also indicated how different risks and protective factors were present in the ecological contexts of children.

Key risks and protective factors for British-Indian children of divorce were systematically considered and policy and practice suggestions made towards enhancing protective factors and minimising risks across different levels and systems. These include analysing risk and protective features for children in an interconnected and integrated manner. Recommendations were aimed at providing accessible and culturally relevant services and practices with children, parents, women, communities and the larger policy level in ways that recognise the wider contexts and support systems that are available and address particular barriers that exist. A case was also made for cultural dialogue to provide services in partnerships with British-Indian families and communities that respects the strength of communities and their influence on individuals and families.

The value of culturally sensitive practices and cultural dialogue practices towards understanding minority contexts and providing meaningful support is also generalisable to other minority groups. For children and families from minority ethnic families, this is particularly important on account of the multiple exclusions they face and the inability of services to provide meaningful support to ensure better outcomes for children and families.

Culturally competent and sensitive practices necessarily mean understanding the particularities of communities, identifying risks and protective features in an integrated manner and providing appropriate services and addressing barriers that groups or communities might face. There is a need to further develop cultural competency among professionals that is based on appropriate knowledge of communities, skills and attitudes that can enable inter-cultural dialogues between families, communities and services. Many values such as education, respect for faith and ethics of care are common value frameworks across cultures. These can serve as starting points for inter-cultural dialogue and partnerships and to negotiate processes by which agreed outcomes can be achieved. Hepburn (2004) adds that working with minority ethnic families with respect and dignity, promoting positive aspects of cultural life and recognising cultural features through working with partnerships is crucial for work with families and children. Encouraging and empowering community systems through integration with other support systems are positive ways to work with communities that respect their histories and cultures towards delivering culturally sensitive and appropriate services.

The role of policy to influence practice and support families within a diverse context remains important to address child and family issues where racial and ethnic differences are sensitive and continue to shape minority experiences. Policy development to further integrate systems of support for families, formal and informal, in ways that meaningfully support their development and address disadvantage are critical to develop capacities and opportunities for all children.

Bibliography

Abbas, T. 2003. The Impact of Religio-Cultural Norms and Values on the Education of Young South Asian Women. *British Journal of Sociology of Education*, 24(4), 411-28.

Abbey, C. and Dallos, R. 2004. The Experience of the Impact of Divorce on Sibling Relationships: A Qualitative Study. *Clinical Child Psychology and Psychiatry*, 9(2), 241-59.

Ahmad, F., Riaz, S., Barata, P. and Stewart, D.E. 2004. Patriarchal Beliefs and Perceptions of Abuse Among South Asian Immigrant Women. *Violence Against Women*, 10(3), 262-79.

Ahrons, C.R. 1980. Divorce: A Crisis of Family Transition and Change. *Family Relations*, 29(4) Special Issue: Family Stress, Copying and Adaptation, 533-40.

Ahrons, C.R. and Rodgers, K. 1987. *Divorced Families: A Multidisciplinary Developmental View* (New York: W.W. Norton & Company).

Amato, P.R. 1993. Children's Adjustment to Divorce: Theories, Hypothesis, and Empirical Support. *Journal of Marriage and the Family*, 55(1), 43-58.

Amato, P.R. 1994. The Impact of Divorce on Men and Women in India and the United States. *Journal of Comparative Family Studies*, 25, 207-21.

Amato, P.R. 1996. Explaining Intergenerational Transmission of Divorce. *Journal of Marriage and the Family*, 58(3), 628-40.

Amato, P.R. and Booth, A. 1996. A Prospective Study of Divorce and Parent-Child Relationships. *Journal of Marriage and the Family*, 58(2), 356-65.

Amato, P.R. and Cheadle, J. 2005. The Long Reach of Divorce: Divorce and Child Well-being Across Three Generations. *Journal of Marriage and the Family*, 67, 191-206.

Amato, P.R. and Keith, B. 1991a. Parental Divorce and Adult Well-being: A Meta-Analysis. *Journal of the Marriage and the Family*, 53(1), 43-58.

Amato, P.R. and Keith, B. 1991b. Separation from a Parent during Childhood and Adult Socioeconomic Attainment. *Social Forces*, 70(1), 187-206.

Amato, P.R. and Keith, B. 1991c. Parental Divorce and the Well-being of Children: a Meta-analysis. *Psychological Bulletin*, 110(1), 26-46.

Amato, P.R. and Perviti, D. 2003. People's Reasons for Divorcing: Gender, Social Class, the Life Course, and Adjustment. *Journal of Family Issues*, 24(5), 602-26.

Amato, P.R. and Rogers, S.J. 1999. Do Attitudes Toward Divorce Affect Marital Quality? *Journal of Family Issues*, 20(1), 69-86.

Amato, P.R. and Sobolewski, J.M. 2001. The Effects of Divorce and Marital Discord on Adult Children's Psychological Well Being. *American Sociological Review*, 66(6), 900-921.

Amato, P.R., Rezac, S.J. and Booth, A. 1995. Helping between Parents and Young Adult Offspring: The Role of Parental Marital Quality, Divorce and Remarriage. *Journal of Marriage and the Family*, 57(2), 363-74.

Anderson, E.R. 1999. Sibling, Half Sibling, and Stepsibling Relationships in Remarried Families. *Monographs of the Society for Research in Child Development*, 64(4), 101-26.

Anisef, P. and Kilbride, M.K. 2001. *Issues of Newcomer Families in Ontario: Introduction to Final Reports*. Canada: Centre for Research and Education in Human Services and Joint Centre of Excellence for Research on Immigration and Settlement.

Astone, N.M., Nathanson, C.A., Schoen, R. and Kim, Y.J. 1999. Family Demography, Social Theory and Investment in Social Capital. *Population and Development Review*, 25(1), 1-31.

Avenevoli, S., Sessa, F.M. and Steinberg, L. 1999. Family Structure, Parenting Practices and Adolescent Adjustment: An Ecological Examination, in *Coping with Divorce, Single Parenting and Remarriage: A Risk and Resiliency Perspective*, edited by E.M. Hetherington (Mahwah, NJ and London: Lawrence Erlbaum Associates), pp. 65-92.

Ayoub, C.C., Deutsch, R.M. and Maraganore, A. 1999. Emotional Distress in Children of High-Conflict Divorce: The Impact of Marital Conflict and Violence. *Family and Conciliation Courts Review*, 37(3), 297-314.

Banhatti, R. and Bhate, S. 2002. Mental Health Needs of Ethnic Minority Children, in *Meeting the Needs of Ethnic Minority Children – Including Refugee, Black and Mixed Parentage Children: A Handbook for Professionals*, edited by K.N. Dwivedi (London and New York: Jessica Kingsley), pp. 66-90.

Banyard, V. and Canter, E. 2004. Adjustment to College Among Trauma Survivors: An Exploratory Study of Resilience. *Research In Brief*, 45(2), 207-21.

Barlow, A., Duncan, S. and James, G. 2002. New Labour, The Rationality Mistake and Family Policy in Britain, in *Analysing Families – Morality and Rationality in Policy and Practice*, edited by A. Carling et al. (London and New York: Routledge), pp. 110-28.

Barn, R. 1993. *Black Children in the Public Care System* (London: Redwood Books).

Barn, R. 2007. 'Race', Ethnicity and Child Welfare: A Fine Balancing Act. *British Journal of Social Work*, 37, 1425-34.

Barn, R. 2008a. Child Discipline and Ethnicity: Contextualising Parental Practices, in *Integrating Diversity the Collected Papers of the 2007 Interdisciplinary Conference*, edited by T.R. Thorpe and S. Singer. (Dartington Hall, Bristol: Jordans), pp. 117-26.

Barn, R. 2008b. Indian Diaspora in the UK: Second Generation Parents' Views and Experiences on Heritage Language Transmission, in *Tracing an Indian*

Diaspora: Contexts, Memories, Representations, edited by A.K. Sahoo et al. (New Delhi, India: Sage), pp. 191-209.

Barn, R., Ladina, C. and Rogers, B. 2006. *Parenting in Multi-Racial Britain* (London: National Children's Bureau).

Barnett, O.W. and LaViolette, A.D. 1993. *It Could Happen to Anyone: Why Battered Women Stay* (Thousand Acres, CA: Sage Publications).

Becher, H. and Husain, F. 2003. *Supporting Minority Ethnic Families. South Asian Hindus and Muslims in Britain: Developments in Family Support* (London: National Family and Parenting Institute).

Beishon, S., Modood, T. and Virdee, S. 1998. Ethnic Minority Families. *Findings*, (No. 398) (York: Joseph Rowntree Foundation).

Benson, M.J. and Deal, J.E. 1995. Bridging the Individual and the Family. *Journal of Marriage and the Family*, 57(3), 561-66.

Berardo, F.M. 1990. Trends and Directions in Family Research in the 1980s. *Journal of Marriage and the Family*, 52(4) Family Research in the 1980s: The Decade in Review), 809-17.

Berger, P.L. and Luckman, T. 1966. *The Social Construction of Reality – A Treatise in the Sociology of Knowledge* (London: Penguin Books).

Berns, R.M. 2007. *Child, Family, School, Community: Socialization and Support* (Canada: Thomson Wadsworth).

Berry, J.W. 2006. Mutual Attitudes Among Immigrants and Ethnocultural Groups in Canada. *International Journal of Intercultural Relations*, 30, 719-34.

Berthoud, R. 1997. Income and Standards of Living, in *Ethnic Minorities in Britain – Diversity and Disadvantage*, edited by T. Modood et al. (London: Policy Studies Institute), pp. 50-83.

Berthoud, R. 2000. *Family Formation in Multi-cultural Britain: Three Patterns of Diversity* (University of Essex: Institute for Economic and Social Research).

Berthoud, R. and Beishon, S. 1997. People, Families and Households, in *Ethnic Minorities in Britain – Diversity and Disadvantage*, edited by T. Modood et al. (London: Policy Studies Institute), pp. 18-59.

Bhardwaj, A. 2001. Growing Up Young, Asian and Female in Britain: A Report on Self-harm and Suicide. *Feminist Review*, 68 (Women and Mental Health), 52-67.

Bhopal, K. 2000. South Asian Women in East London: The Impact of Education. *The European Journal of Women's Studies*, 7, 32-52.

Bilge, B. and Kaufman, G. 1983. Children of Divorce and One-Parent Families: Cross-Cultural Perspectives. *Family Relations*, 32(1), 59-71.

Birgit, E.P. and Birgit, G. 2002. Political Intervention and Family Policy in Europe and the USA – Cultural Change and Family Policies in East and West Germany, in *Analysing Families – Morality and Rationality in Policy and Practice*, edited by A. Carling et al. (London and New York: Routledge), pp. 77-83.

Blumer, H. 1969. *Symbolic Interactionism – Perspective and Method* (New Jersey: Prentice Hall Inc.).

Bose, R. 2000. Families in Transition, in *South Asian Children and Adolescents in Britain: Ethnocultural Issues*, edited by A. Lau (London and Philadelphia: Whurr Publications Ltd).

Box, L., Butt, J. and Bignall, T. 2001. Setting the Context, in *Discussion Paper 1: Black and Minority Ethnic Families Policy Forum* (London: REU).

Bradley, D. 1983. Duress and Arranged Marriages. *The Modern Law Review*, 46(4), 499-504.

Brah, A. 1999. Women of South Asian Origin in Britain: Issues and Concerns, in *Racism and Antiracism: Inequalities, Opportunities and Policies*, edited by P. Braham et al. London (New York, New Delhi: Sage Publications), pp. 64-78.

Brannen, J., Heptinstall, E. and Bhoplal, K. 2000. *Connecting Children: Care and Family Life in Later Childhood* (London: Routledge).

Bream, V. and Buchanan, A. 2003. Distress Among Children Whose Separated or Divorced Parents Cannot Agree Arrangements For Them. *The British Journal of Social Work*, 33, 227-38.

Brewer, M. and Gregg, P. 2001. Eradicating Child Poverty in Britain: Welfare Reform and Children Since 1997, in *The Welfare We Want? The British Challenge for American Reform*, edited by R. Walker and M. Wiseman (Bristol: The Policy Press), pp. 81-114.

Bronfenbrenner, U. 1979. *The Ecology of Human Development: Experiments by Nature and Design* (Cambridge, MA and London: Harvard University Press).

Bronfenbrenner, U. 2004. *Making Human Beings Human: Bioecological Perspectives on Human Development* (New York and New Delhi: Sage Publications).

Brooks, R. and Goldstein, S. 2001. *Raising Resilient Children* (London: McGraw Hill).

Brown, Y.A. 2000. *Who Do We Think We Are? Imagining the New Britain* (London: Allen Lane).

Buchanan, A. 2007. Including the Socially Excluded: The Impact of Government Policy on Vulnerable Families and Children in Need. *British Journal of Social Work*, 37, 87-207.

Buchanan, A. 2008. *Involved Grandparenting and Child Well-being* (Oxford: ESRC).

Buchanan, A. 2009. Grandparents are an Influence for Good. *Society Now*, 3, 7-7.

Buchanan, A. and Flouri, E. 2001. Parental Family Structure and Adult Expectations of Familial Support in Times of Emotional Need. *British Journal of Social Work*, 31, 133-9.

Buchanan, A. and Ritchie, C. 2004. *What Works For Troubled Children?* (Essex: Barnardo's).

Buchanan, M., Maccoby, E.E. and Dornbusch, S.M. 1996. *Adolescents After Divorce* (Cambridge, MA: Harvard University Press).

Bulanda, J.R. and Brown, S.L. 2004. *Race-Ethnic Differences in Marital Quality and Divorce*. [Online. Bowling Green State University, Ohio: Centre for Family and Demographic Research]. Available at: http://www.bgsu.edu/downloads/cas/file35757.pdf [Accessed 5 April 2005].

Burgoyne, J., Ornard, R. and Richards, M. 1987. *Divorce Matters* (London: Penguin Books).

Burman, W. and Turk, D. 1981. Adaptation to Divorce: Problem and Coping Strategies. *Journal of Marriage and the Family*, 43(1), 179-89.

Burman, E., Smailes S.L. and Chantler, K. 2004. 'Culture' as a Barrier to Service Provision and Delivery: Domestic Violence Services for Minoritized Women. *Critical Social Policy*, 24(3), 332-57

Cain, M., Khanam, S.O. and Nahar, S. 1979. Class, Patriarchy, and Women's Work in Bangladesh. *Population and Development Review*, 5(3), 405-38.

Carbone, J. 1996. *Feminism, Gender and the Consequences of Divorce* (Aldershot: Dartmouth Publishing Group).

Cere, D. 2003. Redefining Marriage? A Case for Caution. [Online. McGill University]. Available at: http://voteonmarriage.org/Cere-Redifining%20Marriage%20-%20A%20case%20for%20Caution.pdf [Accessed 17 June 2006].

Chana, P.J. 2005. *Domestic Violence: Impact of Culture on Experiences of Asian (Indian subcontinent) Women* (Vol. Monograph No. 216) (Norwich: University of East Anglia).

Chandrasekhar, S. 1954. The Family in India. *Marriage and Family Living*, 16(4), 336-42.

Chen J.D. and George, R.A. 2005 Cultivating Resilience in Children from Divorced Families. *The Family Journal: Counseling and Therapy for Couples and Families*, 13(4), 452-55.

Cherlin, A.J. 1992. *Marriage, Divorce, Remarriage* (Cambridge, MA: Harvard University Press).

Cherlin, A.J. 2009. The Origins of the Ambivalent Acceptance of Divorce. *Journal of Marriage and Family*, 71, 226-9.

Cherlin, A.J., Furstenberg, J.F.F., Chase-Lansdale, P.L., Kiernan, K.E., Robins, P.K., Morrison, D.R. and Teitler, J.O. 1991. Longitudinal Studies of Effects of Divorce on Children in Great Britain and the United States. *Science*, 252, 1386-9.

Cherlin, A.J, Kiernan, K.K. and Chase-Landsdale, P.L. 1995. Parental Divorce in Childhood and Demographic Outcomes in Adulthood. *Demography*, 32, 299-318.

Cherlin, A.J., Chase-Lansdale, P.L. and McRae, C. 1998. Effects of Parental Divorce on Mental Health throughout the Life Course. *American Sociological Review*, 63(2), 239-49.

Choudhary, J.N. 1988. *Divorce in Indian Society* (Jaipur: Printwell Publishers).

Christensen, T.M. and Brooks, M.C. 2001. Adult Children of Divorce and Intimate Relationships: A Review of the Literature. *The Family Journal: Counselling and Therapy for Couple and Families*, 9(3), 289-94.

Cicirelli, V.G. 1994. Sibling Relationships in Cross-cultural Perspective. *Journal of Marriage and the Family*, 56(1), 7-20.

Clarke, L. and Berrington, A. 1999. Socio-demographic Predictors of Divorce, in *High Divorce Rates: The State of the Evidence on Reasons and Remedies, Reviews of the Evidence on the Causes of Marital Breakdown and the Effectiveness of Policies and Services Intended to Reduce its Incidence*, edited by J. Simons (London: Lord Chancellor's Department. Paper 1).

Clarke, K. and Drinkwater, S. 2007. *Ethnic Minorities in the Labour Market* (Bristol: The Policy Press).

Coleman, J.S. 1987. Families and Schools. *Educational Researcher*, 16(6), 32-8.

Coleman, J.S. 1988. Social Capital in the Creation of Human Capital. *The American Journal of Sociology*, 94 (Supplement: Organisations and Institutions: Sociological and Economic Approaches to the Analysis of Social Structure), S95-S120.

Cooney, T.M., Hutchinson, M.K. and Leather, D.M. 1995. Surviving the Breakup? Predictors of Parent-Adult Child Relations after Parental Divorce. *Family Relations*, 44(2), 153-61.

Crow, G. 2002. Families, Moralities, Rationalities and Social Change, in *Analysing Families – Morality and Rationality in Policy and Practice*, edited by A. Carling et al. (London and New York: Routledge), pp. 285-96.

Culley, L., Hudson, N. and Rapport, F. 2007. Using Focus Groups with Minority Ethnic Communities: Researching Infertility in British South Asian Communities. *Qualitative Health Research*, 17, 102-12.

Damme, M.V., Kalmijn, M. and Uunk, W. 2008. The Employment of Separated Women in Europe: Individual and Institutional Determinants. *European Sociological Review*, 25(2), 183-97.

D'Cruz, P. and Bharat, S. 2001. Beyond Joint and Nuclear: the Indian Family Revisited. *Journal of Comparative Family Studies* 32(2), 167-94.

Daniel, B. and Wassell, S. 2002. *The School Years: Assessing and Promoting Resilience in Vulnerable Children* (Vol. 2) (London and New York: Jessica Kingsley Publishers).

Davis, K. 1950. Statistical Perspective on Marriage and Divorce. *Annals of the American Academy of Political and Social Science*, 272 (Toward Family Stability) 9-21.

DeGarmo, D.S. and Forgatch, M.S. 1999. Contexts As Predictors of Changing Maternal Parenting Practices in Diverse Family Structures: A Social Interactional Perspective of Risk and Resilience, in *Coping with Divorce, Single Parenting and Remarriage: A Risk and Resiliency Perspective*, edited by E.M. Hetherington (New Jersey, London: Lawrence Erlbaum Associates), pp. 225-7.

Department for Children, Schools and Families. 2008. *Children Act 2004 – Guidance*. [Online]. Available at: http://www.everychildmatters.gov.uk/strategy/guidance/ [Accessed 5 June 2007].

Department for Education and Skills. 2005. *Children's Workforce Strategy A Strategy to Build a World-Class Workforce for Children and Young People – Change for Children: Consultation*. Nottingham.

Desai, R. 1963. *Indian Immigrants in Britain* (London; New York and Bombay: Oxford University Press).

Despert, L. 1962. *Children of Divorce* (New York: Vintage).

Department for Education and Skills. 2005. *Children's Workforce Strategy A Strategy to Build a World-Class Workforce for Children and Young People – Change for Children: Consultation*. Nottingham.

Dilworth-Anderson, P. and McAdoo, H.P. 1988. The Study of Ethnic Minority Families: Implications for Practitioners and Policymakers. *Family Relations*, 37(3), 265-7.

Dosanjh, J.S. and Ghuman, P.A.S. 1997. Child-Rearing Practices of Two Generations of Punjabi Parents. *Children & Society*, 11, 29-43.

Dudley, J.R. 1991. Increasing our Understanding of Divorced Fathers Who Have Infrequent Contact with Their Children. *Family Relations*, 40, 279-85.

Dunn, J. and Deater-Deckard, K. 2001. Children's Views of their Changing Families. *Findings* (No. 931) (York: Joseph Rowntree Foundation).

Duran-Aydintug, C. 1997. Adult Children of Divorce Revisited: When They Speak Up. *Journal of Divorce and Remarriage*, 27(1/2), 71-83.

Dustmann, C. and Preston, I. 2001. Attitudes to Ethnic Minorities, Ethnic Context and Location Decisions. *The Economic Journal*, 111(470), 353-73.

Dwivedi, K.N. 2002a. Introduction, in *Meeting the Needs of Ethnic Minority Children – Including Refugee, Black and Mixed Parentage Children: A Handbook for Professionals*, edited by K.N. Dwivedi (London, New York: Jessica Kingsley), pp. 17-41.

Dwivedi, R. 2002b. Community and Youth Work with Asian Women and Girls, in *Meeting the Needs of Ethnic Minority Children – Including Refugee, Black and Mixed Parentage Children: a Handbook for Professionals*, edited by K.N. Dwivedi (London and New York: Jessica Kingsley), pp. 42-65.

Dwivedi, K.N. 2002c. Culture and Personality, in *Meeting the Needs of Ethnic Minority Children – including Refugee, Black and Mixed Parentage Children: a Handbook for Professionals*, edited by K.N. Dwivedi (London, New York: Jessica Kingsley), pp. 283-98.

Edwards, R., Franklin, J. and Holland, J. 2003. *Families and Social Capital: Exploring the Issues* (London: South Bank University).

Eide, P. and Allen, C. 2005. Recruiting Transcultural Research Participants: A Conceptual Model. *International Journal of Qualitative Methods* [Online] 4(2), Available at: http://www.ualberta.ca/~iiqm/backissues/4_2/pdf/EIDE. PDF [Accessed 4 February 2006].

Elder, J.G.H. 2001. Families, Social Change, and Individual Lives. *Marriage and Family Review*, 31(1/2), 177-92.

Emery, C.R. 2009. Stay for the Children? Husband Violence, Marital Stability, and Children's Behavior Problems. *Journal of Marriage and Family*, 71, 905-16.

Emery, R.E. and Dillon, P. 1994. Conceptualizing the Divorce Process: Renegotiating Boundaries of Intimacy and Power in the Divorced Family System. *Family Relations*, 43(4), 374-79.

Emery, R.E., Kitzmann, K.M, Waldron, M. 1999. Psychological Interventions for Separated and Divorced Families, in *Coping with Divorce, Single Parenting and Remarriage: A Risk and Resiliency Perspective*, edited by E.M. Hetherington (New Jersey, London: Lawrence Erlbaum Associates), pp. 323-44.

Equal Opportunities Commission. 2002. *Facts About Women and Men in Great Britain 2002* (Manchester: Equal Opportunities Commission).

Evandrou, M. 2000a. Ethnic Inequalities in Health in Later Life. *Health Statistics Quarterly*, 8, 20-8.

Evandrou, M. 2000b. Social Inequalities in Later Life: the Socio-Economic Position of Older People From Minority ethnic Groups in Britain. *Population Trends*, 101, 11-18.

Evans, J. and Bloom, B. 1996. Effects of Parental Divorce Among College Undergraduates. *Journal of Divorce and Remarriage*, 26(1/2), 69-91.

Evans, M.D.R., Kelly, J. and Wanner, R. 2001. Educational Attainment of the Children of Divorce: Australia, 1940-90. *Journal of Sociology*, 37(3), 275-97.

Evans, M., Eyre, J., Millar, J. and Sarre, S. 2003. *New Deal for Lone Parents: Second Synthesis Report of the National Evaluation* (London: Department of Work and Pensions).

Every Child Matters. 2003 (London: HMSO).

Falk, G. 2001. *Stigma – How We Treat Outsiders* (New York: Prometheus Books).

Family and Parenting Institute, 2008. *Parenting Fund Round 3 Funding* [Online] (Updated 22 October 2008) Available at: http://www.familyandparenting.org/ ParentingFundFunding [Accessed 27 November 2008].

Farver, J.M., Xu, Y., Bhadha, B.R., Narang, S. and Lieber, E. 2007. Ethnic Identity, Acculturation, Parenting Beliefs, and Adolescent Adjustment: A Comparison of Asian Indian and European American Families. *Merrill-Palmer Quarterly*, 53(2), 184-215.

Fateh, T., Islam, N., Khan, F., Ko, C., Lee, M., Mallik, R. and Krause, I.B. 2002. Can Talking about Cultures be Therapeutic? in *Meeting the Needs of Ethnic Minority Children – Including Refugee, Black and Mixed Parentage Children: A Handbook for Professionals*, edited by K.N. Dwivedi.(London, New York: Jessica Kingsley), pp. 130-50.

Faust, K. and McKibben, J. 1999 'Marital Dissolution: Divorce Separation, Annulment, and Widowhood.', in *Handbook of Marriage and the Family*, edited by M. Sussman et al. (New York: Plenum Press), pp. 475-500.

Fawcett, M. 1999. *What Hurts? What Helps? A Study of Needs and Services For Young People Whose Parents Separate and Divorce* (Belfast: Relate (NI))

Feng, D., Giarrusso, R., Bengston, V.L. and Frye, N. 1999. Intergenerational Transmission of Marital Quality and Marital Instability. *Journal of Marriage and the Family*, 61(2), 451-63.

Fergusson, D.M. and Horwood, J.L. 1998. Exposure to Interparental Violence in Childhood and Psychosocial Adjustment in Young Adulthood. *Child Abuse & Neglect*, 22, 339-57.

Ferri, E. 1984. *Step Children: A National Study, A Report from the National Child Development Study* (Berkshire: NFER-Nelson).

Fischer, T. 2007. Parental Divorce and Children's Socio-Economic Success: Conditional Effects of Parental Resources Prior to Divorce, and Gender of the Child. *Sociology*, 41(3), 475-95.

Flouri, E. And Buchanan, A. 2003. The Role of Father Involvement and Mother Involvement. *British Journal of Social Work*, 33, 399-406.

Foner, N. 1997. The Immigrant Family: Cultural Legacies and Cultural Changes. *International Migration Review*, 31(4) Special Issue: Immigrant Adaptation and Native-Born Responses in the Making of Americans, 961-74.

Forehand, R., Brody, G., Long, N., Slotkin, J. and Fauber, R. 1986. Divorce/Divorce Potential and Interparental Conflict: The Relationship to Early Adolescent Social and Cognitive Functioning. *Journal of Adolescent Research*, 1, 389-97.

Foreign and Commonwealth Office. 2008. *Young People & Vulnerable Adults Facing Forced Marriage: Practice Guidance for Social Workers* [Online] (London: Foreign and Commonwealth Office) Available at: http://www. fco.gov.uk/resources/en/pdf/FM-Guidance-Social-Workers [Accessed 10 September 2008].

Freeman, M. 1996. *Divorce: Where Next?* (England: Dartmouth Publishing Company).

Fried, S.T. 2003. Violence Against Women. *Health and Human Rights*, 6(2), Violence, Health, and Human Rights, 88-111.

Furstenberg, F.F. and Cherlin, A.J. 1991. *Divided Families – What Happens to Children When Parents Part* (USA: President and Fellows of Harvard College).

Gans, H.J. 1997. Toward a Reconciliation of 'Assimilation' and 'Pluralism': the Interplay of Acculturation and Ethnic Retention. *International Migration Review*, 31(4) Special Issue: Immigrant Adaptation and Native-Born Responses in the Making of Americans, 875-92.

Garbarino, J. 1977. The Human Ecology of Child Maltreatment: A Conceptual Model for Research. *Journal of Marriage and the Family*, 39(4), 721-35.

Garbarino, J., Abramowitz, R.H., Benn, J.L., Gaboury, M.T., Galambos, N.L., Gabarino, A.C., Grandjean, P.A., Long, F.N. and Plantz, M.C. 1982. *Children and Families in the Social Environment* (New York: Aldine Publishing Company).

Gelles, R.J. 1997. *Intimate Violence in Families* (London, UK; Thousand Oaks, CA and New Delhi, India: Sage Publications).

Gerstel, N. 1987. Divorce and Stigma. *Social Problems*, 34(2), 172-86.

Ghuman, P.A.S. 1999. *Asian Adolescents in the West* (Leicester: British Psychological Society Books).

Giles-Sims, J. and Crosbie-Burnett, M. 1989. Stepfamily Research: Implications for Policy, Clinical Interventions, and Further Research. *Family Relations*, 38(1), 19-23.

Gill, A. and Rehman, G. 2004. Empowerment Through Activism: Responding to Domestic Violence in the South Asian Community in London. *Gender and Development*, 12(1) Diversity, 75-82.

Gingerbread 2005. *About Gingerbread* [Online] Available at: http://www.gingerbread.org.uk/about-us/index.htm [Accessed 30 November 2008].

Gish, O. 1968. Color and Skill: British Immigration, 1955-68. *International Migration Review*, 3(1), 9-37.

Glaser, B. 2002. Conceptualization: On Theory and Theorizing Using Grounded Theory. *International Journal of Qualitative Methods*, 1(2), 1-31.

Glenn, N.D. and Kramer, K.B. 1985. The Psychological Well-Being of Adult Children of Divorce. *Journal of Marriage and the Family*, 47(4), 905-12.

Glenn, N.D. and Kramer, K.B. 1987. The Marriages and Divorces of the Children of Divorce. *Journal of Marriage and the Family*, 49(4), 811-25.

Goel, R. 2005. Sita's Trousseau: Restorative Justice, Domestic Violence, and South Asian Culture. *Violence Against Women*, 11, 639-65.

Gohm, C., Oishi, S., Darlington, J. and Diener, E. 1998. Culture, Parental Conflict, Parental Marital Status, and the Subjective Well-Being of Young Adults. *Journal of Marriage and the Family*, 60(2), 319-34.

Gonzalez-Lopez, J.M. 2002. A Portrait of Western Families–New Models of Intimate Relationships and the Timing of Life Events, in *Analysing families – Morality and Rationality in Policy and Practice*, edited by A. Carling et al. (London and New York: Routledge), pp. 21-48.

Goode, W.J. 1964. *The Family Foundations of Modern Sociology Series* (New Jersey: Prentice Hall).

Goode, W.J. 1993. *World Changes in Divorce Patterns* (New Haven, CT: Yale University Press).

Gordon, J. 2000. Ecological Influences on Parenting and Child Development. *British Journal of Social Work*, 30, 703-20.

Gray, C.B. 2005. Marriage as a Legal Institution: A French Institutionalist Perspective, *Illuminating Marriage Conference*, Canada, 18-20 May 2005 (Canada: Marriage Institute).

Greenberg, E.F. and Nay, R.W. 1982. The Intergenerational Transmission of Marital Instability Reconsidered. *Journal of Marriage and the Family*, 44(2), 335-47.

Grotberg, E.H. 1995. *The International Resilience Project: Research, Application, and Policy.* [Online Resilience Net: University of Illinois: Urbana Champagne] Available at: http://resilnet.uiuc.edu/library/grotb95a.html [Accessed 9 July 2005].

Grych, J.H., Seid, M. and Fincham, F.D. 1992. Assessing Marital Conflict From the Child's Perspective: The Children's Perception of Interparental Conflict Scale. *Child Development*, 63(3), 558-72.

Guru, S. 2009. Divorce: Obstacles and Opportunities – South Asian Women in Britain. *The Sociological Review*, 57(2), 285-305.

Halpern, D. 2005. *Social Capital* (Cambridge, UK: Polity Press).

Handa, A. 1997. *Caught Between Omissions: Exploring 'Culture Conflict' Among Second Generation South Asian Women in Canada*. PhD (Canada: University of Toronto).

Harris, Q. 2000. Psychological Problems in Asian Children, in *South Asian Children and Adolescents in Britain: Ethnocultural Issues*, edited by A. Lau (London and Philadelphia: Whurr Publications Ltd), chapter 12.

Harrison, A.O., Wilson, M.N., Pine, C.J., Chan, S.Q. and Buriel, R. 1990. Family Ecologies of Minority Children, *Child Development* 61(2), 347-62.

Hawthorne, J., Jessop, J., Pryor, J. and Richards, M. 2003. *Supporting Children Through Family Change – A Review of Interventions and Services for Children of Divorcing and Separating Parents* (York: Joseph Rowntree Foundation).

Heath, A. and Cheung, S.Y. 2007. The Comparative Study of Minority ethnic Disadvantage. *Proceedings of the British Academy*, 137, 1-44.

Helweg, A.W. 1979. *Sikhs in England – The Development of a Migrant Community* (Delhi: Oxford University Press).

Hepburn, H.S. 2004. *Building Culturally and Linguistically Competent Services to Support Young Children, Their Families and School Readiness* (Baltimore: The Annie E. Casey Foundation).

Hernandez, D.J. 1997. Child Development and the Social Demography of Childhood. *Child Development*, 68(1), 149-69.

Hess, R. and Camara, K. 1979. Post-divorce Family Relationships as Mediating Factors in the Consequences of Divorce for Children. *Journal of Social Issues*, 35(4), 79-96.

Hetherington, E.M. 1999. Family Functioning and the Adjustment of Adolescent Siblings in Diverse Types of Families. *Monographs of the Society for Research in Child Development*, 64(4) (Adolescent Siblings in Stepfamilies: Family Functioning and Adolescent Adjustment), 1-25.

Hetherington, E.M. 2003. Social Support and the Adjustment of Children in Divorce and Remarried Families. *Childhood* 10(2), 217-36.

Hetherington, E.M., Cox, M. and Cox, R. 1978. *The Aftermath of Divorce*. (Washington D.C.: National Association for the Education of Young Children).

Hetherington, E.M., Clingempeel, W., Anderson, G., Deal, E.R., Hagan, J.E., Hollier, A.E., Lindner, M.S., MacCoby, E.E., Brown, J.C., O'Connor, T.G., Eisenberg, M., Rice, A.M. and Bennion, L.D. 1992. Coping with Family Transitions: A Family Systems Perspective. *Monographs of the Society for Research in Child Development*, 57(2/3), 1-238.

Hill, C. 1970. *Immigration and Integration: A Study of the Settlement of Coloured Minorities in Britain* (Oxford: Pergamon Press Ltd).

Himmelweit, S. 2002. Economic Theory, Norms and the Care Gap, or Why Do Economists Become Parents? in *Analysing families – Morality and Rationality in Policy and Practice*, edited by A. Carling et al. (London and New York: Routledge), chapter 12.

Hiro, D. 1967. *The Indian Family in Britain* (London: National Committee for Commonwealth Immigrants).

Hope, S., Power, C. and Rodgers, B. 1998. The Relationship Between Parental Separation in Childhood and Problem Drinking in Adulthood. *Addiction-Research Report*, 93(4), 505-14.

House of Commons 2004. *Child Poverty in the UK*. Second Report of Session 03-04: Vol. 1 (HC85-1) (London: The Stationery Office).

Howard, S., Dryden, J. and Johnson, B. 1999. Childhood Resilience: Review and Critique of Literature. *Oxford Review of Education*, 25(3), 307-23.

Hutchins, T. and Sims, M. 1999. *Introduction in Programme Planning for Infants and Toddlers: An Ecological Approach* (Australia: Prentice Hall).

Jansen, M., Mortelmans, D. and Snoeckx, L. 2009. Repartnering and (Re) employment: Strategies to Cope with the Economic Consequences of Partnership Dissolution. *Journal of Marriage and Family*, 71, 1271-93.

Jekielek, S.M. 1998. Parental Conflict, Marital Disruption and Children's Emotional Well-being. *Social Forces*, 76, 905-36.

Johnson, M.P. and Ferraro, K.J. 2000. Research on Domestic Violence in the 1990s: Making Distinctions. *Journal of Marriage and the Family*, 62(4), 948-63.

Johnson, P., Thorngren, J. and Smith, A. 2001. Divorce and Family Functioning: Effects on Differentiation Levels of Young Adults. *Family Journal: Counselling and Therapy for Couples and Families*, 9(3), 265-72.

Johnston, R.J. and Roseby, V. 1997. *In the Name of the Child: A Developmental Approach to Understanding and Helping Children of Conflicted and Violent Divorce* (New York: The Free Press).

Joplin, J., Shaffer, M., Francesco, A.M. and Lau, T. 2003. The Macro Environment and Work-Family Conflict: Development of a Cross-Cultural Comparative Framework. *International Journal of Cross Cultural Management*, 3(3), 305-28.

Joppke, C. 1996. Multiculturalism and Immigration: A Comparison of the United States, Germany, and Great Britain. *Theory and Society*, 25(4), 449-500.

Kalsi, S.P. 2003. 'The Best of Both Worlds': Bicultural Identity Formation of Punjabi Women Living in Canada. [Online Canadian association for the study of adult education] Available at: http://www.oise.utoronto.ca/CASAE/cnf2003/2003_papers/psodhiCAS03.pdf [Accessed 5 May 2006].

Kandiyoti, D. 1988. Bargaining with Patriarchy. *Gender and Society*, 2(3) Special Issue to Honor Jessie Bernard, 274-90.

Kannan, C.T. 1978. *Cultural Adaptation of Asian Immigrants – 1st and 2nd Generation* (Bombay: India Printing Works).

Kathane, R.H. 2000. Roots and Origins: Ethnicity and the Traditional Family, in *South Asian Children and Adolescents in Britain: Ethnocultural Issues*, edited by A. Lau (London and Philadelphia: Whurr Publications Ltd).

Kavemann, B. 2004. Children and Domestic Violence. *Fempower*, 8, 1-5.

Keith, V.M. and Finlay, B. 1988. The Impact of Parental Divorce on Children's Educational Attainment, Marital Timing and Likelihood of Divorce. *Journal of Marriage and the Family*, 50(3), 797-809.

Kelly, J. 2003. Changing Perspectives on Children's Adjustment Following Divorce: A View from the United States. *Childhood*, 10(2), 237-54.

King, V., Harris, K.M. and Heard, H. 2004. Racial and Ethnic Diversity in Non-Resident Father Involvement, *Journal of Marriage and Family* 66, 1-21.

King, V. 2009. Stepfamily Formation: Implications for Adolescent Ties to Mothers, Nonresident Fathers, and Stepfathers, *Journal of Marriage and Family*, 71, 954-68.

Kitson, G.C. and Morgan, L.A. 1990. The Multiple Consequences of Divorce: A Decade Review. *Journal of Marriage and the Family*, 52(4, Family Research in the 1980s: The Decade in Review), 913-24.

Kline, M., Johnston, J.R. and Tschann, J.M. 1991. Long Shadow of Marital Conflict – A Model of Children's Post Divorce Adjustment. *Journal of Marriage and the Family*, 53(2), 297-309.

Knapik, M. 2006. The Qualitative Research Interview: Participants' Responsive Participation in Knowledge Making. *International Journal of Qualitative Methods*, 5(3), Article 6. Available at: http://www.ualberta.ca/~iiqm/backissues/5_3/pdf/knapik.pdf [Accessed 15 March 2010]

Krausz, E. 1971. *Ethnic Minorities in Britain* (London: Granada Publications Ltd).

Kroll, B. 1994. *Chasing Rainbows: Children, Divorce and Loss* (Dorset: Russell House Publishing).

Krumrei, E.J., Mahoney, A. and Pargament, K.I. 2009. Divorce and the Divine: The Role of Spirituality in Adjustment to Divorce. *Journal of Marriage and Family*, 71, 373-83.

Lakey, J. 1997. Neighbourhoods and Housing, in *Ethnic Minorities in Britain – Diversity and Disadvantage*, edited by T. Modood et al. (London: Policy Studies Institute), pp. 184-223.

Landis, J.T. 1960. The Trauma of Children When Parents Divorce. *Marriage and Family Living*, 22(1), 7-13.

Lang, K. and Zagorsky, J.L. 2001. Does Growing Up with a Parent Absent Really Hurt. *The Journal of Human Resources*, 36(2), 253-273.

Lareau, A. 1987. Social Class Differences in Family-School Relationships: The Importance of Cultural Capital *Sociology of Education*, 60(2), 73-85.

Lau, A. 2000. Traditional Values and the Family Cycle, in *South Asian Children and Adolescents in Britain: Ethnocultural Issues*, edited by A. Lau (London and Philadelphia: Whurr Publications Ltd).

Lau, A. 2002. Family Therapy and Ethnic Minorities, in *Meeting the Needs of Ethnic Minority Children – Including Refugee, Black and Mixed Parentage Children: A Handbook for Professionals*, edited by K.N. Dwivedi. (London, New York: Jessica Kingsley), pp. 91-107.

Lau, A. and Bond, A. 2000. Children and Families Involved in Children Act Proceedings, in *South Asian Children and Adolescents in Britain: Ethnocultural Issues*, edited by A. Lau (London and Philadelphia: Whurr Publications Ltd).

Link, B.G. and Phelan, J.C. 2001. Conceptualizing Stigma. *Annual Review of Sociology*, 27, 363-85.

Lee, M.Y. 1997. Post-divorce Interparental Conflict, Children's Contact with Both Parents, Children's Emotional Processes, and Children's Behavioral Adjustment. *Journal of Divorce and Remarriage*, 27(3/4), 61-82.

Luthar, S.S., Cicchetti, D. and Becker, B. 2000. The Construct of Resilience: A Critical Evaluation and Guidelines for Future Work. *Child Development*, 71(3), 543-62.

Luthar, S. 1991. Vulnerability and Resilience: A Study of High Risk Adolescents. *Child Development*, 62(3), 600-16.

Maitra, B. and Miller, A. 2002. Children, Families and Therapists: Clinical Considerations and Ethnic Minority Cultures, in *Meeting the Needs of Ethnic Minority Children – including Refugee, Black and Mixed Parentage Children: A Handbook for Professionals*, edited by K.N. Dwivedi (London, New York: Jessica Kingsley), pp. 108-29.

Mama, A. 1989. *The Hidden Struggle: Statutory and Voluntary Sector Responses to Violence Against Black Women in the Home* (London: London Race and Housing Research Unit).

Mathers, N., Fox, N. and Hunn, A. 1998. *Using Interviews in a Research Project* (Nottingham: Trent Focus Group).

Maundeni, T. 2000. The Consequences of Parental Separation and Divorce For the Economic, Social and Emotional Circumstances for Children in Botswana. *Childhood*, 7(2), 213-23.

Maundeni, T. 2002. Seen But Not Heard?: Focussing on the Needs of Children of Divorced Parents in Gaborone and Surrounding Areas, Botswana. *Childhood*, 9(3), 277-302.

McKay, S. and Rowlingson, K. 1998. Choosing Lone Parenthood? The Dynamics of Family Change, Lone Parenthood in the UK, in *Policy Dilemmas and Solutions, Private Lives and Public Responses: Lone Parenthood & Future Policy in the UK*, edited by R. Ford and J. Millar (London: Policy Studies Institute), pp. 42-57.

McKendrick, J. 1998. The 'Big' Picture: Quality in the Lives of Lone Parents, Lone Parenthood in the UK, in *Policy Dilemmas and Solutions, Private Lives and Public Responses: Lone Parenthood & Future Policy in the UK*, edited by R. Ford and J. Millar (London: Policy Studies Institute), pp. 78-103.

McLoyd, C.V., Cauce, M.A., Takeuchi, D. and Wilson, L. 2000. Marital Processes and Parental Socialization in Families of Color: A Decade Review of Research. *Journal of Marriage and the Family*, 62(4), 1070-93.

Medora, N.P., Larson, J.H. and Dave, P.B. 2000. East-Indian College Student's Perceptions of Family Strengths. *Journal of Comparative Family Studies*, 31. 408-24.

Menjivar, C. and Salcido, O. 2002. Immigrant Women and Domestic Violence: Common Experiences in Different Countries. *Gender and Society*, 16(6), 898-920.

Mitchell, A. 1985. *Children in the Middle: Living through Divorce* (London and New York: Tavistock Publications).

Modood, T. 1997a. Culture and Identity. In: *Ethnic Minorities in Britain–Diversity and Disadvantage*, edited by T. Modood et al. (London: Policy Studies Institute), pp. 290-338.

Modood, T. 1997b. Employment. In: *Ethnic Minorities in Britain – Diversity and Disadvantage*. London, edited by T. Modood et al. (London: Policy Studies Institute), pp. 83-149.

Modood, T. 1997c. Qualifications and English Language. In: *Ethnic Minorities in Britain – Diversity and Disadvantage*, edited by T. Modood et al. (London: Policy Studies Institute), pp. 60-82.

Modood, T., Beishon, S. and Virdee, S. 1994. *Changing Ethnic Identities* (London: Policy Studies Institute).

Mohammad-Arif, A. 2000. A Masala Identity: Young South Asian Muslims in the US. *Comparative Studies of South Asia, Africa and the Middle East*, 20(1 and 2), 67-97.

Morrison, D.R. and Cherlin, A.J. 1995. The Divorce Process and Young Children's Well-Being: A Prospective Analysis. *Journal of Marriage and the Family*, 57(3), 800-12.

Morrison, D.R. and Coiro, M.J. 1999. Parental Conflict and Marital Disruption: Do Children Benefit When High-Conflict Marriages are Dissolved? *Journal of Marriage and the Family*, 61(3), 626-37.

Morrison, D.R. and Ritualo, A. 2000. Routes to Children's Economic Recovery after Divorce: Are Cohabitation and Remarriage Equivalent. *American Sociological Review*, 65(4), 560-80.

Mossakowski, N.K. 2003. Coping with Perceived Discrimination: Does Ethnic Identity Protect Mental Health? *Journal of Health & Social Behaviour*, 44(3, Special Issue: Race, Ethnicity and Mental Health), 318-31.

Moxnes, K. 2003. Risk Factors in Divorce: Perceptions by the Children Involved. *Childhood*, 10, 1131-46.

Mullender, A. and Hague, G. 2005. Giving a Voice to Women Survivors of Domestic Violence through Recognition as a Service User Group, *British Journal of Social Work*, 35, 1321-41.

Nain, G.T. 1991. Black Women, Sexism and Racism: Black or Anti-racist Feminism. *Feminist Review*, 37, 1-22.

Neale, B. and Flowerdew, J. 2003. Trying to Stay Apace: Children with Multiple Challenges in their Post-Divorce Family Lives. *Childhood*, 10(2),147-61.

Needle, R., Su, S. and William, D. 1990. Remarriage and Adolescent Substance Use: A Prospective Longitudinal Study. *Journal of Marriage and the Family*, 52(1), 157-69.

Newman, T. and Blackburn, S. 2002. Transitions In the Lives of Children and Young People: Resilience Factors. *Interchange 78*, Edinburgh: The Scottish Executive.

Nock, S. 2001. The Marriages of Equally Dependent Spouses. *Journal of Family Issues*, 22(6), 756-77.

Nye, F.I.1957. Child Adjustment in Broken and in Unhappy Broken Homes. *Marriage and Family Living*, 19(4), 356-61.

Ochieng, B.M.N. 2003. Minority Ethnic Families and Family-Centred Care. *Journal of Child Health Care*, 7(2), 123-32.

O'Neale, V. 2000. *Excellence Not Excuses: Inspection of Services for Ethnic Minority Children and Families* (London: Department of Health).

Office for National Statistics. 2002. *Social Trends 32* (London: HMSO).

Office for National Statistics. 2003. *Social Trends 33* (London: HMSO).

Office for National Statistics. 2004a. *Social Trends 34* (London: HMSO).

Office for National Statistics. 2004b. *Focus on Ethnicity and Identity* (London: HMSO).

Office for National Statistics. 2004c. *Focus on Religion* (London: HMSO).

Office for National Statistics. 2006a. *Focus on Ethnicity and Religion* (London: HMSO).

Office for National Statistics. 2007a. *Focus on Families* (London: HMSO).

Office for National Statistics. 2007b. *Social Trends 37* (London: HMSO).

Office for National Statistics. 2007c. *Population Trends 127* (London: HMSO).

Office for National Statistics. 2008a. *Social Trends 38* (London: HMSO).

Office for National Statistics. 2008b. *Divorces: England and Wales Rate at 29 Year Low* [Online Society ONS] Available at: http://www.statistics.gov.uk/cci/nugget.asp?id=170 [Accessed 27 May 2010].

Office for National Statistics. 2009. *Social Trends 39* (London: HMSO).

O'Neale, V. 2000. *Excellence Not Excuses: Inspection of Services for Ethnic Minority Children and Families* (London: Department of Health).

Owen, D. 1997. Labour Force Participation Rates, Self-Employment and Unemployment, in *Ethnicity in the 1991 Census: Vol. Four – Employment, Education and Housing Among the Minority ethnic Populations of Britain*, edited by V. Karn (London: HMSO).

Parekh, B. 2000. *The Parekh Report: The Future of Multi-Ethnic Britain*. Report of the Commission on the Future of Multi-Ethnic Britain (London: The Runnymede Trust).

Parquette, D. and Ryan, J. 2001. *Bronfenbrenner's Ecological Systems Theory*. [Online National-Louise University] Available at: http://pt3.nl.edu/paquetteryanwebquest.pdf. [Accessed 7 August 2005].

Patel, N., Thomas, P.G. and Bhavnagri, P.N. 1996. Socialization Values and Practices of Indian Immigrant Parents: Correlates of Modernity and Acculturation. *Child Development*, 67(2), 302-13.

Patel, N., Humphries, B. and Naik, D. 1998. The 3Rs in Social Work, Religion, Race and Racism in Europe, in *Social Work and Minorities: European Perspectives*, edited by C. Williams et al. (London: Routledge).

Pett, M.A., Lang, N. and Gander, A. 1992. Later-Life Divorce: Its Impact on Family Rituals. *Journal of Family Issues*, 13, 526-51.

Pettigrew, N. 2003. Experiences of Lone Parents from Ethnic Communities. *Research Report No* 187, Department of Works and Pensions.

Pike, L.T. 2003. The Adjustment of Australian Children Growing up in Single Parent Families as Measured by their Competence and Self Esteem. *Childhood*, 10(2), 181-200.

Pink, J.E.T. and Wampler, K.S. 1985. Problem Areas in Stepfamilies: Cohesion, Adaptability, and the Stepfather-Adolescent Relationship. *Family Relations*, 34(3), 327-35.

Pinto, P.E. and Sahu, N. 2001. *Working with Persons with Disabilities: An Indian Perspective* (Buffalo, New York: Center for International Rehabilitation Research Information and Exchange (CIRRIE)).

Platt, L. 2005. *Migration and Social Mobility: The Life Chances of Britain's Minority Ethnic Communities* (Bristol: The Policy Press).

Platt, L. 2007. Child Poverty: Employment and Ethnicity in the UK: The Role and Limitations of Policy. *European Societies*, 9(2), 175-99.

Platt, L. 2007. *Poverty and Ethnicity in the UK* (Bristol: The Policy Press).

Popay, J., Rimmer, L. and Rossiter, C. 1983. *One Parent Families: Parents, Children and Public Policy* (Occasional Paper No. 12) (London: Ivor Kamlish FSIAD and Associates).

Portes, A. 2000. The Two Meanings of Social Capital. *Sociological Forum*, 15(1), 1-12.

Poulter, S. 1987. Ethnic Minority Customs, English Law and Human Rights. *The International and Comparative Law Quarterly*, 36(3), 589-615.

Purkayastha, B., Subramaniam, M., Desai, M. and Bose, S. 2003. The Study of Gender in India: A Partial Review. *Gender and Society*, 17(4), 503-24.

Putnam, R.D. 2000. *Bowling Alone: The Collapse and Revival of American Community* (New York: Simon & Schuster).

Pyett, P.M. 2003. Validation of Qualitative Research in the 'Real World'. *Qualitative Health Research*, 13, 1170-9.

Qureshi, J., Berridge, D. and Wennman, H. 2000. *Where to Turn: Family Support for South Asian Communities* (NCB/Joseph Rowntree Foundation, London).

Rands, M. 1988. Changes in Social Networks Following Separation, in *Families and Social Networks*, edited by R.M. Milardo (California and London: Sage Publications), pp. 127-46.

Ranga Rao, A.B.S.V. and Sekhar, K. 2002. Divorce: Process and Correlates a Cross-cultural Study. *Journal of Comparative Family Studies*, 33(4). 541-63.

Raj, D.S. 2003. *Where Are You From? Middle-Class Migrants in the Modern World* (Berkeley: University of California Press).

Raoa, N., McHaleb, J.P. and Pearson, E. 2003. Links Between Socialization Goals and Child-Rearing Practices in Chinese and Indian Mothers, *Infant and Child Development*,12, 475-92.

Reitz, J.G. 1988. The Institutional Structure of Immigration as a Determinant of Inter-racial Competition: A Comparison of Britain and Canada. *International Migration Review*, 22(1), 117-46.

Reynolds, J. and Mansfield, P. 1999. The Effect of Changing Attitudes to Marriage and its Stability, in *High Divorce Rates: The State of the Evidence on Reasons and Remedies: Reviews of the Evidence on the Causes of Marital Breakdown and the Effectiveness of Policies and Services Intended to Reduce its Incidence*, edited by J. Simons (London: Lord Chancellor's Department) Paper 3.

Reynolds, T. 2002. Reanalysing the Black Family, in *Analysing families – Morality and Rationality in Policy and Practice*, edited by A. Carling et al. (London and New York: Routledge), pp. 69-76.

Robert, A. 1996. Pathways Linking Parental Divorce to Adolescent Depression. *Journal of Health & Social Behaviour*, 37(3), 133-48.

Rodgers, B. and Pyror, J. 1998. *Divorce and Separation: The Outcomes for Children* (York: Joseph Rowntree Foundation).

Rowlands, A.J. 1981. Recent Development in Shared Parenting and Joint Custody: A Personal View from the Court. *Proceedings at 14th Annual Family Law Masterclass Conference.* Sydney, 10 May 2005.

Roy, S. 1995. Restoring Hope or Tolerating Abuse? Responses to Domestic Violence Against Immigrant Women. *Georgetown Immigration Law Review Journal*, 9, 263-90.

Sanders, J.M. and Nee, V. 1996. Immigrant Self-Employment: The Family as Social Capital and the Value of Human Capital. *American Sociological Review*, 61(2), 231-49.

Schwartz, H. and Jacobs, J. 1979. *Qualitative Sociology: A Method to the Madness* (New York: The Free Press, Macmillan Publishing Company).

Sen, P. 1998. Development Practice and Violence Against Women. *Gender and Development*, 6(3), 7-16.

Shaw, D. 1991. The Effects of Divorce on Children's Adjustment: Review and Implications. *Behaviour Modification*, 15, 456-85.

Shaw, D.S., Winslow, E.B. and Flanagan, C. 1999. A Prospective Study of the Effects of Marital Status and Family Relations on Young Children's Adjustment Among African American and European American Families. *Child Development*, 70(3), 742-55.

Shields, K.M. and Behrman, R.E. 2004. Children of Immigrant Families: Analysis and Recommendations. *The Future of Children*, 14(2, Children of Immigrant Families), 4-15.

Silverman, D. 2000. *Doing Qualitative Research: A Practical Handbook* (London: Sage Publications).

Simons, R.L., Kuei-Hsiu, L., Gordon, L.C., Conger, R.D. and Lorenz, F.O. 1999. Explaining the Higher Incidence of Adjustment Problems Among Children of Divorce Compared with Those in Two-Parent Families. *Journal of Marriage and the Family*, 61(4), 1020-33.

Simpson, B. 1998. *Changing Families: An Ethnographic Approach to Divorce and Separation* (Oxford: Berg).

Singh, R. 1998. *The Cultural Adjustment of Asian Lone Mothers Living in London* (Aldershot: Ashgate Publishing Limited).

Singh, R. 2000. Religious Beliefs and Practices Among Sikh Families in Britain, in. *South Asian Children and Adolescents in Britain: Ethnocultural Issue*, edited by A. Lau (London and Philadelphia: Whurr Publications Ltd), chapter 7.

Singh, G. and Tatla, D.S. 2006. *Sikhs in Britain: The Making of a Community* (London and New York: Zed Books).

Smart, C. 2000. Divorce in England 1950-2000: A Moral Tale? in *Cross Currents: Family Law and Policy in the US and England*, edited by S Katz et al. (Oxford: Oxford University Press), pp. 363-87.

Smart, C. 2004. Changing Landscapes of Family Life: Rethinking Divorce, *Social Policy and Society*, 3(4), 401-8.

Smart, C. and Neale, B. 1999. *Family Fragments* (Cambridge: Polity Press).

Smart, C. and Shipman, B. 2004. Visions in Monochrome: Families, Marriage and the Individualization Thesis. *The British Journal of Sociology*, 55(4), 491-509.

Smart, C. and Wade, A. 2002. *Facing Family Change: Children's Circumstances, Strategies and Resources* (York: York Publishing Services).

Smart, C., Neale, B. and Wade, A. 2001. *The Changing Experiences of Childhood – Families and Divorce* (Cambridge: Polity Press).

Smith, H. 1999. *Children, Feelings and Divorce: Finding the Best Outcome* (London: Free Association Books).

Sobolewski, J.M. and King, V, 2005. The Importance of the Coparental Relationship for Nonresident Fathers' Ties to Children, *Journal of Marriage and Family*, 67, 1196-1212.

Solomos, J. 2003. *Race and Racism in Britain*. (New York: Palgrave Macmillan).

South, S.J. and Trent, K. 1989. Structural Determinants of the Divorce Rate: A Cross-Societal Analysis. *Journal of Marriage and the Family*, 51(2), 391-404.

South, S.J., Crowder, K.D. and Trent, K. 1998. Children's Residential Mobility and Neighbourhood Environment Following Parental Divorce and Remarriage. *Social Forces*, 77(2), 667-93.

Spillman, J.A., Deschamps, H.S. and Crews, J. 2004. Perspectives on Non-residential Paternal Involvement and Grief: A Literature Review. *The Family Journal: Counseling and Therapy For Couples and Families*, 12(3), 263-70.

Srinivasan, S. 1995. *The South Asian Petty Bourgeoisie in Britain* (England: Avebury).

Stewart, S.D. 2003. Non-Resident Parenting and Adolescent Adjustment: The Quality of Non-Resident Father-Child Interaction. *Journal of Family Issues*, 24(2), 217-44.

Strohschein, L. 2005. Parental Divorce and Child Mental Health Trajectories. *Journal of Marriage and Family*, 67, 1286-300.

Swiss, L. and Bourdais, C.L. 2009. Father-Child Contact after Separation The Influence of Living Arrangements. *Journal of Family Issues*, 30(5) 623-52.

Tallman, I., Rotolo, T. and Gray, L.N. 2001. Continuity or Change? The Impact of Parent's Divorce on Newly Married Couples. *Social Psychology Quarterly*, 64(4), 333-46.

Tasker, F.L. and Richards, M.P. 1994. Adolescent's Attitudes Towards Marriage and Marital Prospects after Parental Divorce: A Review. *Journal of Adolescent Research*, 9, 340-62.

Thornton, A. 2009. Framework for Interpreting Long-term Trends in Values and Beliefs Concerning Single-Parent Families. *Journal of Marriage and Family*, 71, 230-34.

Toth, T. and Kemmelmeier, M. 2009 Divorce Attitudes Around the World: Distinguishing the Impact of Culture on Evaluations and Attitude Structure. *Cross-Cultural Research*, 43(3), 280-97.

Trinder, L., Beek, M. and Connolly, J. 2002. *Making Contact: How Parents and Children Negotiate and Experience Contact after Divorce* (York: York Publishing Services).

Tuhiwai-Smith, L. 1999. *Decolonizing Methodologies: Research and Indigenous Peoples* (UK and USA: Zed Books).

Vance, E. and Sanchez, H. 1998. *Creating a Service System that Builds Resiliency.* (North Carolina, US: Department of Health and Human Services).

Vaughan, R. 1991. The Indians: Onward and Upward, in *Ethnicity in the 1991 Census – Vol. 2: The Ethnic Minority Populations of Great Britain*, edited by C. Peach (London: Office for National Statistics).

Waite, L.J. 2000. The Family as a Social Organization: Key Ideas for the Twenty-First Century. *Contemporary Sociology*, 29(3), 463-69.

Waites, C., Macgowan, M.J., Pennell, J., Carlton-LaNey, I. and Weil, M. 2004. Increasing the Cultural Responsiveness of Family Group Conferencing. *Social Work*, 49(2), 291-300.

Walby, S. 1990. *Theorizing Patriarchy* (Oxford: Blackwell Publishers Ltd).

Walker, R. 1985. *Applied Qualitative Research* (Aldershot: Gower).

Walker, R., Logan, T., Jordan, C.E., and Campbell, J.C. 2004. An Integrative Review of Separation in the Context of Victimization: Consequences and Implications for Women. *Trauma, Violence & Abuse*, 5(2), 143-93.

Wallerstein, J. and Kelly, J.B. 1980. *Surviving the Breakup – How Children and Parents Cope with Divorce* (London: Grant McIntyre Limited).

Wallerstein, J.D., Tschann, J.M., Johnston, J.R. and Kline, M. 1989. Family Process and Children's Functioning During Divorce. *Journal of Marriage and the Family*, 51(2), 431-44.

Wallerstein, J., Lewis, J.M. and Blakeslee, S. 2000. *The Unexpected Legacy of Divorce – A 25-year Landmark Study* (New York: Hyperion).

Walzack, Y. and Burns, S. 1989. *Divorce: The Child's Point of View* (London: Harper & Row Publishers Ltd).

Weaver, H.N. 1999. Indigenous People and the Social Work Profession: Defining Culturally Competent Services, *Social Work*, 44(93), 217-25.

Weiss, R.S. 1975. *Marital Separation* (New York: Basic Books Inc.).

Wietzman, L.J. 1985. *The Divorce Revolution: The Unexpected Social and Economic Consequences for Women and Children in America* (New York: The Free Press).

Welsh, E., Buchanan, A., Flouri, E. and Lewis, J. 2004. Father's Involvement and their Secondary School-Aged Children. *Findings* (No. 1904) (York: Joseph Rowntree Foundation).

White, L.K. 1990. Determinants of Divorce: A View of Research in the Eighties. *Journal of Marriage and the Family*, 52(4), 904-12.

Widmer, E.D. 2006. Who are my Family Members? *Journal of Social and Personal Relationships*, 23(6). 979-98.

Wilson, A. 1978. *Finding a Voice: Asian Women in Britain* (London: Virago).

Wilson, A. 2006. *Dreams, Questions and Struggles* (London: Pluto Press).

Winchester, H.P.M. 1990. Women and Children Last: The Poverty and Marginalization of One-Parent Families. *Transactions of the Institute of British Geographers*, 15(1), 70-86.

Woehrer, C.E. 1982. The Influence of Ethnic Families on Intergenerational Relationships and Later Life Transitions. *Annals of the American Academy of Political and Social Science*, 464 (Middle and Late Life Transitions), 65-78.

Wolfinger, N.H. 2000. Beyond the Intergenerational Transmission of Divorce: Do People Replicate the Patterns of Marital Instability They Grew Up With. *Journal of Marriage and the Family*, 21(8), 1061-86.

Wolfinger, N.H. 2003. Parental Divorce and Offspring Marriage: Early of Late. *Social Forces*, 82(1), 337-53.

Wyman, P.A., Cowen, E.L., Work, W.C., Hoyt-Meyers, L., Magnus, K.B. and Fagen, D.B. 1999. Caregiving and Developmental Factors Differentiating Young At-Risk Urban Children Showing Resilient Versus Stress-Affected Outcomes: A Replication and Extension. *Child Development*, 70(3), 645-59.

Younge, G. 2000. South Asians Fly the Flag for Traditional Family Life. [Online The Guardian online,] 18 Dec. Available at: http://www.guardian.co.uk/uk/2000/dec/18/britishidentity.race [Accessed 5 February 2005].

Yount, K. and Li, L. 2009. Women's "Justification" of Domestic Violence In Egypt, *Journal of Marriage and Family* 71, 1125-40.

Zaslow, J.M., Dion, M.R., Morrison, D.R., Weinfeld, N., Ogawa, J., Tabors, P. 1999. Protective Factors in the Development of Preschool Age Children of Young Mothers Receiving Welfare, in *Coping with Divorce, Single Parenting and Remarriage: A Risk and Resiliency Perspective*, edited by E.M. Hetherington. (Mahwah, NJ: Lawrence Erlbaum Associates), pp. 193-26.

Index